2

Growing Up with the Goons

Growing Up with the Goons

Memories, Reflections and Startling Tales from their Children

With a foreword by HRH the Prince of Wales

Andy Secombe

BOOKS

First published in Great Britain in 2010 by

JR Books, 10 Greenland Street, London NW1 0ND

www.jrbooks.com

Picture credits
Page 2 top; Trinity Mirror/Mirrorpix/Alamy; page 3: Keystone/Stringer/Getty Images; page 5: Hulton Archive/Stringer/Getty Images; page 6 top: Popperfoto/Getty Images; page 7 bottom: Topfoto; page 8: Rex Features; page 11 top: John Pratt/Stringer/Getty Images; page 12 bottom: Rex Features; page 15 bottom: Hulton-Deutsch/Corbis. All other photographs supplied courtesy of the author.

ISBN 978-1-906779-89-4

1 3 5 7 9 10 8 6 4 2

Printed by MPG Books Ltd, Bodmin, Cornwall

For Dad. '*Vide 'o mare quant'è bello*'

Contents

Acknowledgements

A book of this nature is a collaborative effort and I'd like to thank all participating Goonchildren for being kind enough to talk to me about their experiences and for allowing me to use some much-cherished family photographs.

I'd also like to thank Richard Sellers' family for giving me permission to quote from his book *PS I Love You*; John Repsch of The Goon Show Preservation Society for his help in tracking down several missing addresses; and Gill Nicholas for supplying me with reams of *Goon Show* facts and figures.

Finally, I'd like to thank Jeremy Robson for having had the good sense to commission this book, and all at JR Books for their patience and gentle guidance.

When I was approached to write the foreword for a book called "Growing up with the Goons" by someone styling himself "Son of Ned", I knew exactly who it was. Andy Secombe, of course, really did grow up with the Goons. I merely grew up with them at a distance, during the 1950's, irresistibly attracted to the hysterical sound effects I first heard on my father's wireless. Before long, I found myself able to imitate many of the voices and probably drove everybody mad in the process. However, when my younger brothers finally heard recordings of the Goon Show for themselves, they thought it must have been me playing all the parts!

The sadness for me was that I only discovered the true joy of Messrs. Neddie Seagoon, Eccles, Bluebottle and Major Bloodnok just as the show was drawing to a close. However, I received a certain amount of compensation by being lucky enough to get to know the remarkable people behind the characters. Whenever they met, they would revert to those characters in a very short time. I remember Michael Bentine telling me on one occasion that when he was flying in the R.A.F. during the Second World War he was so short sighted that he needed a Braille instrument panel. Spike Milligan told me about the endless efforts they made to achieve the right sound effect on one of the shows of a sock full of wet custard hitting someone. Try as they could, they couldn't achieve the right sound. So Spike went down to the B.B.C. Canteen, took off his sock, and asked the lady behind the counter to fill it with custard. But it still didn't sound like a sock full of wet custard hitting someone!

The tragedy, of course, is that these brilliantly funny men are no longer with us to lighten up our lives. But, much as they are missed, their work survives and anyone wanting a respite from today's fashion for the witless humour of cruelty and smut could do worse than seek out the repeats of the Goon Shows on Radio 7.

I am delighted that such a book has been written, having always been curious as to what went on behind closed doors in the households of Milligan, Sellers, Secombe and Bentine. I suppose I had vague notions of anarchic rites being carried out to the accompaniment of galloping coconut shells, raspberries and manic laughter. The reality, I can assure you, was much more bizarre – digging potatoes with explosives being just one example…

As this book testifies, the legacy of the Goons is in safe hands, it lives on in their children and, as long as they survive, Harry, Mike, Peter and Spike will remain: Goon, but not forgotten!

Introduction

Celebrity is a strange thing; being related to celebrity even stranger. One is not quite the thing itself, but forever associated with it. It's a bit like being an historical artefact: a lock of Nelson's hair, perhaps, or a rivet from the SS *Great Britain*.

I was born in 1953, when my father was appearing in a radio programme called *The Goon Show*, which was rapidly gaining a cult following. Little did either of us realise then the colossal impact that show would have on both our lives.

For those not old enough to remember those days, *The Goon Show* was a hugely popular show that changed the face of British comedy for ever. To an audience used to settling down by the radiogram for an easy-listening half-hour in the company of Henry Hall and his band, or cosying up to the genteel humour of Richard Murdoch and Arthur Askey's *Band Waggon* (a comedy and music radio show from the late thirties) and Tommy Handley's *I.T.M.A.* (a popular forties radio comedy), *The Goon Show* was like a naughty schoolboy throwing stones at the headmaster's study window.

Reflecting the attitude of those who had fought in the war towards the idiots who had sometimes commanded them, it lampooned authority and shoved a bayonet into the bubble of middle-class pomposity. In some ways, it followed the formula laid down by those earlier, more reserved shows, in having recognisable characters that returned week after week – it even had catchphrases, but there the similarity ended.

The mad genius behind it – Spike Milligan – put his characters into surreal situations. In what other comedy show might you come across three idiots trying to cross the channel on a piano? Where else but *The Goon Show* could you find a man wearing reinforced concrete socks; a dastardly German plan to make British shirt-tails explosive; and a taxi that sounds like a set of bagpipes? It was hugely inventive, introducing the raspberry to a wide audience, and even adding to the English language with terms such as 'jobsworth', 'lurgi', 'You silly, twisted boy', 'Nurse, the screens!' and 'No more curried eggs for me!'

The musician and comedian Mitch Benn, from Radio 4's *Now Show*, is a fan:

'How many people do you know who refer to being ill as having the lurgi and have no idea that it's a Goon joke? Lurgi has absolutely passed into the idiom…Apparently it's from Milligan misreading the word "allergy". He misread it as "A lergy". I use that without a moment's thought…

'Lurgi is, in fact, an audio disease: eeeeeyackaboo! That's what it sounds like, cured only by playing a brass band instrument.'

The Goon Show was enjoyed by millions, who clustered around their radio sets as eagerly as people today might gather around the television for the next instalment of *Doctor Who* or *Glee*, and still, today, nearly 40 years after *The Last Goon Show of All*, it is loved by people all over the world. Even America has its own *Goon Show* fan club, where the likes of Major Dennis Bloodnok, Grytpype-Thynne, Moriarty, Eccles, Bluebottle and Neddie Seagoon are regarded as heroes, and the men who brought them to life – Peter Sellers, Spike Milligan, Harry Secombe and Michael Bentine – revered as icons.

When I was born, *The Goon Show* was in its second year, Mike Bentine had already left and the show had evolved into the format that it would keep until the end of its long run. It was a few years before I was old enough to understand what all the fuss was about, let alone laugh at the jokes but, by then, sadly, it was over. That didn't, however, stop people from calling me Neddie Seagoon, or quoting large chunks of dialogue at me for years to come. Just the other day, I opened the door to a young postman who had an envelope too big to go through the letter box. As he handed it over to me, a sudden gust of wind whipped it out of his hand and dumped it in a puddle. Quick as a flash, he said, in Little Jim's voice, 'It's fallen in the water!'

That postman could hardly have been out of his thirties, far too young to remember the original broadcasts, so how did he know? It seems that *The Goon Show* has somehow become embedded in the national psyche and it was partly a fascination with the show's enduring appeal that led me to write this book.

Another reason for embarking on this project was a desire to 'come clean' about my heredity, after spending the better part of my life attempting to distance myself professionally from my father. But the main reason was to find out what effect the show had had on those who grew up in its shadow. It wasn't always easy for me and my siblings, so I was interested to find out how the children of the other Goons had fared.

This book has had a long gestation period. I suppose it all began in 2000, when I received a phone call from someone called Dirk Maggs, the man behind *At Last the Go On Show*, a radio documentary marking the 40th anniversary of the show's first series. After a bit of research, I discovered that he was also responsible for *Flywheel, Shyster and Flywheel*, a collection of Marx Brothers' radio scripts originally broadcast in thirties' America on *Five Star Radio Theater*. Most recordings had been lost, so Dirk decided to save them from obscurity by re-recording them with Michael Roberts as Groucho, Frank Lazarus as Chico and Lorelei King playing all the women. These new recordings, put out on Radio 4, had been hugely and deservedly successful, and Dirk wanted to do a similar thing with some 'lost' *Goon Shows*, the recordings of which, although wiped by the BBC, still survived in script form. Although impressed by his credentials, not least by the fact he was a Marx Brothers' fan, when he asked me if I'd like to play Neddie Seagoon, I turned him down flat.

'Thanks, but I have no interest in taking over the family business,' I told him, rather high-handedly.

I had always 'ploughed my own furrow' as a 'straight' actor and had sworn never to go near anything to do with my dad. This attitude stemmed from my watching other children of comedians entering the business on their parent's coat-tails only to end up being vilified and sometimes destroyed by the media. This wasn't always entirely fair as, in many instances, it was the famous parent who had stood behind their unwilling child and pushed.

Agreeing, however, that we should never give the media the opportunity to level the charge of nepotism against us, Dad and I made a mutual non-intervention pact. He would never help me professionally and I would never ask for his assistance. I was also careful to state to whomsoever would listen that I was an 'actor', not a 'turn', and that there was nothing of the 'Variety' performer about me, oh no. Nevertheless, it was for comedy roles I was best known and, for that matter, most enjoyed.

At the time of Dirk's phone call, my father was pretty ill, having recently been diagnosed with cancer and then almost immediately having suffered a debilitating stroke. But when I visited him in hospital and told him about it, his eyes lit up.

'Do it!' he said.

I was shocked.

'*The Goon Show* was the best fun I ever had,' he said, wistfully. 'The scripts were brilliant and walking into rehearsal on a Sunday morning was a joy. Do it, Andy, you'll enjoy it.'

'But people might think I'm capitalising on your name,' I said feebly.

'Nonsense,' he replied. 'You've been in the business too long now for people to think you're taking advantage. Other fathers have companies they can pass on to their sons. All I've got is my career. Think of it as my gift. Look on it as taking over the family business.'

Suitably chastened, I went home and phoned Dirk to ask if he'd recast yet. Luckily he hadn't and, a few months later, I found myself on the stage of the Player's Theatre (where several of the original *Goon Shows* were recorded) in *Goon Again*. With me were the highly talented Jon Glover and Jeffrey Holland, Jon taking all of Spike's characters and Jeffrey playing Peter's. I wasn't the only link with the past, though: Dirk had also persuaded Christopher Timothy (son of Andrew – the original announcer) and Ray Ellington's son, Lance, to join the cast.

It was a great night and I had a ball. Dad had been right, as usual. Sadly, neither he nor Spike were able to make it to the recording, as both were very ill at the time. I took Dad a recording of the show, hoping that it might rekindle some happy memories, but by that time he had slipped into unconsciousness, from which he never re-emerged.

A few weeks after *Goon Again* was broadcast, I was watching a Marx Brothers' film on television with my children and remembered doing the same thing with my father. As he had introduced me to all his favourite comedians – Laurel and Hardy, W.C. Fields, Buster Keaton, Jacques Tati, Groucho, Chico and Harpo – so I, in turn, was introducing them to my boys. I felt as if I was passing on a comedy heritage, one that over the years has kept me joyously amused and given me succour in hard times. I considered my own comedy inheritance, and it occurred to me that I was a member of an élite clan: I belonged to that select group which one of Spike's daughters, Sile Milligan, refers to as 'Goonchildren'. This is how she sees it:

'Being the child of a Goon is like being a member of a private club…I saw Stella McCartney on television one day, and I thought, "Christ, she's one of the Beatles' kids – that's huge!" Then I thought, "Hold on a minute…" Since Dad died, I've realised that it's humungous to be the child of a Goon. I mean, *The Goons* did for comedy what the Beatles did for music.'

I began to wonder what life must have been like in those other Goon households. What was Spike like at home; was he crazy all the time? How was Peter as a father? Behind closed doors, was

Mike Bentine really the lovely gentle man I remember meeting?

This started me thinking. I got back on the phone to Dirk and floated the idea of a radio programme about the experiences of the children of the Goons, exploring the impact those giants of comedy had had on the lives of their sons and daughters.

Unfortunately, because of other commitments, it was impossible to get the idea off the ground until 2006, and then, just when we'd been given the green light, something else intervened to prevent the show going ahead: I got cancer. As I said to Dirk at the time, 'It's all very well following in my father's footsteps, but this is ridiculous!'

It was another two years before I was able even to think about making the programme, by which time Dirk was deeply involved in another project. There was, however, no time to hang about as the BBC were getting impatient, having given us the ultimatum: 'It's now or never!' So, with Dirk's co-producer, David Morley, taking the reins, we went ahead and recorded the show that autumn. *Growing Up with the Goons* went out on Radio 2 on Christmas Day 2008.

Meeting the other Goonchildren to interview them for the programme was a great experience, as we all shared something unique. The programme, too, seems to have gone down well and induced a surge of nostalgia among those of a certain age, rekindling fond memories of clustering round a crackling radio set. After the broadcast, I lost count of the number of people who asked me if I was turning it into a book, saying, 'It would be a perfect present for my father/uncle/grandad/psychiatric nurse...'

My answer was always the same: an unequivocal 'No'. As far as I was concerned, I'd owned up, I'd 'come out' as a Goonchild and that was it – job done. The programme had been made, it was time to move on.

But as I sat in my writing shed and tried to work on my next novel, *The Goon Show* just wouldn't leave me alone. I looked up at my bookshelves, groaning with biographies, CDs and files stuffed with Goon facts and anecdotes: the research gathered for the programme. The thing was, we had recorded such a vast amount of material that many great stories had, of necessity, been excised to fit into the hour-long broadcast slot. It seemed almost criminal to waste all this great stuff. Then there were the people we hadn't got around to talking to in the timeframe granted us by the BBC and, of course, all the photographs that we couldn't use: my dad's archive alone fills three large chests.

I tried to dismiss the thought…I was far too busy. But, annoyingly, the idea wouldn't go away, and continued to buzz around my head like, appropriately enough, a bluebottle. To resolve matters once and for all, I decided the best course of action would be to approach my dad's old publisher with the idea. If he said yes, I would go ahead with it; if he said no, at least I'd tried and could move on with a clear conscience.

Expecting him to dismiss the idea out of hand with a weary groan, I tentatively got in touch with the ever-patient Jeremy Robson, of JR Books. To my great surprise, he thought it was a terrific idea and so, girding my loins, off I went again, filling in all the gaps in the programme, visiting James Grafton, having an audience with Lord Snowdon and, at last, managing to get hold of Richard Bentine. Admittedly, there were still some people it was impossible to get to – some because of geography, some because of other, more personal reasons, but I think there's more than enough here to satisfy the most inquiring mind.

The result of all this enjoyable research you're holding in your hands. Or, as this book is Goon-related, you may well be wrapped in a Union Jack, standing to attention in a bucket of custard and saluting it. But however you look at it, I hope you enjoy it.

1

Army Days

Much has been written about the early days of the Goons and how they met; indeed, three of them wrote autobiographies telling the story themselves. I make no apology, however, for adding to the amount of printed matter on this subject, as I think a brief exploration of the ground out of which *The Goon Show* sprang is essential in a book of this kind, giving insights not only into the behaviour of the men behind the Goons, but also the subsequent experiences of their children. For those of you who don't know the story, what follows will be a bracing and enlightening, whistle-stop tour of the pre-Goon lives of those four famous men and, I think I'm right in saying, the information contained herein is not available all in one place anywhere else. But to those who think they already know the whole story, my advice is to pull up a bollard, sit back and enjoy a long satisfying Gorilla until it passes.

For those old enough to remember the fifties, the words 'It's the highly esteemed *Goon Show*' will have a special meaning. It was with this phrase that my father used to kick off half-an-hour of surreal humour, which was essential listening for people the length and breadth of the British Isles. All over the country, on a Friday evening, people would gather round their radiograms to listen to the latest instalment of the adventures of Neddie Seagoon, Eccles, Bluebottle, Bloodnock, Henry Crun and Minnie Bannister.

After the war, Britain was tired. Crippled by shortages, many of her cities in ruins and up to her eyes in debt, she badly needed cheering up, as testified by the proliferation of radio comedy shows at that time: *Ray's a Laugh*, *I.T.M.A.* and *Variety Bandbox*, to name but three. All these shows were popular, highly regarded and boasted incredibly talented writers and casts. They were also old-fashioned, safe and cosy, the radio equivalent of a grey worsted suit – the sort of thing you could happily listen to with your aged auntie without feeling embarrassed.

But then, in the early fifties, the BBC, without fanfare, unleashed a programme that was to change radio comedy for ever. This was *The Goon Show*, which exploded on to the airwaves in a Technicolor burst of madness, blowing a raspberry at authority and sticking two fingers up at the Establishment.

The comedian, writer and *I'm Sorry I Haven't a Clue* stalwart, Barry Cryer, was an early fan and well remembers those days:

'I was at school and university when *The Goon Show* first came out. *The Goon Show* was our *Monty Python*. I always remember one time in the university union, there were 300 people in this room trying to listen to one radio – it sounds so quaint now. But that was our show, we thought, arrogantly. It was widely popular, we knew that, but it was our show. We'd never heard anything like it – we'd heard *Ray's a Laugh*…and Tommy Handley during the war, and Arthur Askey and all that. They were brilliant, but orthodox, and then we heard this madness going on, this anarchy and we latched on very quickly.

'They'd been in a war – they were rebellious, they had an instinctive anti-authority attitude which the other comedy programmes didn't…and that, of course, appeals to young people – the rebellious side of it.

'It was in a great English tradition of nonsense, sheer nonsense and, of course, as radio it was superb because it was loaded with sound effects and situations you could never have depicted on television.

'Initially it was *Crazy People* on the old Third Programme…I mean, my generation didn't listen to the Third Programme… but suddenly there was this explosion – everyone was going around saying, "Have you heard *The Goon Show*?" And it became a hit very quickly.'

Gill Nicholas, archivist of the Goon Show Preservation Society, was also a fan:

'When we were at school, if you hadn't listened to *The Goons* the night before, you may as well not bother to go to school the next day. We were at the local grammar school and all the talk in the playground was *The Goon Show*. It caused more rows in my home than anything else, because my father couldn't understand a word they were saying – and we only had the one radio. "Why have we got to listen to this rubbish?" he'd say. So it led me to having to go out to work during the summer holidays so that I could buy my own trannie.

'Younger people tuned in a bit more than the older generation, although, funnily enough, my father did get to like them in the end. And then when I went to teacher training college, anybody who had a radio…we all got round to listen to the Goons.'

So how did all this madness come about? What were the circumstances that led to this outburst of anti-authoritarianism? Could such anarchy have originated in the ranks of the British Army? Surely not.

At the end of the war, in the mid-forties, although British squaddies returning home to battered Britain may have found it hard to recognise the country they had left, they too had been changed. After travelling so far and seeing so much, their horizons had been broadened – they had had enough of being told what to do and few were content to slip meekly back into the narrow ways of the lives they had left. They wanted adventure and excitement, and many found it in the entertainment business.

Some had had their first taste of 'treading the boards' in the various army concert parties organised to keep the lads happy while they convalesced or took a well-earned break from hostilities. One such was a Swansea boy named Harry Donald Secombe.

Just before Harry was called up, he was working as a pay clerk at a colliery in south Wales, making up the miners' pay. Now, Dad wasn't blessed with a head for figures and, one day, he got things hopelessly mixed up. As the miners opened their pay packets, many discovered they'd been short-changed. Angry muttering broke out, which soon flared into open hostility. A furious mob surrounded the pay office demanding satisfaction – there was no way out. The fortuitous arrival of the soldiers to come and tell Dad he'd been called up probably saved his life.

Dad's war was pretty busy. Joining an artillery regiment, he was sent to Aldershot to be trained in the dark arts of artillery bombardment and thence to Ditchling in Sussex, where his regiment was employed in an anti-invasion role. There, in a break between scanning the dunes for invading German paratroopers, Dad, having had some amateur theatrical experience back in Swansea, playing straight-man to his sister, Carol, was persuaded to join the local concert party, which was giving a Variety concert in the town hall. He cobbled together an act consisting of impressions of famous radio comedians of the time, finishing with a song.

On the first night, horribly nervous, he popped into the pub across the way to fortify himself. Unfortunately he took things a little too far and, by the time he was due on stage, he was past merry – he was flying. His act was a total disaster and he finished in a heap of hysterical giggles.

The next day, a more sober Secombe was filled with remorse at having let down not only the lady running the concert party, but also his regiment. He was not, however, allowed to brood long on his inauspicious début as a solo comedian, for he soon found himself in Scotland on manoeuvres, wandering the hills around Dunblane, trying to find his way back to base in the middle of the night armed with nothing but a prismatic compass. There, he also received training in assault landings. The war was getting nearer.

On 15 October 1942, Lance Bombardier Secombe of the 132nd Welsh Field Regiment, Royal Artillery, boarded a ship at Greenock, bound he knew not where. All he did know was that he was going to war, and this time it was for real.

The regiment landed at Algiers and was into the action almost immediately. Dad's unit was on the 25-pounder guns, 'The Five-Mile Snipers' they used to call themselves.

The campaign in North Africa was tough; the Germans, led by Rommel, the 'Desert Fox', were well trained, well equipped and not in the habit of retreating. After a bruising encounter with the German's 10th Panzer Division, Dad's regiment was moved down to the Le Kef area, in north-western Algeria, to prepare for the 'big push' that was to drive the Germans out of Africa once and for all.

Reinforcements were arriving all the time, including a detachment of 7.2in howitzers which were to be deployed on a plateau to destroy some enemy gun positions in rock caves deep in the adjacent hillside. Dad and his colleagues were ordered to dig gun-pits for these howitzers, to absorb the recoil of their huge barrels.

Once the pits were dug, Dad retired to a wireless truck, halfway down the steep cliff that led up to the plateau. That night, under cover of darkness, the howitzers were moved into position and settled into the gun-pits dug by my father's regiment. Unfortunately, having been given the wrong specifications, Dad and his oppos hadn't dug the pits deep enough, and so when the first howitzer was fired, its huge recoil caused it to leap out of its pit and career down the cliff.

In the truck, Dad heard the terrifying rumble of the out-of-control howitzer approaching like the wrath of God. His first thought was, 'Now they're throwing guns at us!'

After the gun had hurtled past, a few minutes later, the flap of the truck was thrown back and a white-faced squaddie enquired, 'Anybody seen a gun?'

'What colour?' Dad threw back.

This was his first encounter with a certain Spike Milligan, and

Dad immediately recognised a fellow idiot, but little did he know then the impact on his life this man would have in years to come.

Towards the end of the war, the two would meet up again at a concert party in Italy and then, of course, more significantly, back in England.

But now, after surviving having guns thrown at him by his own side, Lance Bombardier Secombe became part of the huge army which, under Field Marshal Montgomery, pushed the German Army westward across North Africa. Before long, his regiment had reached Sicily, trudging north over the jagged lava beds on the western side of Mount Etna. The fighting here was extremely fierce, but eventually Sicily was taken. Once it was safely in Allied hands the troops were given a welcome respite from combat.

Here, notwithstanding his earlier disaster in Ditchling, Dad managed to get himself attached to the Divisional Concert Party. Performing out of the back of a 3-ton truck, with the legend 'The Sicily Billies – Lava Come Back To Me' on the side, Dad got his first taste of theatrical touring, although his later experiences, trawling round the British Variety circuit, playing theatres in Bolton, Hull, Sheffield and Liverpool, would be very different from the vineyards and olive groves of Sicily. Dad had a great time swanning around the Sicilian countryside, drinking the local wine and chatting up the local girls.

But all good things come to an end and, after four weeks tasting the life of an itinerant Mediterranean entertainer, in mid-September 1943 Dad returned to his regiment at Messina, to move up into Italy. It was supposed to be a simple 'clearing up' operation; the Italians had already surrendered and the Allies thought they'd have a walk-over. Marching into Italy uncontested, they reached Bari on the east coast without incident. But as they pressed on northwards, it became clear that the Germans weren't yet ready to lie down. They made a stand at Termoli, where a vicious battle raged for three days. After this, exhausted and suffering from shock, Dad was hospitalised for five weeks.

It was while he was convalescing in the 76th General Hospital in Trani that he discovered a nearby Italian army barracks had a theatre which was advertising for volunteers for a Variety concert. He applied and was given a spot, and it was these few months with the Trani concert party that convinced him that the stage was his future.

Eventually, the concert party was broken up. Dad was given a medical that passed him fit for active service and was told to report to the Royal Artillery Training Depot at Eboli, near Salerno. Arriving there in November, he immediately sought the man in charge of the local concert party.

He auditioned and got a place in the regular show. This particular concert party was very different from that at Trani, being of almost professional standard, and the audiences they played to demanded new material on a regular basis. The competition to get into the show was stiff and any performer who couldn't keep up with the pace was likely to be replaced – there were plenty more waiting to get in. Dad was soon scraping the barrel of his impersonations; if he didn't think of a new act, and soon, he could well find himself back hurling 25-pound shells at the Germans. It was this pressure and his determination not to be sent back up the line to be shot at any more that led him to develop his Shaving Act.

This simple idea came to him when he was shaving one day in an overcrowded tent. He started messing around to entertain his mates and soon had them in hysterics. In this act, he demonstrated how different people shaved: a small boy playing with his dad's razor; a soldier shaving in a bucket of ice-cold water; someone embarrassed at being watched shaving for the first time; and he'd finish by drinking the soapy water from his shaving mug. It was much funnier than my rather dry description and it was this act which, after the war, got him on to the stage of the Windmill Theatre – that Mecca for young comedians, whose celebrated boast that during the Blitz 'We never closed' was almost as well known as the girls who were the main attraction.

The Windmill Theatre, just off Shaftesbury Avenue, was, in those days, one of the few showcases for up-and-coming comedians in London. But it was best known for its naked showgirls, who would pose in a series of static *tableaux vivants* (under the Lord Chamberlain's rules they were not allowed to move) on a Greek, Roman or nautical theme. Between these tableaux, singers, dancers and comedians would come on and try to entertain the, unsurprisingly largely male, audience. Many famous names started their careers there, such as Jimmy Edwards (RAF ace who won the DFC at Arnhem and would later find fame as the headmaster in the radio show *Whack-O!*), Tony Hancock, Bruce Forsyth, Arthur Haynes, British film star Kenneth More…and another British institution, Barry Cryer:

'The Windmill was six shows a day, six days a week: 36 shows a week – not a bad school. I was hot from Leeds and I – I must have had some real gall – I rang the Windmill (somebody had tipped me off in a pub or something) and they had mass auditions, what we'd now call an "open-mic"; anybody could turn up. It was about ten o'clock in the morning, because the first show was twelve-fifteen, and they'd pack in a load of auditions in an hour and a quarter – wheel you on and wheel you off. And I went on and told some jokes and a voice from the darkness – I couldn't see him – but it was Vivian Van Damm, known to us all as VD. And this voice said, "Know any more jokes?"
"Er, yes, yes…"
"Have you got another song?"
"Yes, but I haven't got any music."
"Ronnie will busk it for you." [Ronnie Bridges, the Windmill's pianist.]
'And then, it wasn't "We'll let you know" or anything, there was just silence. Then, a man called John Law, who was working the show, came and took me away, off the stage and said, "Dressing room 12A."
'I thought, "What's happening?" In the unlikely event of me having had something else to do that afternoon, I would have had to cancel it. I was on stage at half past twelve – in my ordinary clothes. Someone slapped a bit of pancake on my

face, and I did my audition, which was about ten minutes. Then, VD had me in his office between every show that day – five breaks – and he changed my act in one day: "I don't like that joke – here's a better one…That joke's very good, you should finish with that…no, that's wrong, don't do that there…" Wonderful, a masterclass.

'It was a wonderful school…they hadn't come to see you, they'd come to see the strippers, obviously, and they would open newspapers when you came on. That's where I met Bruce Forsyth, in 1957. Bruce was brilliant, but they even did it to him.

'There was a lovely old Geordie comedian, before I worked there, called Jimmy Edmunson, and he walked on in the middle of the afternoon one day and a guy in the front row opened a newspaper, and he said, "Oh, I see you've brought your own comic!"

'But you learned to die with dignity…I suppose it could have been demoralising, but I didn't know any better, really. I was young, it didn't bother me…

'There were "honours" boards outside. Van Damm put the names of Windmill alumni on the boards: Harry Secombe, etc., in gold lettering…VD was very proud of the Secombes and the Hancocks and all the people who did well afterwards…'

Dad auditioned for the Windmill almost as soon as he was demobbed and, on 17 October 1946, he opened in *Revuedeville 187* for the princely sum of £20 a week. And it was at the Windmill, among the sequins and ostrich-feather fans, that the story of the Goons really begins.

Across the street from the Windmill stage door was a drinking club run by a man known as 'Daddy' Allen. Allen's was a popular meeting place for performers trying to break into the big-time, because 'Daddy' allowed them food and drink 'on tick'. Here, struggling young comedians and performers – such as Bill Kerr, Frank Muir, Alfred Marks and Norman Vaughan – would meet and swap stories. And for some of them, life really was a struggle.

My father used to tell a true story which demonstrates to what depths of despair these would-be funny men could occasionally be driven.

A young comedian was so depressed about not getting any work that he tried to kill himself. He locked the door of his flat and stuffed newspaper around it, then he taped up the windows, put his head in the gas oven and turned it on. Seconds later, there was a loud click as the money in the gas meter ran out. Dick Emery pulled his head out of the oven, counted himself lucky, pulled himself together and never looked back.

Also moving in the crowd that frequented Allen's was a young comedy performer called Peter Butterworth. Peter was a lovely man and would later become famous as a regular in the *Carry On* films. He was ex-Royal Navy and, during the war, had been captured by the Nazis in the Netherlands. After escaping from Dulag Luft, near Frankfurt, he was recaptured and placed in Stalag Luft III. It was here, to cover the sound of an escape tunnel being dug by fellow prisoners, he took part in the shows and vaulting demonstrations later made famous in the film *The Wooden Horse*. Peter actually auditioned for the film but was turned down because he didn't look 'convincingly heroic and athletic'.

Sadly, Peter is no longer with us, but his wife, the equally lovely Janet Brown, a Scottish actress and comedienne, probably most famous for her brilliant impersonation of Margaret Thatcher, happily still is:

'Peter and Harry were very fond of each other and had a great rapport, and there's an incident which showed to me how sensitive Harry was, because the outward picture is of this ebullient, wonderful, loveable man.

'We were all appearing together at some theatre, and we'd gone to a big lunch at a hotel. The room in which we were sitting was one half of a much larger room, which was divided by a partition. This partition had a door in it and, during the meal, Pete, unseen by Harry, got up, walked out of our half of

the room, went round the corner and knocked on the door…
Harry leapt up from his chair…and threw back this door.
Unbeknownst to him, behind it, in the other half of the room,
a wedding reception was going on. When Harry opened the
door, it knocked over a table which was laden with food. There
were bits of trifle everywhere…it was a terrible mess. Harry was
so upset that he left, full of apologies and went off to his room
and we never saw him again that day – he couldn't come back,
he felt too badly about it.'

Another regular at Allen's was a wild-haired comedian of Peruvian
descent called Michael Bentine. Mike was in the next show at
the Windmill, in a double-act with a man called Tony Sherwood.
Richard Bentine, Michael's youngest son, recalls:

'Before he joined up, Dad was working with a man called
Tony Sherwood – they called themselves Sherwood and
Forrest. Dad played the drums, Tony played trumpet, I think.
     'In 1942, Dad and Tony went to do a gig in the West End,
as a sort of last farewell before Tony went off on his RAF
training, and the club got bombed – flattened. The sirens had
gone off and everyone was moving towards the cellar doors
when the bomb went off. Tony was blown down into the cellar,
Dad was blown across the club, so they literally both had to be
dug out of the rubble. Dad walked back home the seven miles
or so from the West End to Castelnau by Hammersmith
Bridge, covered in dust, completely deaf in one ear – he just
wanted to get back and tell his parents that he was OK. But
when he got there, to his absolute horror, he saw the whole
building had been gutted.
     'Pop and Grandma had been bombed the same night. His
mum and dad were sitting inside this completely destroyed
building drinking cups of tea waiting for him to come home
– hoping that he would come home.'

According to Harry, Sherwood and Forrest's act was performed entirely in cod Russian. Dad watched their dress rehearsal at the Windmill and laughed until his sides ached. Going backstage afterwards to congratulate them, Dad and the wild-haired Peruvian clicked immediately and, from then on, the two of them were to spend many hysterical hours in each other's company, at Allen's or Lyon's Corner House.

Mike's background was about as different as you could get from my father's. Claiming to be the only Peruvian born in Watford, he had been to Eton and, after a short stint in the ARP, had volunteered to join the RAF. Unfortunately, his Peruvian heritage counted against him with the xenophobic Aircrew Selection Board and, although he was never actually turned down, he wasn't accepted either, at least not until he was arrested as a deserter.

Mike said that he applied to the RAF 'about once every three months' and, while waiting in vain for the men in blue to respond, on a whim, he applied for a job as an actor. Never having had any experience at all in this field, he somehow landed a job in Frank Forbes Robertson's company. After a short and disaster-filled stint at the Prince of Wales Theatre, Cardiff, he was even more surprised to be offered a place in the company of that great actor-manager, Sir Robert Atkins.

After a season touring around Manchester, the company moved to London, playing a season at the open-air theatre in Regent's Park, and then on to the Westminster Theatre, near Victoria station. It was here, one evening, waiting to go on as Lorenzo in *The Merchant of Venice*, that Mike was accosted by two RAF service policemen and arrested as a deserter. It was only the intervention of Robert Atkins himself that prevented them carrying him off there and then. As it was, he was allowed to finish the play, while the burly policemen stood guard in the wings. At RAF headquarters, still dressed in his Shakespearean doublet and hose, Mike tried to explain that there had been a mistake, but the policemen wouldn't listen. Frustrated by their pig-headedness, Mike then insisted on speaking to the Peruvian ambassador.

Richard Bentine takes up the story:

'Having spent most of 1941 and '42 volunteering for every service and being turned down because he was a Peruvian, Dad was arrested as a deserter on the London stage while appearing with Helen Cherry, who eventually became Mrs Trevor Howard. Dad reckons he was the first person to have been paraded as a deserter in doublet and hose for about 400 years. They took his sword away so he wouldn't do himself an injury. He went ballistic and insisted on the Peruvian ambassador being called. He was Dad's godfather and didn't take too kindly to being called at three in the morning because he was on the nest at the time with his latest mistress.'

The ambassador, who well knew the story of Mike's repeated but fruitless attempts to join the RAF, duly arrived and proceeded to lambast the hapless policemen, threatening to close the port of Callao to British shipping unless 'Miguel Bentin' was released immediately.

The red-faced policemen obliged and, 10 days later, Michael was admitted to the RAF, as Aircraftsman Second Class, Bentin, M.J. He was inducted by A.A. Gilligan, who, at the time, was captain of England's cricket team.

Richard Bentine says:

'As Dad tells the story, A.A. Gilligan was sat there at aircrew induction in the middle of Hyde Park, and he went, "Were you at Eton? Good heavens! Were you a dry bob?" Which meant, were you a cricketer?

'And Dad said, "Yes."

"Bowler or batsman?"

"Bowler, medium-pace in-swing."

"Well, we must have you in the RAF."

'Dad said he could have been the illegitimate son of Adolf Hitler and would still have ended up in the RAF, just because he could play cricket.'

However, not long into his training, in preparation for his being sent overseas, Mike received a triple-booster inoculation – anti-tetanus, -typhoid and -typhus – which, unluckily for him, was from a contaminated batch. He and two other young officers immediately fell ill with a high fever. One of the other officers died, the other was invalided out of the service, but Mike survived almost intact, except for his eyesight, which had been permanently damaged.

Richard Bentine recalls:

'That was spring 1943. Summer '43 they tried to invalid him out. Gilligan again interviewed him and said, "What do you want to do? You've been through hell, we'll quite understand if you want to leave." Then he actually said, if I remember correctly, "So sorry, Michael, these things happen. You do know there's a war on?"

But Mike stayed in the RAF and, no longer able to be considered for flying duties, went to Cosford officer training and was subsequently seconded to RAF intelligence. He was attached to a Polish squadron at Hemswell and charged with teaching the aircrews how, when and where to drop airborne mines.

From Hemswell, Mike was posted to Wickenby in the run-up to the great bombing offensive of 1943–44.

According to Richard Bentine:

'He went across on the second-wave Normandy beach-head to oversee the installation of radar. They were setting up forward positions to set up airfields as they moved through France and Belgium. There were a couple of times when the airfield wasn't necessarily as liberated as it could have been. Several times he found himself parading through a town that had Belgians at one end and still had Germans at the other. In one village in Belgium, he was looking around, everything was very quiet and he got the head man of the village to produce any guns that they had. Out of this pile of armaments, Dad chose the best pieces, then took the bolts out of the rest and threw them down the town well. Heading back out of the village he met an American armoured division coming up the road.

"Where have you been?" they asked.

'When he told them, they said, "We haven't taken that village yet."

'After a two-day battle, Dad was one of a group who debriefed the German commander of the Panzer division which had been completely hidden in the woodlands surrounding this village, who said, "Yes, I remember you came into the village, trying to entice our fire. But no, we did not reveal our positions. You cannot fool us!"

Michael finished the war as one of the senior British officers at Belsen.

Richard Bentine adds:

'I think that was the final straw. He never talked about the war at all until I was about eight, when he published his first book…Sometimes I'd meet people who would come up to me and say, "Oh, I knew your dad during the war…" and in the course of the conversation I'd find another story that wasn't in the book.

'One of the most interesting ones was from a woman who contacted my mother after Dad died. She said during the war she'd arrived here as a refugee with her mother – her father didn't survive the walk out of Holland or Belgium or wherever they'd come from. She'd been brought up by her mother, who had remarried and settled in Norfolk. And for years, her mother had always kept an airman's flying jacket and used to tell this story about this airman who had been driving past a line of refugees walking down the road, and he'd stopped his jeep because he saw this woman carrying a little baby and she didn't have a proper coat. And he took his flying jacket off and gave it to her and said, "You'd better have that for both of you." Then he got back in the jeep and drove off. And the identity tag in the jacket was Flight Officer Michael Bentine…I didn't know that as a story, but that's Dad…he was a very unassuming hero.'

Back home after a long physical and mental recuperation, Michael met up with his old school friend, Tony Sherwood, with whom he dreamed up the mad Cossack act which my father saw at the Windmill. But after their stint at the 'Mill, work proved hard to come by and, after Tony decided to take up an offer of two years' free tuition at the Guildhall School of Music, Mike went solo, but didn't have much luck until he hit upon a crazy idea, with a little help from his brother.

Richard Bentine continues:

'Back from the war, Dad didn't want to kill anyone any more, or be involved in anything that had anything to do with killing, which is why he picked up with Tony Sherwood again. But after Tony went off to Guildhall in 1947 or '48, Dad had a fight with his brother, pushed him over and he fell back and broke a chair. And his brother stood up with this broken chair-back and, holding it like a machine-gun, said, "I ought to shoot you for doing that." And Dad thought, "What a brilliant idea – I wonder how many uses I can find for a broken chair-back?" And that's how he developed his chair-back act. I suppose that is just as weird as Harry's shaving act. Where do things like that come from?'

This very clever act consisted of Mike stumbling on stage clutching the back of a chair and delivering a monologue as a character that would later, in *The Goon Show*, develop into mad professor Osric Pureheart. During the course of the monologue, the chair-back served as a flag, a plough, a machine-gun, the bars of a prison, handcuffs and even a comb. Later, he also worked a sink-plunger and vacuum-cleaner pipes into the act, but what exactly he did with them I have no idea. According to my father, his act was incredibly physical.

I remember Dad telling me that he once watched Mike's act from the wings during a show in which they appeared together. This particular night, Mike, who apparently shunned underwear, split his trousers during the strenuous routine. But as this happened during the part of the act where he'd stuck the sink-plunger on his face, completely covering his nose and eyes, he was unaware of this fact until the laughs he had been getting were replaced by gasps. 'He was very well-endowed,' my father said.

Mike, as this story and the title of his autobiography, *The Long Banana Skin*, attest, was spectacularly accident prone. In his book *Arias and Raspberries*, Dad tells a very funny story about one of their outings together:

'Mike was always good company, so when one Sunday, early on in our acquaintance, he invited me to spend the day with him at the house of a recently acquired girlfriend, I accepted readily.

'She lived with her family in the outer suburbs of London and, as neither of us had a car, we took the train. It was a lovely summer afternoon, and the house was quite grand. The company consisted of the girl's mother and father and an aunt, who were all dazzled by the brilliance of Mike's conversation.

'Throughout a beautifully cooked meal, he regaled us with stories of his days in repertory with Robert Atkins, and when it came to playing a spot of croquet on the lawn, he beat everybody, performing wonders with his mallet. At tea, which was sumptuous and extremely filling – especially after our huge lunch – he enthralled us with tales of his adventures in the air force. By the end of our visit everyone, including myself, was captivated by Mike's wit and eloquence.

'Farewells were said, and then the three ladies decided to walk us to the station, leaving the father behind. Mike enlivened the short walk with descriptions of ballets he had seen and, as we walked on to the gravel leading to the station platform, he decided to show us Nijinsky's famous leap as performed in *The Spectre of the Rose*.

'He took a little run and leapt into the air. Unfortunately, the amount of food Mike had consumed throughout the day – the roast beef and apple tart at lunch and the pastries and the boiled ham at tea – proved too much and, as he took off, he gave vent to a blast from his nether regions. It was gargantuan, and had it been properly harnessed it would have propelled him over the roof of the railway station. It seemed to me the shock of it actually delayed his return to earth, exactly like Nijinsky's celebrated leap.

'I immediately collapsed into hysterics against the wall of the station, and the three ladies, who were standing watching arm in arm, abruptly turned around and began to walk off without a backward glance. Mike followed them for a few steps, making little raspberry sounds with his mouth in a vain attempt to convince them that he had made the sound from that end. But their retreating backs offered no forgiveness.

'He turned to where I lay, kicking my heels in the gravel in helpless, uncontrollable laughter and, seeing the funny side of the incident himself, he joined in the hysteria.'

After their meeting at the Windmill, Mike took my father to a pub in Victoria, called Grafton's, of which more later.

It was around this time that Spike Milligan re-entered my father's life. His war years are, of course, well documented in his brilliant series of autobiographies, from *Adolf Hitler: My Part in His Downfall* to *Peace Work*, but, just for the record, here's a brief resumé.

Terence Alan Patrick Sean Milligan was born on 16 April 1918 in Ahmednagar, India. His father, Leo, was an NCO serving in the British Army. Spike received a fitful education at Roman Catholic convent schools in Poona and Rangoon, where the nuns used to beat him. But in 1933, when he was 15, Ramsay MacDonald's government imposed a 10 per cent cut on the armed forces, which forced the Milligan family, already in financial straits, to come back to England where Leo hoped to find more lucrative employment. They settled in Catford and Spike resumed his education at St Saviour's in Lewisham.

Before war broke out, Spike was pursuing a musical career, as a trumpet player and vocalist. But after being called up, Gunner Milligan – 954024 – found himself serving with the First Army in North Africa and Italy. Soon after being promoted to Lance Bombardier, he was blown up by a mortar shell in the terrifying Monte Cassino offensive. It was this incident which he blamed for his later psychiatric problems.

Steve Punt, writer, comedian and one of the presenters of Radio 4's long-running *Now Show*, says:

'*The Goons* was long finished by the time I developed an interest in comedy. But I'd read Milligan's war books before I got a chance to hear a lot of *The Goons*. So I always heard it in the context of knowing Milligan's background and what he'd been through in the war, and therefore how liberating it must have felt. Because you get a great sense from the books of the amount of black humour that went on in the forces. The war produced an awful lot of humour, but not much of it was broadcast because it was all too tasteless. People were terribly over-sensitive; the BBC was terribly over-sensitive, but the actual fighting men themselves dealt with it with a lot of really black comedy. Comedy is always a way of dealing with bad things. And so there had been in the war a whole sub-genre of dark humour of which, you can imagine, Milligan was probably the leading exponent.'

After being hospitalised for a leg wound and shell shock, Spike spent time at a rehabilitation centre in Italy. As the war neared its close, he worked as a wine waiter and clerk in an officer's club, before being 'discovered' playing his trumpet by a Sergeant Phil Phillips, who invited him to join a band called the '02E'.

When the war ended, Spike stayed in Italy, joining the Central Pool of Artists as a trumpeter. While there, hanging around, waiting to be told where exactly he was to play his trumpet next, he was whiling away the time fooling around on a borrowed guitar when he was again discovered, this time by a tall fiddle player called Bill Hall.

In a very short time, Spike and Bill were joined by Johnny Mulgrew on double bass, to form the Bill Hall Trio. The trio – all excellent musicians – would stumble on stage dressed as tramps and perform a series of superbly crafted comedy numbers.

Also in the CPA was a small Welsh entertainer, named Secombe, H., part-time gunner and full-time lunatic. At that time, the Shaving Act was in its early days, and delivered at a pitch and speed comprehensible only to bats and amphetamine junkies. When Spike saw it for the first time, he thought my dad was an imported Polish comic.

The Bill Hall Trio became one of the biggest hits of the CPA and, even after being demobilised, the trio remained in Italy, performing in Bologna, Florence, Naples, Bari, Capri, Padua, Venice…they even crossed the border into Austria and played the State Opera House in Vienna.

On their return to England, the trio was signed up by theatrical agent Leslie MacDonnell, who got them work on the Variety circuit and even a booking at the London Palladium. But this brief flirtation with stardom didn't last long and soon the trio was back on the road: Glasgow, Dublin, Golders Green, then overseas once again, to Germany, Italy and Germany again. But Spike, beginning to realise they were going nowhere and fed up with the constant touring, left the trio.

By this time, Spike had already got back in touch with Harry and, after being taken along to Grafton's, had been introduced to Jimmy, Mike and Peter.

Jimmy Grafton now took Spike under his wing and got him his next job, with yet another three-piece. 'The Anne Lenner Trio' consisted of Anne, who sang, accompanied by Spike and Reg O'List (another army pal) on guitars. Jimmy wrote an act for them and the trio was booked for a revue called 'Swinging Along', which was touring Germany. Spike found himself back on the road once again.

When the tour finished, Spike headed straight to Grafton's

and, in another example of Jimmy's generosity, was given an attic room over the pub. It was during his residency there that the other Goons christened him 'The Prisoner of Zenda'.

The Anne Lenner Trio didn't last long and, after it folded, Spike, with Jimmy's support, developed his first solo act which he took on the road – back to Germany!

Home again, and this time to stay, Spike wrote an act for the now unemployed Reg O'List and his girlfriend, Jennifer Lautrec. Sadly, they bombed, thus ending the brief career of Reg O'List and Jennifer.

On a more encouraging note, Jimmy Grafton had been commissioned by the BBC to write a series for Derek Roy and asked Spike to write it with him. Derek Roy was just the kind of 'safe', middle-of-the-road comedian Spike would later come to revile. But, back then, he couldn't afford to be choosy and writing for Roy was the beginning, proper, of Spike's professional writing career. The show was called, cringingly, *Hip Hip Hoo Roy*, and, later on, Spike actually appeared on it, unleashing a pre-Goon Eccles on an unsuspecting public. Roy also hosted *Variety Bandbox* on alternate weeks, which was a show that gave many stars their first break, including Michael Bentine, Tony Hancock, Morecambe and Wise, Harry Secombe, Peter Sellers and Harry Worth.

Charles Chilton, probably best known for creating the radio science-fiction programme *Journey into Space*, and for being the inspiration behind the show *Oh! What a Lovely War*, was an early *Goon Show* producer. He remembers:

'I worked with Spike quite a lot before *The Goon Show*…I did a programme called *The Bowery Bar*, which was based on a bar in the Bowery in New York in the early days of the century. And the chap I'd chosen to star in it was appearing at the London Palladium and did an act like Al Jolson. I thought he was good and would do fine. So we got this show going…

'I got Spike to write the script and we rehearsed and everything, and ten minutes before we're due on air we can't find the star – he's disappeared! So everybody goes looking for him…he wasn't in the pub, or anywhere you'd expect. And I found him locked in the men's lavatory – he was scared out of his mind and wouldn't come out. And I said, "Well, you must, we're on the air!" and he said, "I can't do it! I can't do it!"

'And I was wondering what we were going to do, and Spike said, "I'll do it!" And so, Spike Milligan did it. And that was his first appearance on radio as a performer…the show ran for weeks after that, with Spike writing the scripts and starring in it.

'He was wonderful to work with: inspired, eccentric…of course he was blown up in the war, and that affected him a bit, and when he used to feel whatever it was inside of him coming on, he would go and lock himself in a padded room at the top of his house. Then he'd send his wife telegrams, saying things like: "Where's the tea?"

'He was very particular about everything: about his writing and about every aspect of the show. I did a few programmes with Spike after *The Goons*. I remember one of them was called "The Prime Minister's Trousers". [This was an episode of the series *The Omar Khyyam Show* that went out on the BBC in 1963/64.]

The last member of the foursome that was to become the Goons was Airman Richard Henry Sellers. His parents called him Peter after his stillborn, older brother – a weird enough start to a life that would just keep on getting weirder.

Descended from boxer Daniel Mendoza on his mother's side (a heritage of which he was extremely proud), Peter was born on 8 September (a birthday he shared with my father) in 1925, in Southsea, where his parents (Peg and Bill) were appearing at the King's Theatre. Peter himself made his theatrical début on that stage when he was just two days old, in the arms of the star of the show, Dick Henderson (father of Dickie), who led the audience in a chorus of 'For He's a Jolly Good Fellow'.

Born into a theatrical family, Peter spent the early years of his life on the road, touring the halls in a number of revues during the last days of music hall. Forced to stay in a collection of grotty digs with damp sheets and mouldering wallpaper, Peter hated this time. He hated the smell of greasepaint and size (a glaze painted onto theatre sets) – the quintessential aroma of theatres which, funnily enough, my father loved. Above all, he hated the constant travelling and longed for a place to call home.

As befits Peter's contrary character, despite his dislike of life on the road, Sarah Sellers – his daughter with his first wife, Anne – recalls the nostalgia he felt for those days:

> 'He used to talk a bit about school and sometimes places he had lived – he liked to take you on tours of places he'd lived and things like that. So he was quite sentimental, and he also had some great aunts who lived up in Southport, near Blackpool…they were characters, and they were connected with the music-hall side of things…they were important to him and he kept in touch with them.
>
> 'I can remember them being at the Dorchester before Dad's funeral and they were probably in their eighties then, and they were looking around for rich Arabs. They loved it there!'

Notwithstanding his professed hatred of this time, it was his experiences on the road during the dark, dying days of music hall that would provide Peter with an endless source of character material. The weird and wonderful creatures who peopled that now vanished world – the faded old actors and ageing hoofers, the jugglers, acrobats, fire-eaters and sword-swallowers – were stored away in the 'dressing-up box' of his mind and, out of this jumble of accents, voices and funny walks, he would assemble the many brilliant characters which populated his later work.

The actor Lionel Jeffries, with whom he worked on the classic Ealing comedies, *Two Way Stretch* and *The Wrong Arm of the Law,* said of his mimicry that it was so perfect it was if he had a tape recorder between his ears which had instant playback.

Although young Peter longed for stability, he never found it.

The constant movement of his early life left him with a wanderlust that was impossible to satisfy. Even at the height of his fame, when he could afford to live wherever he chose, he never settled anywhere for long.

The same restlessness seemed to infuse every part of his life. Lord Snowdon, who was to become a good friend and who trailed Peter around London and the countryside on many a jaunt, said, 'He'd never stay anywhere for long…it was infuriating.'

The only constant in Sellers' life was his mother, Peg. Peg claimed Peter as her own, even keeping him at a distance from Bill, his father. Although the theatres and the digs may have changed (even Bill came and went from time to time, disappearing whenever he got tired of his wife's offhand treatment), Peg was always there. She was the archetypal overbearing mother, in whose eyes Peter could do no wrong, and she was the person, everyone seems to agree, who was responsible for Peter's absolute inability to forge a healthy relationship later in life.

Sarah Sellers observes:

'In the Geoffrey Rush film [*The Life and Death of Peter Sellers*], I think it [Peg and Peter's relationship] was perhaps pushed a little too far. They did have a love-hate relationship and she was a typical Jewish mother: the sun shone out of his backside…

'It was perhaps a little bit unhealthy, but he was an only child and you often find that somebody that's an only child has been spoilt in a particular way and been allowed to get away with things and hasn't learnt to share. But because of her theatrical background, it was all a bit more exaggerated.

'She was quite a dominating person. She was a character, and she had a cupboard that had treasures in it, called a "mush" cupboard – whatever that might mean – but there were always little silver trinkets in there. I have fairly fond memories of her. In fact, being an antique dealer, I find it quite interesting…

'She was a knocker, she used to go round knocking on

people's doors and try to get antiques to sell and so it's kind of in the blood – so I have followed in the family tradition…'

Dad said that during rehearsals for *The Goon Show*, Peter would ring his mother several times a day and, if you happened to pass him while he was on the phone, it was as if he were talking to a lover. The conversation would be peppered with 'darlings' and 'loves' and kisses blown into the receiver. The rest of the gang also thought it odd, but no one ever said anything. Despite what they'd been through during the war, their closeness and the outrageous pranks they occasionally pulled on each other, this was the fifties after all and, to all intents and purposes, a society still based on Edwardian sensibilities: one just didn't meddle in another chap's business.

Compared to the experiences of the other three, Peter's war was a doddle. When war broke out in 1939, Peg took her darling Peter to Ilfracombe, to be away from the bombs, and it was here that young Sellers learned to play the drums. His father, Bill, got himself a job playing piano with 'Waldini and his Gypsy Band' at the Victoria Pavilion. The exotically named Waldini was, in reality, Wally Bishop, a silent movie accompanist from Cardiff. Peg took tickets and Peter helped out backstage, but after Peter and a local boy won a talent contest with a ukelele double-act, Bill offered to pay for music lessons for Peter on an instrument of his choice – he opted for the drums. He was set up with Waldini's drummer and it wasn't long before he was in the band himself. Now he had a proper trade and, by all accounts, was very good.

But even Peg couldn't prevent the war catching up with Peter and, in 1943, not long after his 18th birthday, Peter was conscripted into the Royal Air Force. Confined to ground duties because of his bad eyesight, Peter was the lowest of the low, an aircraft-hand, his job being to look after the planes, making sure they were ready for service. But Peter soon became bored both with pushing bullets into planes' wings and the company of the technicians and fitters he now found himself among – he wanted out. Of course, there was no way that the Royal Air Force was simply going to let him go, not even faced with the indomitable Peg's powers of persuasion, so he had to find a different line of attack.

Even though it was clear Peter had a facility for mimicry – he could do all the voices of all the characters in *I.T.M.A.*, for example – he still thought of himself primarily as a drummer. The impersonations were something he did just for fun and to entertain his fellows. And so it was as a drummer that he applied to join Ralph Reader's *Gang Show*.

There is a famous story of his first meeting with Ralph Reader. Peter was in the NAAFI, waiting to audition and, in the meantime, entertaining a group of airman with his impersonation of Reader, singing 'We're Rolling Along on the Crest of a Wave'. Apparently it was going well and he had all the other airmen helpless with laughter when, suddenly, they stopped laughing, stood to attention and saluted. Peter kept going for a little while before finally realising that something was up. Turning round, he came face-to-face with Ralph Reader himself, who'd been standing behind him for some moments.

It says something for Peter's ability at mimicry even then, and not least Reader's sense of fair play, that Reader hired him on the spot. Peter was back in showbusiness.

The *Gang Show*s were a mixture of sketches and musical interludes, cast from members of the RAF to entertain the chaps both at home and abroad. Sellers soon found himself touring India, playing the drums and doing impersonations. But he found it hard to confine his play-acting to the stage and, by his own account, for a bit of fun, used to borrow costumes from the *Gang Show* wardrobe, 'age up' with a bit of make-up and visit the local officers' mess as a variety of Flight Sergeants, Air Commodores and, once, a Sikh officer. If he'd been caught, he would have been in serious trouble but, having the luck of the devil, he always managed to get away with it, as he also did with his occasional dabblings in the black market.

Having had the time of his life out in India, at war's end Peter came back to cold, cash-strapped Britain and tried to get a job. It was a hard slog and work was intermittent. During this time, apart from the odd gig as a drummer, he did stints as a fairground barker, an entertainments officer at a holiday camp and even dusted off his ukelele skills, doing George Formby impressions in a show with Dorothy Squires who, after he'd bombed on the Monday night, saved him from getting the sack. Finally, Peter took along his ukelele and his impressions to an audition for the Windmill and got the job.

Revuedeville, however, proved not to be the entrée to stardom Peter had hoped for. After his six-week stint, he was back on the street looking for work yet again. In desperation, he phoned Roy Speer, the producer of *Show Time* – a radio programme which featured a lot of new comedy acts – pretending to be comedian Kenneth Horne, and singing the praises of a new comic called Peter Sellers. Speer was completely fooled until Sellers confessed that it was, in fact, him.

Although Speer called him 'a cheeky young bastard', he gave him an interview and Peter came away with a booking on *Show Time*.

Now, at last, his career began to take off. Becoming a regular on *Show Time*, appearances on *Henry Hall's Guest Night*, *Workers' Playtime* and *Variety Bandbox* followed. Once his talent for mimcry had been discovered, he was soon in great demand and went from show to show. It was during this feverish round of radio performing that Sellers finally ran into my father and Mike Bentine in something called *Third Division*, produced by Pat Dixon and also featuring Robert Beatty, Robert Moreton, Benny Hill and Patricia Hayes, written by Frank Muir and Denis Norden. Sadly, nothing of this show remains, save a sketch which was a send-up of the travelogues about exotic places often shown between the newsreels in picture-houses and called *Balham, Gateway to the South*. This was later re-recorded by Peter on the album, *The Best of Sellers*, produced by George Martin.

Mike and Harry immediately recognised Sellers' wild talent and a sense of humour that chimed with their own, and it wasn't long before Peter was invited to Grafton's to meet Spike.

Richard Bentine remembers:

'I always got the impression that, out of all of them, Peter was a little bit sheepish as he was the youngest and was the one who'd never seen active service. In a way, the fundamental fact of being through a war – being shot at, shelled, wounded, dropped behind enemy lines, and just having to pick up a gun and shoot somebody – really affected Mike, Harry and Spike in a way that Peter never experienced…They had all suffered.'

Now all the actors were assembled and the stage was set. Four comedians in a pub – it sounds like a recipe for disaster, but it was in Grafton's that the Goons began to take shape.

2

Grafton's and KOGVOS

Grafton's was a pub in Strutton Ground, Westminster. Built in 1848, it was originally called The King's Arms, but that changed in 1861. I'll let James Grafton, Jimmy Grafton's son, explain:

'A labourer named James Grafton 1st (I'm James Grafton 5th) was employed there as what was then termed "pub servant". Through his endeavours, he managed to buy the fixtures and fittings and become licensee and landlord in 1861. Although the pub was officially known as The King's Arms, the locals came to refer to it as Grafton's, which it soon officially became until May 1973, when my father and I left it. It then became Finnegan's Wake and is currently The Strutton Arms.

'*Goon Show* history will always refer to the pub as The Grafton Arms for some reason that no one has ever been able to discover. This is the name of a pub in Grafton Street, just off Tottenham Court Road and nothing whatever to do with the Goons.'

I'm afraid I, too, have been guilty of spreading that untruth – sorry, James.

I suppose now would be a good time to explain the term 'Goon'. This has nothing at all to do with World War II German guards, and everything to do with Popeye.

Harry, Peter, Michael and Spike were cartoon fans and regularly visited the cartoon cinema around the corner from the

Windmill, on Piccadilly Circus. There they would sit and rock with laughter at the antics of Tom and Jerry, Daffy Duck and Bugs Bunny. Popeye, too, was a favourite and it was this cartoon that featured large, dim-witted beings covered in hair and with big noses. These characters were called Goons and, as all four men felt a particular affinity with these simple, small-brained creatures, they appropriated their name.

Charles Chilton, an early producer of *Goon Shows*, recalls:

'We used to work in the Paris Theatre a lot, and we'd have lunch, then we'd all go down to the newsreel cinema, and in those days, newsreel cinemas ran newsreels and cartoons, and the reason we went was because Spike wanted to see Woody Woodpecker. And if you listen to the Goons, you can hear Woody Woodpecker in there quite often. It was this kind of humour that he went after.'

But back to Grafton's. Pay attention now, this gets a little confusing…Jimmy (James Grafton 4th) had inherited the pub from his father (James Grafton 3rd) who had inherited it from his father before him (James Grafton 2nd). Still with me?

James Grafton 5th takes up the story:

'My father had always wanted to write, but his father was a very strong character and wanted him to go to catering college, which he did. And then he became a commis waiter at Simpson's not long before the war. He was always a bit of a show-off and once, when he was serving soup, he put the ladle in the soup tureen and, with a big flourish, lifted the ladle high in the air…unfortunately, the other commis waiter hadn't put the plate underneath!'

After clearing up the soup, Jimmy was called up:

'He was a very serious soldier – at Arnhem, he got the British to fire on his own position because the Germans were right on him…that episode is in *A Bridge Too Far*…he was convinced that was the end of his life. He had to do it because otherwise the Germans would have got a lot further on…

'He got shell shock and ended up going to a hospital in the north of England somewhere…Then, in 1946, newly demobbed from the army, with a wife and two small children to support, he launched himself on the dual careers of pub landlord and radio scriptwriter.

'My father had always been a bit of a writer…it was while he was waiting to be demobbed that he got started, putting on shows for other men waiting to be demobbed. His father – James Grafton 3rd – had been killed during the war by a bomb, so my dad, being the first-born twin [Jimmy and his brother, Peter, were born 20 minutes apart], inherited the pub and therefore had an income. As far as I know, Dad had met somebody from the BBC during the war, which allowed him to get involved there and, by 1948, he was writing for *The Forces' Show, Workers' Playtime* and *Variety Bandbox*, the show during which he established a rapport with Derek Roy – a South African comedian. Derek subsequently introduced him to a friend of his called Michael Bentine…'

So that's how it all began…although Richard Bentine has a slightly different version of the story:

'Out of all the Goons, Dad and Harry were the ones who worked together first, if I remember correctly, because Harry was doing *Variety Bandbox* and Dad was writing bits and pieces for Harry. He and Dad ended up getting more laughs than the star of the show, and they got the note from the writer who said, "Why don't we meet for a drink?" That writer was Jimmy Grafton.

'I'm such a fan of my dad and I always take great pride in saying this, but he was genuinely the nicest person I think I ever met. He was also fond of your dad – they had similar laughs: they would both sort of explode. So Jimmy invited them down to Grafton's and they met up there.'

Whatever the actual sequence of events, the upshot was that Harry and Jimmy hit it off immediately. Dad, always on the lookout for new material, recognised a good thing when he saw it and Jimmy was soon writing for him. Later, he would become his agent and manager and the two remained firm friends, right up until Jimmy's death in 1986.

Soon, Spike had joined Mike and Harry at Grafton's and, before long, he was actually living there, sharing an attic room with Jimmy's pet vervet monkey called Johnny. The attic was right above the bar and Johnny, according to Spike, used to pee through a grille in the floor which opened over the food counter, leading Spike to warn his friends, 'Don't touch the soup!'

James Grafton continues:

'Spike came to live in the pub in 1951, when I was eight, and slept in the attic on the PSM (the Piss-Sodden Mattress – that's what we called it) and paid for his rent by working behind the bar. The monkey used to spend the days sitting on the hot-water tank in the kitchen and he allegedly used to pee into the Brown Windsor soup, although I never saw it happen.

'We also had a dumb waiter inside the bar and, one night, when Spike was working behind the bar, I put Johnny the monkey inside the dumb waiter and sent it down – Johnny leapt out and ran along the counter drinking everybody's drink.'

Having Spike Milligan as a house guest might seem to many people an invitation to madness and mayhem, but according to James and his sister Sally, he was a gentle, compassionate man and remarkably well-behaved.

Sally Grafton remembers:

'Because we used to have chimneys in the pub, Spike used to make up these stories about the Hobbley-Gobbley Men who lived up the chimneys, and they used to come down and do things, none of which I can now remember.

'Alfie from the Boneyard was like the bogeyman. He used to come along at night and take your bones out if you were naughty. Spike was very good with children. He had many childlike qualities. He could be a bit frightening when he got into one of his moods, but we never saw much of that – he used to lock himself away upstairs – he never really visited his moods on us.'

But when he wasn't making up stories for James and Sally, Spike was in the bar doing daft things with Harry, Mike and Peter. These four ex-servicemen shared a love of the absurd, and soon the nascent Goons had begun improvising wild sketches to bemused punters after hours at Grafton's.

Sally Grafton continues:

'I was really a bit young to understand a lot of what was going on. I was aware of them being there obviously, and of them being funny, but they were all surrogate uncles, really. Uncle Harry, Uncle Spike, Uncle Mike and Uncle Peter at a distance. Peter, if he wasn't being a character, wasn't very interesting at all. He was rather dull, but the others weren't.'

Although Peter was as much involved as the others in the tom-foolery that went on at Grafton's, he was the least approachable. Neither James nor Sally developed a relationship with him anywhere near as close as that they had with Spike and the others. Even to my father, who both admired and loved him, Peter was unfathomable. Dad once described him as 'a strange, distant, lonely man who, when he wasn't working, had all the charisma of a tax inspector'.

James Grafton is also able to offer his perspective:

'Peter was very remote, you could never get close to him at all; whereas Spike obviously, your father, very obviously, and Michael Bentine were all wonderfully approachable.

'I met him many, many years later...I was about 21 and

Peter had the Penthouse Suite at the Dorchester and my father asked me if I could take a script round to him…so I drove round there.

'I told them at reception, "I've got to take this up to Mr Sellers…"

'These days, they'd never have let you get near him, but then they said, "Yes, Penthouse, up you go…"

'Anyway, I knock on the door and Britt Ekland opens it – Peter's not there. So she says, "He'll be back in a minute, do come in." I thought I'd died and gone to heaven.

"Would you like a drink?" She poured me this enormous whisky, so I stayed there for about half an hour, talking to her.

'And in the end, when Peter still hadn't turned up, I gave her the script and said, "Thank you very much, but I ought to be going…" while I could still stand.

'So, I'm walking round the corridor at the top of the Dorchester and I see Peter coming the other way. "Hello, Peter," I said, "I've just left some scripts for you from my father…"

'He said, "Thank you," and carried on walking. Then he turned round and said, "Just a minute! It's James, isn't it?"

'Then he went into one of his things…"Hello, old man, how are you?" he put his arm around me…he went into a different persona. So there I am, back in with Britt, having another large whisky! Lovely experience…she was gorgeous.

'But that's as much as I know about Peter – he was totally remote.'

But when all four of them were together it was, apparently, a riot. What they actually got up to in the pub after hours is now lost in the mists of time, but Janet Brown, who, along with husband Peter Butterworth, was a Grafton's regular, gives us a flavour:

'Jimmy was a very affable fellow…I think Spike actually lived there…I can see Harry coming in…he always made us laugh so much when he came in, he would start demonstrating how different people walked: a night watchman going home, and somebody coming out of a shop... And then Peter Sellers, who was quite plump at the time, and he said to me that he was on a diet, and then he went over to the bar and got himself two scotch eggs and I thought, "What a weird diet!"

'Spike was there, of course, but I don't recollect so well what he got up to in the pub, I remember him more from various shows that we did...And Mike did this thing: he'd pretend he had a glass eye and he'd tap it with a coin...He got up to all kinds of weird things like that. I suppose that, at the time, you just accepted it because it was all to do with the Goons – they were all mad.'

At that time the pub was frequented by the up-and-coming of the comedy world: Alfred Marks, Tony Hancock, Sam Kydd, Dick Emery, Eric Sykes, Peter Butterworth, Graham Stark and Richard Hearn – better known as Mr Pastry. With their peers as an audience, the four started improvising mad routines, some of which Jimmy recorded on a clunky, reel-to-reel tape-recorder. With this wonderful new toy, they used to play a game called 'Tapesequences', a form of the old game of 'Consequences'. Someone would murmur the beginning of a story into the microphone, then pass it on to the next person. The next person would hear only the final sentence recorded by the previous person and had to take the story on from there. Then the mic was passed on again...and again...At the end, the whole would be played back, to much hilarity. Sadly, these tapes are now lost, but James Grafton recalls:

'Dad was a gadget freak, he had a wristwatch tape-recorder that used to record along a wire. You had the recorder itself in your pocket and the wire went down the arm into the wristwatch. He also had an old Grundig tape-recorder and, during closing time, it was on the bar. And that's when they used to do it. I was too young, really, to appreciate it...

'My dad was a night person...and there would always be a

whole load of ideas coming forth all at the same time and that was the way they used to write *The Goon Show*…I used to sit in on some of the later meetings and I couldn't stop laughing… they used to go off at so many tangents…completely lose the plot. That's the way Dad always used to write until Spike took everything under his own wing…'

Another game they indulged in was making up limericks. The most famous they produced goes like this:

There was a young man from Cathay,
On a slow boat to China one day,
Got trapped near the tiller
By a sex-crazed gorilla –
And China's a bloody long way!

Jimmy Grafton – now christened KOGVOS: Keeper Of the Goons, Voice Of Sanity – saw an opportunity. With all this raw talent hurtling around his pub, he suggested they harness some of the madness, shape it into a script and try and get the BBC interested. Bear in mind that radio comedy of the time was nothing like what the Goons were doing. Steve Punt observes:

'The thing that fascinates me about it now, knowing a bit more about comedy history, is that radio comedy had only been around for about 13 years before *The Goon Show* started, because before 1938, the only comedy that was on the radio was Variety – people doing their act on a bill, like a Variety show transferred to the radio. There wasn't a proper comedy series, in the sense that we know it: regular cast, same writers, same characters…that didn't happen until 1938, which is amazing. So, radio comedy was still a very young genre, and the rules weren't established.

'*I.T.M.A.* was the big show of the forties, and then *Much Binding in the Marsh,* coming out of that. So by the time *The Goon Show* started, radio comedy was still very much open to experiment – nobody really knew the rules. *The Goons* did take the idea of the central figure and lots and lots of characters coming in and out as in *I.T.M.A.*, which had also used the device of the door opening and closing…but, of course, the big difference was that *The Goons* had a much smaller cast. They had that feeling of a bunch of blokes who'd got together in a pub and knew all the silly voices that each other did. And Milligan was custom-writing this stuff for his friends: "I know you can do, this, this and this voice…and you can do this voice, this voice and this voice, so let's just have fun!" And I don't think there's been another show I can think of where the writing is that integrated with the performers.

'The reason why it's a great show as opposed to just a good show, is that it has a quality that's very rare. I think *Python* had it and probably *The Young Ones* had it, and maybe early Vic Reeves had it…and that's the quality of a private joke going public. Most comedy writers will think, "Now, what sort of joke tends to work here? What makes people laugh? How can we craft these jokes?" There's nothing wrong with that – that's the craft of comedy writing. But *The Goon Show* was very much: "This is what makes us laugh, and maybe it'll make you laugh as well." And I think it's a very brave thing to do. It's one of those very rare programmes where you get a glimpse into what is essentially a private world and it tends to create – when it works – really great shows.'

This was the ground – the Strutton Ground, if you like – out of which *The Goon Show* sprang. But although the conception may have been fun, *The Goon Show* did not have an easy birth.

3

Introducing Those Crazy People, the Goons!

As Sellers was the most well-known of the group, Jimmy and Spike concocted a scenario around him to be called *Sellers' Castle*. Set in a crumbling stately home owned by 'the twenty-second *(FX: SHOT. SCREAM)*, I beg your pardon, the twenty-third Lord Sellers...', it featured Milligan as an Eccles-type butler, Bentine as a mad professor who did unspeakable things in the basement and my father as the singing protégé of impresario Alfred Marks. Also in the cast were Robert Moreton, Peter Butterworth, Janet Brown and Andrew Timothy. Timothy (who, incidentally, was the father of Christopher and, rather more interestingly, the man after whom I was named) was a well-known radio announcer, brought in by Jimmy to give the show a certain BBC gravitas.

Sellers' Castle was recorded in a tiny Soho studio sometime in 1950 and obviously made a huge impression on the young Janet Brown. When I asked her about her involvement, she could remember absolutely nothing about it.

The recording was duly handed over to BBC producer, Roy Speer, whom Jimmy knew well. Speer was interested and, a few days later, just to make sure the whole thing wasn't a load of drunken ad-libbing by a group of mates, invited the cast to come and read the script to him. He was impressed enough to schedule the recording of a pilot, in a proper BBC studio.

Anyone who has listened to a *Goon Show* cannot fail to notice the rapport between the performers and the audience actually present in the theatre. Comedy such as the Goons' cannot exist in a vacuum; it depends for its life on live performance, feeding off the audience reaction.

Unfortunately, the task of producing the pilot fell to Jacques Brown, a man with strong views on radio comedy, one of which was that it should not have to rely on a studio audience.

Bobby Jay, an early studio manager on *The Goon Show*, perfectly sums up why a live audience was, and remains such an important part of radio comedy: 'The audience was tremendously important – a live audience was what you wanted. It's no good having one that sits there quietly while you go through a lot of funny remarks, because no one has told you that it's perfectly acceptable to laugh and enjoy yourself.'

Jacques Brown, however, unable to grasp this simple fact, recorded the pilot in a cold, empty studio, totally devoid of atmosphere. This lifeless recording was then passed, without reference to Jimmy Grafton, to the programme planners. Unsurprisingly, *Sellers' Castle* was turned down flat and Jimmy never talked to Jacques Brown again.

Trying to get a foot in the door of the BBC must have seemed like a daunting task. The 'gods' of comedy then were people like Tommy Handley and Ted Ray – middle-aged men in three-piece suits who purveyed safe, middle-class humour to middle-England. How could four, young, anarchic ex-squaddies hope to penetrate the cosy, wood-panelled corridors of the BBC?

Steve Punt who, with the popular and subversive radio show *The Mary Whitehouse Experience*, also came up against the BBC's withering disdain, sums up how it feels to be a young comedian, daunted by the corporation's comedy heritage:

'Another of the fascinating things about the Goons is the generation gap, because I think, certainly for my generation, we always saw the Goons in middle age, because they all were when I was a child: on *Parkinson* or whatever…but actually, of course, during *The Goon Show*, they were young men, which explains its enormous appeal to teenagers, like my dad.

'Radio shows tended to be recorded in proper theatres…one was a converted cinema – a place called the Paris, which was a wonderful place – we did *The Mary Whitehouse Experience* there, just before it closed. My mum and dad used to go there to watch the recording of *Beyond our Ken*. It was a truly wonderful building and absolutely reeked comedy history. But it was actually an awful place to record as a young comic, because it pushed its history in your face, because you would walk down the stairs and, at every step, on the wall there'd be a picture of Tony Hancock, then the Goons, then Kenneth Horne, and it really felt like it was saying: "You really shouldn't be here. Do you have any idea what this building has done?" But it was a great place…because it had a low ceiling, it sat about 300, it wasn't so big that the laughs start to take up too much air time, it was just the right size and had a terrific atmosphere. And because it was a converted cinema rather than a theatre, it also had a very low stage, so the audience weren't having to stare right up at the performers. So the audience and performers were perfectly positioned in relation to each other.'

Happily, after the *Sellers' Castle* débâcle, the Goons found other champions. Pat Dixon, who had already worked with Harry, Peter and Mike, was one.

Charles Chilton recalls, 'Pat Dixon was an Oxford don and he used to have wonderful ideas for programmes, do two or three of them and get tired. So somebody else would take them over and he'd think of something else.'

Peter submitted a tape to Dixon on which he'd recorded some Goon-like exchanges with Spike, and Dixon went back to the planners to persuade them to give the Goons a second chance. Eventually, fed up with Dixon's constant badgering, the powers that be relented and, in February of 1951, another pilot was scheduled.

Bobby Jay was present at that recording:

'I think it was called *Crazy People* in those days…and it was marvellous, because they just knew they were on to something that was going to be very, very interesting. And, of course, it was the start of what somebody once called *The Go On Show*.

'I remember that the first one – Pat Dixon was actually producing it – was just a trial. And, after we'd finished recording, with all its crazy gags and everything, he just turned to the mic and said to the people who'd been listening [presumably the BBC commissioning editors], "Look, this is not me, this is not the sort of show I want to be involved with… So, if you don't mind, I think it should go to a person who can best do it – somebody who is mad enough to take it on." Which, of course, was Dennis Main Wilson…'

Main Wilson (christened Main Drain by the Goons for his seemingly inexhaustible ability to sink pints of Guinness) was another regular at Grafton's and already a huge fan of these four wild men.

The pilot was a success and the first series was scheduled for May of that year. This series was billed by the BBC, in their wisdom, as *Those Crazy People, the Goons*, describing them as 'the Junior Crazy Gang'. But by the second series, the BBC, bowing to pressure from its creators, had the good sense to re-brand it *The Goon Show*, despite some crusty, senior executive insisting on calling it, *The Go On Show*.

Steve Punt observes:

'American radio comedy, which was very influential because of the war, tended to be very smart, lots of wit and one-liners, lots of double-acts with clever cross-talk. But I think the British, as ever, were into something slightly weirder and more surreal and messier, and using the fact that all the Goon performers, away from *The Goons*, were all Variety performers as well, so they all had these individual skills that they specialised in. Like

Secombe's shaving act, which, when you think about it, is tremendously contemporary. I've seen acts at Jongleurs [a famous London comedy club] like that – you can imagine now, seeing somebody shaving in the style of different people, as a totally contemporary comedy idea…'

The first six episodes were written by Jimmy, Spike and Larry Stephens – one of Tony Hancock's writers, and vastly more experienced than Spike – and were a far cry from later *Goon Shows*. They were, in essence, a series of unconnected sketches with musical interludes performed by the Ray Ellington Quartet, The Stargazers and Max Geldray. Even Dad got in on the act, belting out Italian arias. In one early recording, he sings 'Vesti la Giubba', the tragic aria from *I Pagliacci* where the Clown – his heart broken from learning that his wife plans to run away with her lover – prepares to go on stage and do his comic turn. 'Ridi Pagliaccio' (laugh, clown) he sings, sobbing all over the microphone – all in all, a strange choice of song for a comedy show.

The contemporary comedian and performer, Mitch Benn, says:

'You get the impression that they were adrift in search of a format for the early shows, and I suppose they thought, "Well, if Harry wants to do a bit of *I Pagliacci*, let him and see what happens…"

'Now, when you listen to them, the Max and Ray interludes do seem pretty incongruous, but then, 10 years later, *Round the Horne* was putting the Frazer Hayes Four on in the middle. It was just what you did in radio – you didn't do half-hour straight comedy, you had musical interludes, because the whole thing's coming out of Variety, isn't it? Even Pete and Dud used to have people like Lulu on. Right up until the seventies, with *The Two Ronnies* bunging Barbara Dixon on in the middle of it. And later still, *The Young Ones* had bands on: Dexy's Midnight Runners would suddenly materialise in the kitchen. But that, apparently, was to get more money – if they stuck a band on they qualified as light entertainment and got more money.'

In the early shows, Sellers was the main 'turn' and performed, amongst other things, a Bloodnok monologue; Spike was Eccles and other assorted idiots; Mike did a routine as his mad professor, now christened Osric Pureheart; Andrew Timothy announced; and, when he wasn't singing, my father spouted reams of high-pitched gibberish. In later series, you'll note that there is no opportunity for Harry to exercise his top Cs, nor does he sing on any of the records the Goons made, because at some point in the early fifties he signed exclusively to Philips, the terms of his contract forbidding him from singing for any other record label.

There was also a 'spot FX' man in place during the recordings, to perform on-the-spot sound-effects. Steve Punt explains:

'On radio, not only can you use sound, but the audience can see how the sound is made. This is something, tragically, which has changed…nowadays there is very little of what used to be called spot effects, which is basically a bloke at the side of the stage surrounded by coconut shells and sheets of corrugated iron and, literally, a box with gravel in it. The spot FX man was sort of part of the show.

'One of the things I love about *The Goon Show* is that it sounds like they're enjoying themselves. There's often corpsing…there's often off-mic laughing. There's often bits left in where you can hear people off-mic talking, or making comments to each other, because things didn't tend to be edited that closely.'

Bobby Jay was occasionally called upon to play the role of the spot FX man. He says:

'Spike was marvellous, we got on very well, because he used to think up crazy things, thinking that we would never be able to provide them. But we always did, and it was always a bit better than even he thought of, and he loved that.

'Once I had to run up and down a flight of stairs for what seemed like five minutes, in order that Spike could come in and say, "That's funny – I live in a bungalow!"'

The second series followed more or less the same format, but was to be the last in which Mike appeared. There has been much speculation over the reasons for Mike's departure, and the whole affair seems to be cloaked in an impenetrable mist, something which Barry Cryer believes, too:

'Yes, there is a wonderful mist around it. Sadly, I think there was a big ego clash there. Mike thought he was underrated as one of the creators of the style...and I think there was a resentment that everybody went, "Milligan, Milligan, Milligan..." and all that...Then Mike went to the US to do something and, when he came back, I think they'd drafted Graham Stark in. It was like – the door was closed, he wasn't in *The Goon Show* any more.'

This account chimes with what James Grafton remembers:

'He left *The Goon Show* because he was too much competition for Spike, basically. Spike just left him out. Mike went to America and, when he came back, his place just didn't exist any more. They did have their creative differences...they were very much on the same track, when you think about what Mike did later: *Potty Time* and *It's a Square World*.'

Here's what my Dad says about it in the second volume of his autobiography, *Strawberries and Cheam*:

'As the second series wore on, Mike Bentine began to show signs that he was not too happy with the way things were going. When we all sat around discussing ideas for the show, he and

Spike used to throw off ideas for scripts like sparks from a Catherine wheel and it became inevitable that when some of these ideas actually appeared in the script, both would claim authorship. This led to some friction, and Dennis Main Wilson, the producer...did not seem to be able to control us. After all, we were all about the same age and, like most ex-servicemen, were not too willing to accept authority. We had had enough of that.

'I was not privy to the other reasons why Mike decided to leave *The Goon Show*. My Variety commitments took me all over the country, and the only time I met the others was on the Sunday of the recording, so I was not aware of any power struggles that might have been going on.

'Looking back on those days, I realise that I must have been surprisingly naïve. In any event, I was sorry to see Michael go.'

Maybe there was an element of creative rivalry between Spike and Michael; it's also been suggested that Peter was jealous of Mike because he'd been to Eton and made Sellers feel inferior. But whenever explosively creative people get together, sparks will fly. Whatever it was that Michael found so discomfiting, it was proving a drain on his nerves and he was nervous enough as it was. Janet Brown remembers working with him, saying, 'I do know that when Mike and I did the odd broadcast he'd break out in such a rash...with the concern, I suppose.'

Charles Chilton knew Michael well, and worked with him regularly after the *Goons*. He adds, 'Bentine didn't get on somehow...I don't know, he didn't get on with Spike or something, and so...I did another series with Mike on radio and, meanwhile, *The Goons* got going, without Michael Bentine...very few people remember now that he was ever in the show at all.'

Which I think is a shame. It is true that Mike and Spike had different ways of working; Mike's later work tends more to the visual, whereas Spike's comedy remains rooted in wordplay.

Richard Bentine also remembers this critical difference, adding, 'In the same way that Spike revelled in delivering a gag that had no visual element at all, Dad was almost the reverse – he loved having a gag that in script terms had one word and he'd have to explain to the director why it was going to be funny.'

Mike, in his autobiography, *The Long Banana Skin*, says he left of his own volition, 'falling on his sword' because it seemed that in comedy terms three was a magic number, viz. the Marx Brothers; the Ritz Brothers and the Three Stooges. I think this is an unlikely reason to leave a show that's just starting to make ground. But, whatever his motivation, it's probably too late now to get to the bottom of Mike's departure. His going, however, seemed to leave no lasting scars. He later made a 'guest appearance' in one *Goon Show* and the four of them continued to meet as friends.

But Mike's departure didn't stop the squabbling and a lot has been made, by journalists and biographers alike, of the 'violent animosity' between Peter and Spike, something that Charles Chilton remembers, too:

'Peter Sellers was a bit eccentric and, of course, as he became more famous he became more and more…I wouldn't say troublesome, but difficult. I remember one time, he and Spike had a row and they wouldn't talk to each other. So when we were checking the script before the broadcast, Peter would say to me, "Would you tell the author that I can't say this stupid line here."

'And I'd say to Spike, "He says he can't say this stupid line."

'And Spike would say, "He'll say it and like it."

'And this was the atmosphere before we went on the air. Of course, Harry used to giggle all the time when all this quarrelling was going on. He used to go into the corner and laugh his insides out. "Listen to them, listen to them!" he used to say…

'The rehearsals were fun. Some people said that they were sometimes better than the actual show. They were hysterical sometimes, and usually when Milligan and Sellers didn't agree, they were most hysterical of all.'

It's true that Spike was not always the easiest person to work with but, as Jane Milligan – Spike's daughter with his second wife, Paddy – explains, his frustrations were always about getting it right:

'I still feel like Dad's arguing with the BBC from his grave! I remember him getting a bit grumpy if things weren't right, or props were wrong, or sounds were wrong, which I'm sure was very similar in *The Goons* – very frustrated about things being wrong. And looking at the scripts now, I just find it fascinating how organised they were: all the characters were there in the scripts, and effects and sound, and orchestra…I love the organisation behind this chaos – brilliant.'

Barry Cryer knew both Peter and Spike:

'I never saw any animosity between Peter and Spike. I saw Spike over in the corner, not communing with Peter much, but I didn't attribute anything serious to that, it was just that Spike was locked into his thoughts and worried about what he was going to do next…Peter seemed to love every minute of it.
  'When I used to go to recordings…Peter was over the moon. And it's very interesting, later in life – Hollywood film star and everything – Peter would love to turn the conversation to *The Goon Show* and say, "That was a happy time." He was like a kid during *The Goon Show*.'

My sister Jennifer, who, as a publicist, worked with Dad, Spike and Peter, was well placed to observe their relationship: 'They were kind of like brothers in a way. I'm sure there's was a bit of 'Oh, bloomin' heck, what's he said now?' that used to go on between them, but at heart, I think, they appreciated each other's friendship and humour.'
  But I'll leave the last word on this famous rivalry to someone closer to the action, Sile Milligan:

'When we were young, our two families [the Milligans and the

Sellers] were very intertwined, and we spent a lot of time together, and I think the reason being that, when parents get on, if they've got kids of around the same age, they just get stuck together and they have to deal with it. But we did get on with Peter's kids and while the adults were doing their thing, the kids were playing somewhere else.

'Then Peter "went away" – he split up with Anne [his first wife], so their family environment must have become a bit dysfunctional. Dad used to meet Peter all the time…I'm sure it's recognised now, but long before it was generally recognised, Dad realised that Peter had to be a manic-depressive…they used to phone each other up and go, "I'm bad…meet you at Ronnie Scott's…"

'Peter and Dad got on well and I think a lot of it was due to this thread of depression – and they'd try and pull each other out of it. But from what I read in the newspapers, they hated each other and Dad was always trying to kill Peter…it's all just a load of magnified crap. I'm not saying that things weren't said…but it's like the wife walking into the kitchen and saying to her husband, "I hate you, I'm going to kill you!" and then the next day he dies accidentally and, of course, then it's the wife who must have done it because the day before she threatened to kill him. There were times of love/hate between Peter and Dad, but nothing massively antagonistic.'

With Bentine's departure, *The Goon Show*, as most people remember it, began to take shape. Peter Eton, ex-Royal Navy, took over production from Dennis Main Wilson and proved to be much harder to please than the easygoing Wilson. He was, in fact, just what the Goons needed, bringing a sense of order to the chaos, making them rehearse properly, teaching them proper microphone technique and pushing them to give of their very best. Under his guidance, the show grew, reaching a standard none of them ever believed possible, with Charles Chilton observing:

'*The Goon Show* was well in advance of anything else, and

Spike wouldn't let anything go that wasn't absolutely right. Sometimes the effects weren't good enough, so he'd re-record them, doing them all with his mouth. They were all done from the throat and things like that.

'I don't think we were aware that it was going to be as important as it turned out to be. And some, Peter Eton for example, didn't seem to be affected by it at all. Peter Eton had lost a leg at Dunkirk, but he was a very good producer. He was very calm, and limped around with his one leg, telling people off – his other leg lying in the English Channel somewhere.'

Steve Punt also has his own take on the contemporary nature of *The Goon Show*:

'I think that *The Goons* was more grounded in contemporary culture than one actually thinks. It's never thought of as a satirical show, but actually a lot of the stories are based around spoofing current films and political events.

'There's an amazing one from early 1955 which is all about the stars of ITV and it's a parody of Orwell's *1984*. The BBC is the "Big Brother Corporation" and the show is called *1985*, because it was recorded in 1955. The thing is that BBC television had done a famous version of *1984* on the telly just a few months earlier, which had caused a very big stir at the time – the famous last scene with the rats (in Room 101). I think Peter Cushing was in it. And a rat on the telly in the mid-fifties, when it was still Sylvia Peters and *Muffin the Mule*…If you were used to *Pinky and Perky*, an actual rat on your screen was quite shocking. So it was a big thing at the time.

'The show is full of contemporary references and references to contemporary celebrities. There's a running joke of Room 101 being a place where all these terribly traditional Home Service radio programmes are continuously played at you. They're all obviously the kind of programmes that Milligan couldn't stand, like Wilfred Pickles and things like that…I don't know what the equivalent would be nowadays, but it's a bit like you're sitting there bombarded with *Antiques Roadshow* or something…This, for Milligan, summed up the old world BBC…'

The Goon Show continued to grow in sophistication; the same characters started to appear week after week, becoming more defined; the sound effects grew in ambition and complexity; The Stargazers were axed and my father gagged, reducing the musical interludes to two, which were supplied by Ray Ellington and harmonica player Max Geldray. And now the show had a single plot, revolving around a central character.

Steve Punt identifies this 'new age' of comedy, and the ages of the comedians, as being hugely significant:

'*The Goon Show* was very young comedy, as compared to *I.T.M.A.* – Tommy Handley was middle-aged. So, all of a sudden, along come the Goons…none of whom are that established, and they arrive as a group. This must have felt at the time very much like the kids taking over the asylum…

'Sellers, particularly, was very young – about 23, 24. And up at the top of the BBC were people who'd been there in Lord Reith's era and they really didn't like it. They didn't understand it and it felt like a mess to them. It didn't have the reassuring figure at the centre. It did, but the figure at the centre was just as insane as everybody revolving around him…'

The figure at the centre was a character called Neddie Seagoon, played by my father in a manic, high-pitched tenor. Incidentally, Neddie's voice is high-pitched for a good reason. Dad's singing teacher, Maestro Manlio di Veroli – who was a contemporary of Gigli – took a dim view of Harry's vocal shenanigans in *The Goon Show*, informing him that if he was determined to carry on messing around like that, the only way of protecting his voice was to place it high in the tenor register to keep it 'off' his vocal chords. It seemed to work.

Neddie was the idiot around whom the plots revolved and was

the driving force behind what coherent narrative there was. Informed by Spike's wartime experiences and the characters of the officers and men he served with, Neddie is an odd mixture of patriotism, heroism, stupidity and avarice. Neddie will do anything for money and because of this is always falling foul of the dastardly Grytpype-Thynne and his sidekick Moriarty.

Mitch Benn remembers:

'Harry had the most important and least flashy job. Partly because, apart from a few minor characters, Harry only gets to do Neddie. Milligan gets to do all his silly voices: Eccles, Minnie Bannister, etc., and Sellers gets to do his dazzling array of characters: one of the best excuses to show off a comic performer has ever had…

'Harry would occasionally turn up as random Welshmen. But the thing about Neddie's voice is that it's the hardest voice to do…mainly because it's not a voice that anybody's putting on – it's just Harry given full rein. But he's a fantastic character, Neddie, because he's the quintessential British hero – the heroic idiot. *The Goons* is unimaginable without Neddie.'

Sarah Sellers also notes the dynamic, contemporary style that characterised the show:

'It was fun and it was cutting edge…it's hard to put oneself in that place, but after the war years and everything, then suddenly there was this wacky humour that…I suppose it did have boundaries, but it seemed like it didn't at the time…They could really take the piss out of anything and they did, so it was new and fresh.'

During the fourth series, Andrew Timothy departed, saying that he 'feared for his sanity', and Wallace Greenslade stepped into the breach. Incidentally, during the second series, Spike really was in danger of losing his mind after suffering a mental breakdown due to the enormous pressure of having to come up with original scripts, week after week. Jimmy Grafton and Larry Stephens stepped in and continued writing the scripts while Spike took a well-earned rest. Spike soon felt well enough to resume writing duties, but not performing. Sellers took over Spike's parts and both Dick Emery and Graham Stark were drafted in from time to time to help out, although I do remember Dad telling me that there was more than one occasion when all the parts were played by him and Sellers alone, but which shows they actually were, I'm afraid I no longer remember.

I'm not sure exactly when or how the famous 'warm-up' started. This was a string of mad routines performed before the recording, to get the audience 'in the mood'. One of these routines was 'Braces-O', which consisted of Dad coming on stage, taking his place at the microphone and, accompanied by Ray Ellington's pianist, Dick Katz, starting to sing 'Falling in Love with Love'.

After a few bars, Peter would come on, remove Dad's braces and walk off-stage with them. Then, as Dad continued, Spike entered, took an exaggerated bow and, as he sang the final top notes, Dad would step forward and pull Spike's trousers down. Apparently, at one recording, Spike forgot to wear underpants, which provoked gasps from the audience, especially as that afternoon it consisted mainly of nuns.

Another bit of warm-up madness, which was filmed for posterity before *The Last Goon Show of All*, was the brandy and milk routine, where Dad, once again at the microphone singing, arms outstretched, had a pint pot thrust into his hand by Peter. Then Spike came on, poured half a pint of milk into it, followed by half a bottle of brandy. They then rushed off-stage to drink it.

Sometimes, the laughs they got during the warm-up would be sneaked into the programme with a bit of subtle editing. Charles Chilton recalls:

'They stuck to the script more or less. Spike knew that the show could be edited, so sometimes he would do outrageous things in order to stir the audience up and get a good laugh. Sometimes we used laughs for gags which were actually laughs that we'd got for something else that we couldn't broadcast – usually something a bit "off colour". So we used to do a bit of editing there – put a very good laugh to a pretty weak joke.'

Charged with the onerous task of making sure that everything was in place before a recording, the life of a studio manager on *The Goon Show* was fraught with difficulty. But, as Bobby Jay remembers, it wasn't only the lads who were capable of causing him distress:

'Peter would always want to play the drums during the warm-up, and so they had to be set from the beginning, on rostra. I remember once, before the recording, I was making sure the rostra were in the right place, because the boys used to muck around a lot…and I stamped on one of these rostra and it moved slightly. So, in order to get something to wedge it in place, I went to the cupboard where we used to keep all sorts of rubbish – leads, bits of equipment, etc. – and I opened the door to find a producer and his female assistant…they definitely looked as though they didn't want to be disturbed. Huge embarrassment!'

Life at the BBC back in the fifties certainly sounds like a lot of fun!

Barry Cryer, a young, eager *Goon* fan during the show's heyday, was actually present at several of the recordings:

'I saw a recording of *The Goon Show* at the Camden Palace…I saw them more than once, but memory plays tricks…I think they worked at the Playhouse, down Northumberland Avenue, but Camden Palace sticks in my mind…

'There was a lot of messing about and a lot of editing after, I suppose, but they were pretty disciplined on the whole, and Harry steamed it through…What I loved was hearing him laughing in the background…he still loved listening to the others – typical Harry.

'The atmosphere at these recordings was like a party – a terrific atmosphere. I didn't expect that atmosphere at a radio show. It communicated with the audience…and we were the faithful, you know. It was great, you could smell it.

'I never met them in those days, I was just an oik around the place…just a fan. It was Harry I met first…and then Spike, then Mike and I never really got to know Peter, but then, who did?'

By Series Four, Jimmy Grafton's name had disappeared from the writing credits and, from then on, more and more of the scripts were written by Milligan alone. Larry Stephens continued to contribute from time to time, and the names of other writers also occasionally appeared in the credits, such as Eric Sykes, who was Spike's colleague at Associated London Scripts. Steve Punt says of the writing process:

'You don't know quite where this stuff comes from. There's a tremendously complicated mix of stuff going on in Milligan's mind. And another thing that's very noticeable…is that he hadn't really served a writing apprenticeship. Most people who wrote radio comedy had come up writing little spots and sketches for people…Muir and Norden, for example, had been around writing jokes for people for years – terrific writers – but they had served an apprenticeship before they started doing *Take it From Here*, whereas Milligan had spent two years after the war touring in a jazz band. He'd had a breakdown in Italy after being shelled, and then he lived in a pub. Then there was that amazing era of slouching around London in a duffel coat under rationing, trying to get work…auditioning at the Windmill…And, suddenly, *The Goon Show* seems to have sprung out of all that virtually fully formed. So Milligan didn't know the rules, much to his benefit.'

All the major characters were gradually becoming household names. Their voices and catchphrases – 'You've deaded me!'…

'He's fallen in the water!'…'No more curried eggs for me!' – could be heard in school playgrounds and university halls the length and breadth of the country…and beyond.

In 1954, the BBC Transcription Service started recording the shows and passing them on to organisations in other countries and thence to a worldwide audience. It was probably this, more than anything else, that was responsible for triggering the collapse of the British empire.

Steve Punt says:

'There is, I suppose, as a result of that generation that came out of the war, this great feeling of camaraderie about *The Goon Show* and it's a show – I don't know whether it's because it's an all-male show that it particularly appeals to men, but most of the famous fans do seem to be men – that shows men in a rather good light, in the sense that it's a terribly non-threatening, friendly place to be.

'It seems to be a product of that generation who had met in the worst possible conditions, where any one of them could have been killed the next day and, because of that, there's this terrific feelgood factor about it. Life is here for living: let's just do silly voices and have fun.

'And, above all, there's the voices…because when you say *The Goon Show*, the first thing people think of is the voices. They were, I suppose, party-piece voices that everyone of my dad's generation could do – and would…and still do. And they passed them down through the generations. There are probably people out there who occasionally lapse into those voices possibly without even knowing quite where they come from, it's that embedded in the national consciousness.'

With each series, the programme continued to grow in popularity. But whatever it was that made it such a popular show, Bobby Jay is certain it wasn't down to the efforts of the BBC:

'*The Goon Show* was immensely important – there was nothing like it before…it was called *Crazy People* and they were crazy people.

'I would like to think that the BBC's attitude to comedy changed with *The Goon Show*, but I don't really think so…I don't suppose they even listened to it, frankly, but they were still surprised that it was getting a lot of popularity – they couldn't quite understand why.'

With the popularity of the Goons steadily increasing, outside the show the three performers continued to succeed as solo artistes. Harry branched out sideways into more radio, taking over from Tony Hancock as Archie Andrews's teacher in the hit show *Educating Archie*. Archie was the dummy of ventriloquist Peter Brough. You might think that having a ventriloquist on radio is missing the point, but Dad always maintained that radio was the best thing that could have happened for Peter Brough. Notwithstanding Mr Brough's shortcomings in the ventriloquial art, *Educating Archie* was a huge success and, for a couple of years in the early fifties, Dad would record both *The Goon Show* and *Educating Archie* on the same Sunday.

Spike and Peter were also making a name for themselves outside the Goons, despite occasional bouts of bad behaviour, as Janet Brown recalls:

'I can remember I was with Spike in Southampton and Spike didn't like the audience and he went up and locked himself in his dressing room and played his trumpet – he wouldn't come out. On another occasion, he told an unappreciative audience in Coventry, "I hope you get bombed again!"

'Peter was a wonderful performer, but he did get very bored in theatre, doing the same thing night after night. One night, when appearing in a show called *Brouhaha* at the Aldwych Theatre, he was so bored that he took his camera on stage and started taking pictures of the audience.'

Also in Coventry, Peter once walked on stage with a gramophone and a chair and, instead of going into his act, said to the audience that he had just bought a record that he'd enjoyed so much, he wanted to share it with them. It was an EP of Wally Stott playing Christmas songs. He put the record on the turntable, sat down and listened, humming along. Once it had finished, he got up, bowed, and left the stage.

And it wasn't only the Goons themselves who enjoyed playing practical jokes, as Janet Brown recalls:

'I remember when I was appearing at the Met, Edgware Road, this story was going round backstage that two very important Arab princes were in one night. We could see these two figures, dressed in Arab robes, sitting in one of the boxes. So the cast gave their all for these Arab potentates and, after, we were presented to them, only to find, under the robes, Ray Ellington and Max Geldray.'

The Goon Show continued, more or less in the same format, until its demise in 1960. The show was scheduled to end after the ninth series but, due to a public outcry, Milligan produced another six scripts for Series Ten. There were 'specials' to follow, including *The Last Goon Show of All*, but the last *Goon Show* proper, which ended the tenth and final series, was originally broadcast on the 28 January 1960, entitled *The Last Smoking Seagoon*.

4

Early Days

So, during all the feverish activity around the birth of the Goons, what was going on behind the scenes?

In 1949 – when, between bouts of looking for work, Secombe, Bentine, Milligan and Sellers were meeting occasionally at Grafton's and entertaining the punters after hours – my sister, Jennifer, was born in my grandparents' council house in West Cross, Mumbles.

The night she made her entrance, Dad was appearing at Feldman's Theatre, Blackpool, with another ex-serviceman-turned-comic, Tony Hancock. Between shows on the Monday night, Dad received the news of the arrival of his first-born. Understandably keen to celebrate, he arranged with Tony to go out after the second show. Unfortunately, by the time the two of them left the theatre, all the pubs and restaurants were closed and the only place they could find open was a fish and chip shop. They celebrated Jennifer's arrival with haddock and chips and foaming glasses of Tizer – in my father's own words, 'an aggressively non-alcoholic beverage'.

I followed my sister four years later, on 26 April 1953. By the time of my arrival, my grandparents had moved to a new house just around the corner, in Heathwood Road, roughly the mid-point between Swansea and the Mumbles Pier on the South Wales coast. From my gran's front window, over a patch of waste ground we used to call 'the field', which in summer was knee-deep in grass and butterflies, there was a wide view of Swansea

Bay. To the east, at the far end of one curving arm, lay Swansea Docks, and beyond, Port Talbot Steel Works, where my grandfather, 'Bampa' Jim, worked. At dusk, it was possible to see the red flash as they opened the great furnace doors to the sky – this was Gran's cue to get Bampa's tea on. To the west was the distant pier with its lifeboat station and, on stormy days, Jen and I would gaze longingly up at the grey sky, praying there'd be an emergency and that the rocket would go up – the signal for the lifeboat crew to assemble. Once we'd spotted the red flare, we would fix our eyes on the distant pier and wait for the splash of the lifeboat as it hurtled down the slipway and crashed into the sea, with no thought then either about the brave souls risking their lives on the lifeboat, nor those to whom the crew was racing to save from a watery grave – to us it was all just adventure.

But quite apart from the excitement provided by its attendant lifeboat station, Jen and I had a lot to thank that pier for. It was at a dance there, in 1946, that a recently demobbed serviceman with a Canadian accent, wearing a checked shirt and chewing imaginary gum, had first invited the young Myra Joan Atherton on to the floor. Luckily, for me – and, indeed, my siblings – she accepted. The Canadian turned out to be a local boy called Harry Secombe – a struggling comedian – who only adopted the accent because he thought it would make him appear more attractive. What effect he thought the checked shirt would have, we can only guess at.

After the dance, which went well – Dad was always light on his feet – the two arranged to meet the next day at the Plaza cinema in Swansea.

But waking the next morning with a hangover, Harry – having removed his army-issue, wire-framed glasses before the dance to improve his chances – worried that the girl he'd arranged to meet the night before, attractive through a softly enhancing myopic haze, might not turn out to be the beauty he'd imagined. So, 20 minutes before they were due to meet, Harry turned up at the cinema.

The Plaza had a portico in the classical style, supported by several stout pillars, and it was behind one of these he hid to wait for her. If he liked what he saw, he'd stay. If not, he'd creep quietly home and have an early night. He waited… and waited. Finally, ten minutes after the film had started, she still hadn't appeared. Resigning himself to a lonely walk home, he stepped out from behind his pillar only to see Myra step out from behind hers. It was obvious these two were made for each other.

The life of a second-spot comedian in post-war Britain was not a glamorous one. Apart from the difficulty in getting around the country, which necessitated long, tedious journeys on draughty, uncomfortable trains, the theatre audience could not always be relied upon to be supportive once you actually got there.

In Bolton, during the first house on a Monday, after walking on stage with his shaving kit, Dad greeted the audience with his usual, cheery opening line: 'Hello, folks! I've only just arrived in the theatre. The train was late and I haven't had time to shave yet. So, as I'm doing it, I'll give you some idea of how other people shave…' and he went into his act.

The audience, however, taking him at his word, were mutely furious with this young upstart for not having the decency to shave before coming on stage to entertain them, and sat watching Dad's manic routine in stony silence. He walked off to the sound of his own footsteps to be met by the theatre manager, who paid him off there and then, telling him, 'You'll not shave in my bloody time!'

Then there was the problem of having to contend with truly awful digs ruled over by steely-eyed landladies with a less-than-flattering opinion of 'theatricals'.

However, after his season at the Windmill, work began to pick up, enabling Harry to buy Myra an engagement ring.

He was not an instant hit with his prospective in-laws, Myra's grandmother stating forcefully, 'I'm not having any bloody actors in shiny suits in this house!' But he did manage to pass the more important audition with Jim and Flo, Myra's parents, and eventually managed to bring the whole family round with the sheer force of his personality.

Harry's parents, Fred and Gladys, however, were immediately charmed by their boy's new love, and welcomed her with open arms.

They were married on 19 February 1948 at St Barnabus Church, Sketty, in Swansea, then spent a week's honeymoon in distant Penzance, which was as far as they could go without actually leaving the country. But they weren't allowed long to enjoy wedded bliss as, shortly after, Harry embarked on tour with *Forces Showboat*, a drag show featuring a very young Danny La Rue in the chorus. Dad, I hasten to add, was the 'straight' comedian and was not required to drag up.

When Jennifer was born, unable to afford a permanent base of their own, Mum and Dad took her on the road with them. Looking after a small child in a constant procession of digs, however, was not easy, and soon Harry and Myra decided that until they could afford their own home it would probably be best if Mum and Jen stayed with her folks in the Mumbles, leaving Harry to traipse round the country alone, coming back to visit at the weekends.

My sister Jennifer recalls:

'My earliest memory is of watching the world through a brown-tinted car window. This must have been during Dad's early touring days when he had an old banger [an Austin Atlantic] that he used to drive Mum, me and all our paraphernalia around the Variety theatres that then proliferated all over the country.

'From those earliest days, I remember following trails of sequins to the chorus girls' dressing room, later returning to Dad's room wearing full stage make-up, complete with false eyelashes and wig. I used to be very indulged by the chorus girls and boys when I was very little.

'One act, The Edericks, who were on the bill with Dad in Sheffield, made me a pink tulle ballet dress with a satin bodice, a tiara and wand. The dressmaker (the wife of Sidney Fisher, Dad's tailor), who used to make evening gowns for Mum, made me a Cinderella outfit from the gaudy silk remnants of the stage clothes she made for her celebrity clients. With a dressing box like that it's no surprise that I created the theatrical persona "Hellie Morgan" and had devised an act by the age of two. Apparently, Hellie was very entertaining one New Year's Eve when she went round all the tables finishing up all the leftover drinks.

'I can't remember many of the digs we stayed in – thankfully – but I do remember some of the things that happened while we were renting. We were in a flat in Blackpool... Gran Atherton was staying with us and I'd dropped some biscuit crumbs on the carpet. She fetched the Ewbank carpet sweeper to pick them up, but found that it wasn't working properly. Thinking it needed emptying, she opened the underneath of the contraption and suddenly a nest of mice rushed out and ran in all directions across the room. My grandmother and mother turned into screaming banshees, jumping from chairs to tables, and I was left with a rodent phobia.'

By the time of my arrival, however, Dad's fortunes were on the up. With his matchless comedy timing and glorious voice, he was moving steadily up the bill on the Variety circuit and starting to make an even bigger noise in radio in a curiosity on the BBC Home Service called *The Goon Show*. Today, this would be a bit like The Prodigy turning up on Radio Three, and there were many who bemoaned the passing of a more genteel humour, personified by shows such as Kenneth Horne and Richard Murdoch's *Much Binding in the Marsh*, which was set in a fictional RAF base.

The success of *The Goon Show* finally enabled Dad to buy a home of his own, and soon we had waved goodbye to Swansea and set off on the road to London, where Jennifer found herself completely at home:

'Apparently I knew my way around London when I was very young. We used to stay at the Averard Hotel in Bayswater, and when Bampa Jim and Gran Atherton came up to visit, they would take me out for the day to give Mum a break.

'Their first time in the city they got lost and couldn't find the way back to the hotel. As soon as I realised what was going on, I stood at the kerb, raised my hand to hail a black cab and announced to the driver, "The Averard Hotel, please."

We eventually settled in a place called Cheam, on the edge of Nonsuch Park in Surrey. Back then, Cheam was a pretty little village with three pubs, an ironmonger's, a cricket ground and not much else. Neighbouring Sutton was the main shopping centre, with a high street boasting a Boots the Chemist, a Sainsbury's (with marble counters and gleaming red bacon-slicers) and a very grand Odeon Cinema – now demolished – which once hosted a Beatles concert. But even then it was hardly what you'd call bustling. All that's changed now, of course, with the steady encroachment of Croydon, which has thrown its arms around the once leafy suburb and now grips the area in a concrete embrace.

Jennifer also remembers our early days in Cheam:

'The Goon Show was a background to my childhood. I don't really remember going to the shows…but I have vague recollections of mad shadowy figures: Spike, Peter and Mike, and certainly them being very much Dad's best friends and the people he would see a lot of.

'I suppose there were two radio programmes that had a direct effect on me as a child: one was The Goon Show, because people would blow raspberries at you at school and you'd get called Seagoon and things like that. The other was the Hancock show [Hancock's Half Hour] because of course we lived in Cheam, so we used to get a lot of mail addressed to "Tony Hancock, Railway Cuttings, care of Harry Secombe, Cheam".

My earliest memories of Cheam are of sitting in my pram in the garden of our house. It was a large, five-bedroomed, thirties-built, mock-Tudor pile which, I'm afraid to say, I never really liked. My friends' houses always seemed much more exciting, many of them having three storeys and seeming to go on for ever, with lofts and attic rooms above and damp, forbidding cellars – possibly haunted – below, promising all sorts of scary adventures. Our house, a squat, two-storey edifice with no secret staircases, sliding panels or priest holes, and with nothing remotely otherworldly about it, seemed tame by comparison.

It did, however, have one interesting quirk: in the brickwork at the back was a series of jagged holes which, according to the previous owner, was the result of a passing Messerschmitt using the house as target practice during the Battle of Britain. That aside, it had little to commend it, apart from one glorious feature that made me forgive it almost everything: a vast and magnificent garden. Here, I spent many contented hours exploring, climbing trees, falling into rose bushes, having races with my boxer dog, Jimmy, and, much later, happily ripping up the lawn in my go-kart – much to my mother's chagrin.

It was also in this garden that I learned to fly. I'd become obsessed with a television programme called *The Adventures of Superman*, the original series with George Reeves in the title role. 'Faster than a speeding bullet, he can leap tall buildings in a single bound!' ran the voice-over under the opening credits. After watching Superman flying effortlessly over Metropolis, I became convinced that I, too, could fly, and that all I needed was the right outfit. Stealing one of my mother's tea-towels, which I tied around my neck for a cape, I also borrowed her kitchen stool as a 'launch pad' and spent hours in the garden, leaping off it, chanting Superman's catchphrase, 'Up, up and away!' believing that, at any moment, I would take off and soar into the clouds. My mother, preparing lunch, would watch from the kitchen window, smiling patronisingly at my futile attempts at flight.

But once, after turning away from the window for a few minutes, she returned to find me gone. Feeling a small tremor of panic, she rushed out into the garden. I was nowhere to be seen, the only evidence of my presence the abandoned stool now lying on its side. Tentatively, she looked up into the sky, half expecting to see a small figure dressed in shorts, with an Irish linen cape bearing the legend 'Souvenir of Blackpool' around its neck, streaking through the blue. Much to her relief, all she saw were blackbirds.

What had actually happened was that Jimmy, my dog, taking his cue from me, had leapt the tall fence around the garden and escaped into the road. I had followed to bring him back. When I arrived at the front door, Jimmy at my side, I was met by my ashen-faced mother. It took half a gallon of hot, sweet tea to calm her down.

Mum and Dad lived in that house in Cheam from the early fifties, right up until the eighties, and through the years we watched the area become busier and more suburban. Our house on Cheam Road became a landmark in a changing landscape, even the bus conductors called the stop opposite our front door 'Harry Secombe's Corner'!

Because of the usually frenetic nature of his working life, Dad liked to keep things at home as simple as he could, avoiding stress at all costs. Once he was settled in a place he was very difficult to move – 'If it ain't broke, don't fix it' was his motto. This, however, was not the attitude of Michael Bentine, as his son Richard observes:

'We moved to Esher when I was about three – I was born in 1959. Dad and Mum lived in Cheyne Walk when my elder brother and sister were born and, from there they moved to Sheen, near Richmond Park, living there for about five or six years – I was born in that house. And then when I was about two, Dad was coming back from some show and drove through Esher and thought, "I get good vibes from this place," so he pulled over to an estate agent and saw this house in the window – this was very typically Dad. They bought the house in Esher for something like £8,500 in 1962 and then proceeded to spend £4,000 on it, and Dad's accountant said, "You know, you'll never get your money back!"

'My parents left Esher in something like 1988 or '89. We'd all flown the coop by then. We all flew the coop as soon as we could, actually, because Dad was all for pushing us out, preferably with a one-way ticket and a packed suitcase: "Go, go…you can always come back!"

During the fifties and early sixties, much as I loved the large garden in Cheam, I didn't have a great deal of opportunity to use it. While Dad was performing in summer season in some far-flung corner of the country, Jen and I would usually be packed off to Swansea to spend the long summer holidays with Gran. But just occasionally, Dad would take the whole family with him.

One such summer, Dad was appearing at the Britannia Theatre on Great Yarmouth Pier, with Ronnie Corbett, Harry Worth and comedienne Audrey Jeans. He rented a house for us in the countryside beyond Yarmouth's sprawl, directly opposite a farm run by a very friendly family who let Jen and I ride their horses, feed their chickens and play in their monster haystacks. We spent practically every day there, being 'helpful', but more than likely getting in the way. But they were lovely people and didn't seem to mind.

Apart from the days spent on the farm, there are three incidents that stick in my mind from that summer. One is meeting 'King of Skiffle' Lonnie Donegan, who must have been appearing in a nearby theatre. He came round to the house for lunch one day and, despite the fact that he was probably the most famous man in Britain at the time, I remember taking an instant dislike to him, possibly because he said a very rude word to me. He'd arrived in a brand-new, red Alfa Romeo and, after lunch, found me dancing the feet of my brand-new, wooden 'Pelham' puppet on its bonnet. He got very upset – I can't think why.

The second thing I remember from that summer is something that still causes me the odd tremor of anxiety. During the evening, being a backstage 'tart', I would usually hang out at the theatre – both Ronnie Corbett and Audrey Jeans were fun to be around and I'd always got a buzz from being in a theatre. When I wasn't bothering the other stars of the show, I would sit in Dad's dressing room and watch television on a portable black-and-white set.

There is an unwritten rule in the theatre: never touch someone else's props. Unfortunately, in this particular show, Dad had some very enticing props indeed, one of which was a flintlock pistol, used in a sketch with Ronnie Corbett. They played two soldiers in Bonaparte's army who ended up fighting a duel. I can't now remember exactly how the sketch went, but it involved them shooting at each other – hence the pistol. The pay-off was Dad, thinking he was unscathed, drinking a glass of water which then flowed out of his costume from numerous bullet holes.

Dad's pistol, loaded with blanks, was always kept in a shoulder bag which was part of Dad's costume and, one night, although it was strictly forbidden, I took it out to look at it. I knew better than to pull the trigger, but I liked the way it looked and felt in my hand, and I played with it absent-mindedly, while engrossed in a new and rather scary science-fiction TV series called *A for Andromeda*, featuring a very young Julie Christie.

Dad, being a seasoned pro, always checked his props at the half, but as it was quite a busy show for him, he never came back to the dressing room until the interval, doing his costume changes side-stage. Once the show had gone up, his dresser would occasionally appear, dump Dad's discarded costumes, and scoop up armfuls of new ones to hang on a rail in the wings.

This particular night, as I toyed with the pistol and watched the cloned Julie Christie try to escape her human captors, to my horror, I heard the beginning of the Napoleonic sketch over the tannoy. I went cold. What should I do? Run to the side of the stage and try and get the pistol to him? How? The sketch had already started and neither Dad nor Ronnie came off during it. I froze in awful indecision, listening fearfully to the sketch as it unfolded over the crackly tannoy. The moment was coming up where Dad would reach into his bag to produce the gun. I cringed, not knowing what was going to happen. There was a long pause while Dad rifled through the bag. Then I heard him say, 'BANG!' and blow a raspberry, explaining, 'I should have had a gun, you see…' Then, luckily, I heard Ronnie corpse and the audience follow suit. When Dad came back to the dressing room, I sheepishly handed him the gun, saying, 'Sorry.'

He ruffled my hair and said, 'It's all right, son.'

Ronnie stuck his head into the dressing room.

'Sorry, Ronnie,' I said.

'Oh, I thought it went better than normal, didn't you, Harry?' he replied, but I think this was for my benefit.

Dad sat at the dressing table and looked at me in the mirror with his mock-serious 'And what are we going to do with you?' face on. 'That's why I always say don't touch the props,' he said. Then, seeing how mortified I was, he gave me a ten bob note and told me to go and get an ice cream.

The third thing I remember about Yarmouth is that it was on the stage of the Britannia Theatre that I made my début one Saturday matinée. I had already made an impromptu appearance on the stage of the Palladium, of which more later, but Yarmouth was where I made my theatrical début proper.

It was during a magic act. I forget now the name of the magician, but I had watched his act time and again from the wings, trying and failing to work out how he did things like make all those bottles and glasses appear from his hat, and how he managed to make his magic wand fly all over the stage. But, failing to penetrate the mystery of his magic, I settled instead on watching the children he would invariably invite from the audience to come up on stage to assist him. It seemed to me they never gave the appropriate responses to his questions during, for instance, the Chinese Sticks illusion.

This trick consisted of the magician holding two sticks, side by side in one hand, a long cord hanging out of one and the end of a cord just protruding from the other. Pulling down on the short cord appeared to make the long cord go up into the handle of the other stick. At this point, the magician asked his young assistant if he or she knew how it was done, and they would invariably reply in the negative, at which point he would separate the two sticks, revealing that they were not connected in any way. This always got a nice reaction, but it struck me that it would get a far better one if the child said he knew exactly how it worked, and explained in detail where he thought the cord went – up through the handle of one stick and out through the aperture in the other – especially if the child then reacted accordingly to the 'reveal'.

I begged my Dad to let me go out front and volunteer to be the magician's assistant. Dad wasn't too keen; apart from the fact that he wasn't a great fan of kids on stage, he didn't like the thought of his son possibly destroying a fellow performer's act. But I was whiningly persistent and, in the end, after first checking with the magician that he wouldn't mind, Dad relented. So, the next matinée, I was planted in the audience and waited for the summons to the stage. I was beside myself with excitement and, when the moment actually came, I mounted the short flight of steps from the auditorium with eager anticipation.

But when I reached centre stage and turned and looked out at the audience, I very nearly wished I'd never embarked on such a foolhardy enterprise – it was a full house and they were all looking at me. But I'd gone too far now to back down.

'And what's your name?' the magician asked, thrusting a microphone in my face.

My mouth was dry and my lips stuck to my teeth. 'An…' I began and choked.

'Sorry,' the magician smiled at the audience, 'I didn't quite catch that.'

I glanced to the side of the stage to see that Dad, Audrey Jeans and Ronnie Corbett, as well as sundry members of the chorus, were standing in the wings to watch my performance. I took a deep breath, cleared my throat and tried again. 'Andrew,' I said a little more convincingly, and was gratified to hear my amplified voice ringing off the back wall of the theatre.

'And how old are you, Andrew?'

'Ten.'

'Ten? Good, so you should be able to work out how this trick is done…' and he went into the Chinese Sticks routine.

When he asked, 'And how do you think this works?' I gave him a very detailed answer.

'Well,' I said, 'That cord goes up into the stick there, then it goes along the handle, then across into the other handle, then down the other stick and it comes out there.'

I got a round of applause – things were going well.

Then the magician, rolling his eyes at the audience as if to say, 'We've got a right one here,' pulled the two sticks apart and got a huge reaction – far bigger than normal. I felt vindicated. But now for the *pièce de résistance*: *my* big reaction. I opened my mouth, stepped back in amazement and threw my hands in the air. I caught sight of Audrey Jeans in the wings, crying with laughter, and I immediately blushed, feeling perhaps I'd overplayed it slightly.

My mother has somehow got it into her head that I ruined that magician's act, but the magician himself said he'd be happy to have me as an assistant any time I wanted. If it had been up to me, I would have been on every night, but Dad, firm in his belief that children and showbusiness don't mix, was against it. So I was left to watch disdainfully from the wings as a procession of child assistants came and went, none of them, in my opinion, coming anywhere near my class.

Blackpool summer season was another occasion we all spent the holiday together. This time the house we rented came complete with a pool and a housekeeper. The pool was nothing more than a glorified hole in the ground and was usually full of worms and dead frogs, but the housekeeper, Mrs Eastwood, was a real, salt-of-the-earth, solid, dependable North Country treasure. She would turn up very early every morning and burst into the bedrooms to start cleaning and dusting, announcing her presence with the phrase, delivered in a broad and booming Lancashire accent, 'I'll not wake yer!'

But, as I've already said, most summers, Jen and I would be

packed off to Gran and Bampa Atherton's in Swansea. Jennifer remembers:

'Before we moved to Cheam in 1953, the Secombe family hadn't owned a home of its own. We literally lived from digs to digs, but Swansea was always our base. We stayed with Mum's parents in West Cross. This was our holiday haven after we moved to Surrey.

'We'd travel down by steam engine from Paddington Station. Gran would always pack a picnic of cold roast chicken, ham sandwiches, boiled eggs and lots of pop. You, Andy, would usually eat yours while sitting in the overhead luggage rack. We always got a carriage to ourselves.

'Sometimes we'd drive down to Swansea with Aunty Elsie and Uncle Walter in their Hillman. It took such a long time – we'd leave Cheam early in the morning and never arrive until night-time. I used to love the sight of the twinkling lights over Swansea Bay as we dipped down the hill into the town.

'If we were lucky, Bampa Jim would take us cockling at the weekends in Lilliput Bay. We'd go down at low tide, Bampa carrying a spade and sack and me with my little pail and plastic rake. He'd show me the bubbles at the edge of the tide and the worm casts in the soft sand which were a sure sign that cockles were just under the surface. We'd carry our haul back to the house and, after Gran had washed them, soaked them, discarded the dead ones and cooked the fresh ones, we sat down to a teatime treat of fresh cockles and thinly sliced bread and butter. The last time I was on Lilliput Bay there was a sign preventing cockling because of contamination.'

Sometimes Mum would come with us or, if Dad was feeling lonely or if she just needed a break from her demanding kids, she would join him for a while, leaving us in Gran's tender care. We didn't really mind, there was too much to do: days would be spent cockling, digging for rag worms, playing in the street with the other kids, catching butterflies in the field, or swimming in the icy-cold, opaque waters of the Bristol Channel. More exotic holidays in the Mediterranean and Caribbean were to come, but I'll never forget those summers in Wales, and Jennifer, too, remembers them clearly:

'Swansea allowed us much more freedom than we ever had anywhere else. We would rush outside after breakfast, call at my best friend Sandy's house down the road and then cross over the main road to the beach.

'Lilliput Bay had a great view to the right of the Mumbles Pier and to the left of St Thomas' docks. We'd spend all morning on the beach, waving to the passengers on the Mumbles train (and sometimes trying to derail it by putting sand on the tramlines), jumping off tall concrete blocks on to the sand – left-over Second World War coastal defences – and creating knee problems for the future.

'We'd be called in to lunch by Gran at about one o'clock, bolt down our "dinner" of faggots or sweetbreads or laverbread and bacon and then go out to play again.

'There was a huge field in front of Gran's house and we used to make camps in the long grass and plot how we could catch one of the wild ponies that used to trot down from the Mayals to graze. Our plan always fell down when we tried to work out how we'd get the pony back to Cheam. It was a bit far to go on horseback.

'When it grew dark, Gran would call us in for supper. There was a fish and chip shop called Dick Barton's over the road on the estate and Gran would send us there every Friday to get our haddock and chips. Another treat was an Eynon's pie (but never on a Monday).

'I remember one day when Dick Barton's was closed and we were so disappointed that Gran cooked us home-made fish and chips and wrapped them in newspaper. Gran was a great cook and would have been a brilliant manager of a short order café. If she saw a visitor coming up her road she'd nip into the kitchen, whip up a sponge cake and have it in the oven before they reached the front door.'

The Mumbles train was a tram which ran along the coast. Starting out from Swansea, it went through Brynmill, Blackpill, West Cross, Oystermouth and Norton, finally stopping at Mumbles itself. Near here, there was a ruined Norman castle and, more interestingly for us, a Forte's ice-cream parlour, where Gran would indulge us with huge, sticky Knickerbocker Glories.

Cyril Seacombe (sic) was Dad's uncle, and an inspector on the Mumbles train. If he ever got on when we were on board, he would give us great ribbons of tickets which we would drape round our necks like scarves. Apparently, he was also a dab hand on the musical saw – such a talented family.

Jennifer adds:

'Dad rarely came down to Swansea in the summer – obviously because he was always appearing in a summer season. If ever he did, it would be on a Sunday. It was always so exciting to wake up on a Sunday morning, look out of the window and see Dad's car parked outside. He was like Father Christmas – every time he came down he would bring us presents, and one time he brought us a real live puppy. Jim was a brindle-and-white Boxer dog who had been picked up by Dad while doing a week in Dudley. He was the most loveable and exasperating dog I've ever encountered. He had more bounce than should have been allowed and managed to drag Bampa Jim (the name duplication often caused confusion at home) from West Cross to Blackpill along the beach before slipping his collar and running back home.

'When Dad came down on Sundays, we would go and see our Bampa Fred and Gran Secombe in Derwen Fawr. They had a bungalow and Gran used to make dark Bisto gravy and was always knitting something. Her face always lit up when she saw Dad. I delighted in the stories she used to tell me about what he did when he was a little boy.

'Bampa Fred would make coins appear from behind your ears and then make them disappear again. He also used to quote long monologues or lines from amateur dramatic plays he'd appeared in. "Farewell, Quintas, may we meet again in happier times," he would suddenly declare, apropos of nothing.

'When Mum came down to join us in the Mumbles, we went to a different beach in Gower every day. She would pile all the Heathwood Road kids into the car, load the boot with a picnic and off we'd go to Horton or Caswell, Langland or Oxwich, Pobbles or Three Cliffs. I think Crawley Woods was one of my favourites because the sand dunes offered great opportunities for rolling contests and for spying on courting couples. On the way home after a day on the beach, we would stop for a "99" at Shepherd's Shop in Parkmill (where Mum used to live during the war when her house in Courtney Street was bombed in the three-night blitz) and sometimes call at Jones the Farm to get some double cream. While Mum caught up on the latest gossip we would play in the hay barns, swinging from beam to beam and dropping down on to the cushioning bales.'

The Gower beaches were fabulous. We'd arrive and dive straight into the bone-deadeningly cold sea, screaming with the shock. But after five minutes we were completely numb and happy to spend hours in the freezing water.

When we'd eventually tired of splashing around, we'd thaw out on the beach with the picnic: corned beef sandwiches, chicken drumsticks, boiled eggs and sticks of celery dipped in salt, washing it all down with bottles of dandelion and burdock.

On the way back from the beach, skin prickly with salt and sand, we'd stop at Shepherd's Shop – an Aladdin's cave selling everything from pickled beef to buckets and spades – and get ice-creams. Then, if we were really lucky, on the way home we'd pull up outside a pub on the downs high above Swansea Bay.

In those days, children weren't welcomed into the bar, so, as the grown-ups slaked their thirst inside, Jen and I would sit in the car, sustained by packets of Smith's crisps and illicit glasses of bitter shandy, which would be smuggled out to us on a tin tray. As we sipped our shandies and crunched our salty crisps, we would watch the colour bleed from the landscape as the sun dipped slowly into the wide, blue bay. To this day, every time I watch a sunset, I can still taste the salty crunch of those thickly cut crisps and the wonderful sweet-and-sourness of the shandy.

The street in which my grandmother lived was a real old-fashioned, open-door, nosy-neighbour street. People were always coming and going and everyone knew everyone else's business. I might be viewing those days through the rose-tinted goggles of nostalgia, but I do remember a lot of laughter. All the kids, too, were friendly; we used to move round in a pack and, apart from the odd grazed knee from falling off home-made go-karts (no brakes) and once getting a severe telling-off for trying to make gunpowder in the back yard of the local police station, we never really got into any serious trouble, as Jennifer says:

'Those times in Swansea were a focal point of a golden childhood. I still feel a sense of belonging and homecoming whenever I go back to Swansea. There's something very comforting in seeing again the same views, unchanged since childhood, and hearing the melodic sing-song Swansea accent. We felt safe in Swansea. Everybody knew who we were and looked out for us, but I was more likely to be recognised as "Myra's daughter" or "Harry Secombe's eldest".'

When I think back on those days I remember them as sunshine, laughter and butterflies, although there was one incident which still gives me the odd shiver in the dark hours of the night. It was my first experience of the envy with which some people viewed my secondhand celebrity status. Thankfully a rare occurrence, I was, however, to encounter this attitude from time to time for many years, especially during Dad's glory days.

I must have been about seven years old and had gone to see Robert, a boy who lived at the top of the street. He was really Jen's friend, because he was that much older than me, but he had a quick wit and was fun to hang around with; I was actually a bit in awe of him because he seemed so grown up. What he thought about me trailing after him like an eager puppy, he was too polite to say.

One day, I went round to his house, on what pretext I can't remember, but was shown in with, 'Oh, Andy, come in, my uncle's here – he wants to meet you.' I think Mrs West worked during the day and I don't remember ever meeting Robert's father, so the three of us were alone in the house.

At 16, Robert's uncle was only a few years older than Robert, and I was surprised that it was possible to have an uncle so young, seeing as most of mine were, to my youthful eyes, old men – well into their 40s. He was quite tall, had small, mean eyes, a thin mouth and a wiry frame and, next to him, Robert looked slight and rather apologetic. He was wearing a dark grey suit several sizes too big for him and oozed a swaggering menace. I didn't like him the moment I set eyes on him. But, brought up to be polite, I said, 'How do you do?' and offered my hand.

He stared at me for a moment like I was raw meat, then seized my hand and put me in a half nelson. 'I've heard about you, Secombe boy,' he said, grinning. 'You and your kind need taking down a peg or two.'

I tried to ask him what he meant about 'my kind' but as he had his arm around my throat, I could only gurgle. After dragging me all over the room, he eventually flung me on the sofa and sat on me heavily, announcing, 'Eleven stone of bone and muscle. How does that feel, eh?'

I couldn't answer because my face was buried deep in the cat-smelling sofa cushions. While I was stuck there, gasping for breath, he calmly rolled a cigarette and chatted amiably to Robert about this and that. Once Robert's uncle had finished his cigarette, he got off me and pulled me to my feet. By now I was justly terrified and wondered what he would do next. Looking into my frightened eyes, he said, 'So, we've got him at our mercy, Robert. What shall we do with him, eh?'

I thought Robert would come to my aid, tell his uncle to stop being so daft and let me go, but he just shrugged. Obviously his uncle was much cooler than me and he thought if he protested he'd be considered a wuss.

'Tell you what,' said the grinning thug, 'let's lock him in the kitchen and think about it.'

I was shoved into the small, linoleum-floored room at the back of the house but, before leaving me, the uncle made sure I couldn't escape by sliding home the bolt at the top of the back door, which was way out of my reach. Then he bent down and looked into my face with an evil glint in his eye. 'You stay here and think about everything that could happen to you. We'll be back in a bit.'

He went back into the sitting room, rubbing his hands with glee, closing the door behind him. I had no intention of hanging around while this teenage psychopath decided whether he was going to slice me up and bury me in the garden or encase me in cement and throw me off Swansea Pier in a suitcase, so I looked for a way out. The window above the sink was a possible route, but using it would mean clearing all the junk off the kitchen windowsill, which would make an awful noise and take time I probably didn't have. Then I saw the solution. Quickly clambering up on to the draining board, I found that if I clung to the side of the kitchen window with my right hand, I could lean out and just reach the door-bolt with my left. With trembling fingers I drew it back, hoping that my tormentor wouldn't hear the *snick* as it came free. Then I leapt to the floor, yanked open the door and ran back to Gran's as fast as I could. Dashing into the house, I went straight to the living room, threw myself on the sofa and curled up into a ball, half expecting a knock on the door at any moment.

Gran came and found me. She could see I was in a state, but I was so frightened I couldn't speak. She made me a thick slice of bread and dripping with a smearing of Bovril over the top – my favourite. I sat and ate it staring fearfully out of the window, lest my torturer came along the street looking for me. Luckily, he didn't. Luckier still, I never saw him again, but I never dared go round to Robert's again.

I learned two very important lessons that day: 1) witty doesn't always mean wise; and 2) you can always find a way out of a bad situation if you look for it.

5

School

My sister and I went to a tiny primary school in Ewell, a village next door to Cheam, on the other side of Nonsuch Park. The school was called Girton House and was in a converted detached house on a street of similar houses in a quiet residential area. I didn't know it then, but it was actually part of the vast Stoneleigh Estate, built during the thirties over what once had been the grounds of Henry VIII's Nonsuch Palace. What I *did* know was that I didn't like it, and it fixed the idea in my mind that school was the opposite of fun.

The school was run by Mr and Mrs W. L. Burton-Jenkins. He reeked of cheap cigars and, with his yellow-stained beard, nicotine-streaked hair and the vast swell of his belly straining at the waistcoat of his three-piece tweed suit, reminded me of a giant badger.

She was an ample woman, her bosom jutting out in front of her like a mantelshelf. Not to be outdone by her tobacco-stained husband, she seemed to have a cigarette welded to her bottom lip, the ash from which would fall into the dark, forbidding depths of her cleavage, never to be seen again.

My first meeting with Mr Burton-Jenkins was not all that I could have wished for. I was four years old and it was my first day at school. I remember standing on the pavement next to a silver birch, staring through a white picket fence at a pebble-dashed house surrounded by more children than I had ever seen assembled in one place. They were laughing and playing and seemed to be having a good time, but nothing would induce me to join them; no one had offered me a suitable explanation as to why I couldn't just stay at home and watch *Picture Book* and *Rag, Tag and Bobtail* and read my *Rupert Bear* annual, as I had always done. I clung stubbornly to my mother's legs as Jennifer tried to pull me inside, complaining bitterly that I was going to make her late. Eventually, after promises of sweets and presents and trips to Battersea funfair, I was at last coaxed through the small, white gate, entering the building arm-in-arm with Jen.

The moment I got inside, however, my nerves got the better of me and I desperately needed to pee. Jen showed me to a small lavatory set under the stairs in the entrance hall. I dutifully entered the small cubicle and was in the middle of relieving myself when the door burst open and Mr Burton-Jenkins walked in, immediately filling the small room with his presence and the acrid smell of cigars. I squashed myself into the space between the toilet and the wall, too terrified to speak. Because he had entered the tiny room backwards, Mr Burton-Jenkins hadn't seen me and proceeded to undo his flies. But then, when he turned and found himself looking down on a small child, his eyes widened in shock. I, however was fixed on the large, terrifying thing he held in his hand, which was at my eye level. He growled something unintelligible, hurriedly re-fastened his fly and exited. I was left shaking, with pee all down my left leg. It was an inauspicious start to my school career, but things were to get much, much worse.

There was one teacher in particular at that school who seemed to take great delight in 'taking me down a peg or two'. I can't remember her name, but she was tall, always dressed in black and had a long, hawk-like nose. She also taught maths, which had long been a Secombe failing. Dad had never got the hang of it and, in my absolute incomprehension of how numbers worked and what they did when you put them together, I saw myself as upholding a long and noble tradition. This tall, raptor-like woman, however, took a different view and seemed to be forever keeping me in at break times to 'practise my numbers'. This either involved reciting my times tables or, even more inanely, writing my numbers to her satisfaction – 2s were not allowed to have loops and 4s had to be closed at the top. I lost interest in maths from that moment. If it was all just about how you wrote your numbers, I didn't see the point – I still don't. Which, I suppose, is my revenge on that hideous woman: I wasn't going to let her teach me anything.

Then, when I *was* allowed out, there was playtime. Having never before encountered large numbers of children, I was understandably shy and bewildered by the myriad games of tag, cowboys and indians and marble shoot-outs going on all over the playground. However much I might have wanted to join in, my timidity held me back. So, clinging to the known, I hung around Jen and her mates, standing and watching as they played hopscotch, skipping, or arcane clapping games with uncountable rhythms. Jen was family and, in the new and puzzling world of education, a safe place. This, unfortunately, did not suit the ideas of a certain maths teacher.

One day, I was sitting in a corner of the playground with Jen and her friends, chatting, when she came stalking across the gravel straight towards me.

'Right,' she said, grabbing my left arm and pulling me to my feet none too gently. 'Time you made some friends of your own.'

Dragging me away from my sister, screaming, she then tried to foist me on several groups of boys already deeply involved in well-established games. The boys, naturally, shied away from this squawking child like horses from a forest fire, and ultimately the teacher and I were left in the centre of the playground, united by the uncertainty of where to go next, while a stunned and silent crowd of children looking on from a safe distance.

Humiliated and embarrassed in equal measure, I twisted myself free from the hatchet-faced woman's grasp and made a break for it. The crowd parted before me to reveal the playground fence, which I ran to, burying my tear-stained face in the rough wood, as if it might be possible to disappear into the narrow gaps between the larch-lap. Jennifer ran up to comfort me but was told sharply to 'Stay away!' and was forbidden to come near me during playtime until I'd made friends of my own. Of course, since making such a spectacle of myself, no one would come near me and, after this incident, I wandered the playground friendless and alone for probably no more than a week, but to me it felt like years.

I was eventually befriended by a group of boys, more out of pity than because I matched up to their ideal of the perfect playmate and, as I sensed their charity, I never really felt I belonged.

The gang's leader was a tall, imposing boy with a loud voice. In profile, if you squinted, he looked a bit like Dean Martin. Unfortunately, completely lacking Dino's sense of humour, his favourite pastime was playing war games. These were usually based on famous films he'd seen, such as *The Battle of the River Plate* or *The Dambusters*. Try as I might, I could never really let go and abandon myself to the fantasy of these games like the other boys seemed to be able to do. This was, I suppose, partly because I hadn't yet learned how to be with children of my own age, and partly because I hadn't seen any of the films. But, mainly, the difficulty I found with these games was that they all seemed so childish – the boys running around as aeroplanes, their arms outstretched, making 'Ack-ack-ack-ack-ack' noises, then, after being 'hit', pirouetting like a ballet dancer and tumbling to the tarmac in a simulated explosion. Or manning imaginary anti-aircraft guns and barking out lines like, 'Take that, you filthy Hun!' It also began to dawn on me that whatever film it was we were supposed to be re-enacting, the action was always the same: some boys would take the role of Messerschmitts or Spitfires and indulge in dog fights, ack-ack-acking all over the playground sky, while others would stay on the ground, manning the anti-aircraft guns.

I would half-heartedly join in, but I couldn't help but feel rather silly. When, at the end of one particularly fierce battle, the whole gang lay 'dead' and our leader started humming 'The Last Post', I giggled, thinking it was a joke. It wasn't, and he was deeply upset. This incident ignited a simmering resentment between us which boiled over a few days later and ended with my being expelled from the gang.

I have never found it easy to make friends, but I don't think I can lay the blame for this exclusively at the feet of my maths teacher. My inability to integrate socially must, at least in part, stem from having had a slightly unusual upbringing, making it sometimes difficult to relate to other children and, I should imagine, difficult also for them to relate to me. Now, having met the children of the other Goons, I wish I'd got to know them earlier; at least we'd have had something in common.

Jennifer offers one reason why we never really spent time with the other Goonchildren:

'I don't remember us having much to do with the other Goons when we were young. I think it was mostly a geographical reason – Peter Sellers and Spike Milligan lived near each other in north London, while we lived in Cheam.

'There is a piece of folklore that has been handed down that Spike once managed to lose me in Hyde Park. It was on one of those visits to the Averard Hotel and I was a precocious child, walking by the age of nine months and running by the age of ten months.

'Apparently Spike hadn't been prepared for my amazing speed and I shot off while he wasn't paying attention. I was found very soon afterwards in the middle of a bed of red tulips. What was Mum thinking of?'

Sarah Sellers also reflects on this idea of us sharing a 'bond' of sorts:

'Michael was very good friends with Sean Milligan, so there was that connection…Sile and Jane live in North London and although I don't see much of them now, I feel a kind of bond with them…they know the sort of childhood we had. It was pretty unique really, to have parents that are that wacky.'

Richard Bentine was also friends with the late Michael Sellers:

> 'Michael always used to arrive at various events in a pair of shorts and a Hawaiian shirt, as he was diabetic. He could break into a muck sweat walking down the road in winter. Nice guy. Sarah, I haven't seen for years, but they were the Sellers children we grew up with...'

But making friends wasn't my only problem. My maths teacher aside, there were others of the school staff who made me feel uncomfortable, especially a male teacher who insisted on calling me 'Neddie Seagoon'.

I would politely correct him, informing him that, in actual fact, my name was 'Andy Secombe' but he would simply laugh and blow a raspberry (ineptly, I thought). I was sure he was mad. Then strange things started happening in the playground: older children would come up to me and start talking in funny voices, bandying about vaguely familiar names such as 'Bluebottle', 'Eccles' and 'Bloodnok'.

Sarah Sellers continues:

> 'I don't think I did get any of that. I went to a very sort of progressive school...also there were a lot of kids there of other celebrities...And I was so used to Dad doing voices all the time anyway...and I do live in a bit of world of my own anyway, so I probably wouldn't have noticed!'

It may sound odd, but back then, I had never heard an episode of *The Goon Show*. I can only surmise it was because Dad was always careful to keep his work separate from home life, both he and Mum wanting us to have as normal an upbringing as possible. But now, despite their best efforts, we were inevitably starting to feel the impact of Dad's career on our lives.

There was one, relatively low-key, family foray into the limelight when I was almost three years old. This was a newspaper advert for Gibbs toothpaste. In the finished ad, all the family members are shown smiling happily while holding tins of Gibbs toothpaste – 'Gibbs in a tin lasts twice as long as toothpaste in a tube!' runs the strapline.

But the day of the shoot itself wasn't much fun for anyone, least of all the crew, who turned up to find that Jennifer had just lost her two front teeth – not good for a toothpaste advert. The picture of her that eventually appeared was retouched to give her a full, gleaming set of gnashers.

Even though I wasn't much more than a baby, I do vaguely remember spending much of the day screaming and being generally uncooperative under the hot lights. Dad, who had an incredibly sticky forehead on which he could – and frequently did – stick a whole set of cutlery, tried to keep me happy by sticking a tin of Gibbs toothpaste on it. And that, of course, is the shot they used in the advert.

We never did anything like it again. Dad maintained it was because he didn't want to expose us to public scrutiny, but I suspect the real reason was that we were just too difficult to control.

However, by the time my sister Katy came along, in 1967, Dad had obviously abandoned any pretence of keeping his children out of the public eye, and her first day at school started with a photo-call, which she remembers to this day:

'I remember my first day at school – I went to a school called Thannington, which was round the corner from Girton House, which by that time had stopped being a school. And I remember that day as being the first time I felt pressure – I felt I had to perform. It's bad enough going to school anyway… but there was a whole of pack of press photographers there to record it. I remember feeling pressed for time because I think we were late and I wanted to get to school and all the photographers were like, "Oh, just another one – over here, Katy!"

Michael Bentine, however, never had any qualms about getting his family in on the act, which, as far as Richard Bentine was concerned, had certain benefits:

> 'Potty Time was my holiday job. When it was originally on BBC it was called Michael Ben-Tea-Time, which was another version of Crackerjack, in the sense that there was a game in the middle and had lots of screaming children...I remember once my whole school got to go...So I was considered OK.'

Although it seemed perfectly normal to me that a host of the celebrities of the day – Alma Cogan, Frankie Vaughan, Tommy Cooper, Eric Sykes and Stanley Baker to name but a few – should be regular visitors to our house in Cheam, I began to be dimly aware that this was not the everyday reality of my school friends. I learned early on that to talk about such things could bring accusations of showing off, so most of the time I kept quiet. This was an experience shared by Sarah Sellers as well:

> 'That was just the way it was, and that's the way it always was. Perhaps, rather, it was a realisation that not everybody else was the same...The things that were different were that you'd go places – restaurants for example – and there was always a table. And you never had to queue to go into anything; there was never a problem getting seats for anything – all those kind of things that were different to other people's experiences.'

James and Sally Grafton, sitting in their father's pub, watched the celebrities come and go with an unjaundiced eye. James says:

> 'All sorts of people were regulars at Grafton's: Richard Hern – also known as Mr Pastry – was often in there, as was Tony Hancock, Graham Stark, Dick Emery, Sam Kydd, Hattie Jacques, Alfred Marks and Dora Bryan. My mother used to breed poodles and Dora had the male – so she was around

quite a lot. But you never really knew who you were going to meet. I came home from school one day and there was my dad sitting talking to Lionel Jeffries.'

Sally Grafton adds:

'We grew up with people like that coming in all the time – we thought it was quite normal. I used to sit in the sitting room and do my homework and try and cut myself off, but occasionally people would come in and talk to me. I do remember Jon Pertwee eating all my sandwiches. The cook always used to make me tomato sandwiches – it was always very dangerous to tell the cook you liked anything, so I had tomato sandwiches for tea for ever.

'One day, Jon was there and he was in the sitting room having a cup of tea and he saw my tomato sandwiches and went, "Oh, tomato sandwiches, lovely!" and ate most of them. I was far too polite to say anything.'

But sometimes the people one met were far too special to be kept to oneself, even if the reaction you wanted failed to materialise, as Richard Bentine sadly recalls:

'Peter and Britt Ekland came round for dinner one night, and the next day I went into school and said, "Not only did I have dinner with Britt Ekland last night, but she came upstairs to have a look at my train set."

'And they all said, "Who's Britt Ekland?"'

Peter's son, Michael, sadly died of a heart attack in 2006 at the young age of 52. But, before he died, he wrote a memoir about his life with Peter in the book *P.S. I Love You* in which, amongst other things, he talks about some of the very special guests who showed up at his house from time to time:

'Princess Margaret and Tony came to another party at Elstead and Dad gave me a box of tricks so that I could provide the cabaret. I was far from being properly rehearsed but Spike and Michael Bentine gave me a helping hand behind a collapsible screen and at the end of the evening Princess Margaret was telling Father that Tommy Cooper would soon be facing competition.'

Had it not been for the questions raised by those odd experiences at school, I might have remained in ignorance of my father's trade for years. It wasn't until I started asking my mum, 'Who is Neddie Seagoon? What is this thing called *The Goon Show*, and why does everyone laugh when they talk about it?' that I learned the truth.

I suppose, thinking it was about time that we knew what our father did for a living, Mum took Jen and me to a theatre in London. It must have been sometime in the late fifties at what was probably the Camden Theatre. I remember the stage was flanked by potted palms and, between them, in front of a full orchestra, three men, one of whom was my father, were doing the strangest things: strutting up and down doing silly walks, pulling faces and making funny noises into microphones. I was too young to understand most of the jokes, but the audience had no such problem and were rocking with laughter. And then it hit me, the secret that the whole world seemed to know: my father was a professional idiot.

Sile Milligan remembers:

'When we went to primary school – I went to a convent – there was just no question about who you are, it was just: "Do you go to church? Can you do italic writing? Can you do your maths and Latin and do you go to confession every Saturday?" And that was the end of it; it doesn't matter who your dad is. So that was all cool and OK.

'But when I went to senior school and there were all these posh birds and 95 per cent of them were Jewish, there was definitely a bit of…people thought he was anti-Semitic [he wasn't] but there were a lot of questions about it until they worked out that I was OK and everything was cool. Of course, I had to do ten minutes entertaining everyone before registration happened, but, hey, a small price to pay to not be knocked down dead by all the Jewish girls in the school.'

I was never bullied badly at school; in fact, I was generally very popular with my fellow pupils – it was the teachers who were the problem, many of them judging me on my father's professional persona, seeing a rebel who had to be tamed before he caused too much disruption.

In the early sixties, I moved from Girton House to a prep school in Epsom. This was an all-boys, *Tom Brown's Schooldays* sort of place, complete with sixth-form bullies, sadistic teachers who could hit a misbehaving boy smack on the nose with a board duster at 40 paces, and a headmaster convinced of the character-building qualities of corporal punishment. It was also an institution which, in my view, laid an unhealthy emphasis on outdoor sports.

Before school started, we would assemble for morning prayers. We miserable, pasty-faced, grey-jumpered boys would shuffle into the school hall to stand before the stage on which the black-gowned masters, looking like a flock of emaciated crows, would gaze down on us contemptuously with bloodless eyes. And as Mrs Bruce, the music teacher – the only one in the entire school who had an ounce of humanity in her being – hammered away on the slightly out-of-tune upright piano, we would mumble our way through 'O God Our Help in Ages Past' or 'Jerusalem' and then fall silent while the headmaster – a bullish man with high blood pressure and a complexion to match – would read the morning prayer or, worse, ramble on for several minutes with a prayer of his own devising which would contain words such as 'Duty,' 'Service', 'Sin', 'Hell' and 'Damnation', but never 'Love' or 'Forgiveness'.

Needless to say, I hated this school with a passion and walked through its portals on a Monday morning with a mixture of fear and loathing.

My brother David, born in 1961, and now a respected photographer, also went to a rather snooty public school, in Leatherhead, but for him it wasn't just the teachers who were the problem – he got it in the neck from all sides:

> 'Many of my fellow pupils regarded me with a kind of sneering attitude, so I kept my head down...But then I was already interested in photography, which encourages you to stand outside and be an observer...I was never actually beaten up for being Harry Secombe's son – it was more a kind of low-level hostility.
>
> 'I remember someone saying to me once, when I'd said something about being fed up with it, "Well, imagine what it would be like if you were Harold Wilson's son."

I suppose it's all a matter of degree.

But we weren't the only Goonchildren to suffer at school. Michael Sellers also had problems:

> 'I had a bad time at Frensham's [Frensham Heights, near Elstead]. The other kids would break anything I had; personal possessions in my room would be vandalised and even rulers and pencils were snapped into pieces. One or other of the kids would say, "You can afford it. Your dad's rich." Even the teachers seemed to think that I had been born with a silver spoon in my mouth.'

My sister, Katy, after her all-too-public entrée into education, didn't exactly escape scot-free, either:

> 'The first time I realised my father didn't have a normal nine-to-five job, I remember very clearly: I was in an art class, and this hideous girl called Katrina picked a fight with me...I must have been about ten...and she picked a fight with me. She was a bit confrontational anyway...and she said, "What does your dad do? At least my dad builds bridges. Your dad doesn't do anything."

'And I remember this sense of absolute fury…but I didn't know how to respond because I did feel she had a point. I was aware of what he did but, as far as I was concerned then, he was in his pyjamas 'til noon at least. He had these really hideous shorty pyjamas, they were vile. So I just thought he was really lazy. I didn't know that he was working 'til two o'clock in the morning – I think he was doing a lot of cabaret at the time. Nowadays I'd say, "Don't be so ridiculous, my father brings laughter to many people." But you don't say that sort of thing when you're ten. So I remember a feeling of inability to express myself, but feeling really cross about it at the same time…'

I remember Dad wandering about the house in those pyjamas. He would usually lounge in bed until lunchtime, either reading or making phone calls, when the house would resound to calls of 'Hup!' which was his customary way of ending telephone conversations with family and friends. Why he did this I never thought to ask and, looking back at it now, I suppose it was rather odd, but back then it seemed a perfectly natural and normal thing for him to do.

Even without a famous name, Sally Grafton also had problems at school and, echoing my experience, it was the teachers who proved the most problematic:

'When I went to St Paul's school, I don't think they really approved of showbusiness. My friends thought it was quite good – they used to come to the pub and thought it was quite exciting – they thought we were quite bohemian.

'One of the things I remember quite vividly is, because my route home from school went past the theatre – which was then the television theatre – I used to go to rehearsals. I used to sit in the front stalls and do my homework. And then, when it moved to Shepherd's Bush, that was only a short walk away from school, so I used to do the same and come back with father. They were shows like *The Billy Cotton Band Show* and,

of course, all the shows with Harry – they were the best because he got the best guests.

'I remember one show with Richard Burton, Donald and Glyn Houston, Ivor Emmanuel and just about any Welsh person you could think of. That was quite something. The one I liked best was Glyn Houston – he was the nicest to talk to. I also remember meeting Max Bygraves, much later on, and he said to me, "I hope your first son's a boy."

'But just before I left school, we all had to have an interview with the head teacher – or the "high mistress" as she was known – and she asked me what I wanted to do. And at that stage I thought I'd like to be a floor manager, and a director eventually. And it met with considerable disapproval.'

The knowledge in those early days that my father was public property was bitter-sweet – although proud that he was so obviously loved and revered, I was also a bit jealous. This feeling was compounded by the fact that in those days he was a somewhat shadowy figure: off on the road during the week, and back only fleetingly at the weekends. If we were lucky, we would catch an exciting glimpse of him between his arrival home and his departure for the studio on Sunday morning. Seeing him after the dull, grey conformity of our school week was a bit like an exotic bird of paradise turning up in the middle of Cheam High Street.

Because he was only around intermittently, the glimpses we had of him were all the more special. I don't remember him reading to us when we were very young, although apparently he did, but I do remember a number of colourful ditties he taught us. One, to the tune of 'The British Grenadiers' went like this:

There was a Scots Highlander at the battle of Waterloo,
The wind blew up his petticoat and showed his toodle-oodle-oo,
His toodle-oo was dirty, he showed it to the Queen,
The Queen she gave him sixpence to go and wash it clean.

Pretty highbrow stuff. But of all the slightly naughty rhymes he taught us, my favourite was:

> Mum's out, Dad's out, let's be rude: pee, po, belly, bum, drawers.
> Run around the garden in the nude,
> Pee, po, belly, bum, drawers.
> We'll poke our tongues out at everyone we meet,
> Write rude words up and down your street:
> Pee, po, belly, bum. Pee po, belly, bum. Pee, po, belly, bum, drawers.

I insisted my two boys learn the latter as soon as they were able, and I got into awful trouble with a rather uptight mother whose young children they then taught it to. I hate to think what she'd have done if they'd come out with any of the others.

When Dad was around, the atmosphere had a charged, tingly feeling, as if there was electricity in the air. I remember Jen and I waking in the early hours of a Sunday morning and, a good 20 minutes before he arrived home, being aware of something like an approaching hurricane moving towards us through the night. It was the sound of a large engine overlaid with a high-pitched giggle and a liberal helping of raspberries. At last, this strange, larger-than-life creature would explode into the house with a 'Hello, folks!', a raspberry and a quick burst of an Italian aria, which would instantly bring Mum's displeasure down on his head.

'Shh, you'll wake the kids!'

But we were already awake and bounding downstairs, hungry for our share of Dad's energy. There would follow a magical half-hour, where he would regale us with stories of things that had happened during the week, illustrating them with impressions of the people he'd met, doing their walks, their voices. We were an appreciative audience and used to roll around on the floor, giggling. Then Mum would drag us back off to bed and we'd try to sleep. The next morning we might catch a brief glimpse of him before he went up to London to rehearse and record *The Goon Show*.

By the time he got back late on Sunday night, exhausted, we would already be in bed. When we left for school on Monday morning, if we were lucky he'd stand on the doorstep and wave us off in his pyjamas, much to the delight of the neighbours and passing commuters. But by the time Jennifer and I got home from school, he'd be gone. Without him there, the house would seem cold and empty, and we'd long for the next weekend. Meanwhile, Dad would be back on the road, heading for his next booking in Wolverhampton, Oldham, Leeds or Blackpool. Ah, the glamour…

Janet Brown observes:

'I remember Harry telling me…of leaving every Monday and going off to do his next tour…and I understand this, because having done lots of Variety, you're on the move all the time. And on this occasion, he was telling me how he'd come home and how he'd got out of the taxi and how he'd walked up the path and Myra and the family were there and they put out their arms to welcome him back and he turned round to go back and get his case and the children burst into tears – they thought he was leaving again. I thought that was so sad…'

Dad may only have been there fitfully at the very beginning, but when was around, colours shone brighter, the sky was that little bit bluer and you had the feeling that anything could happen, and it usually did.

Sometimes when he'd been away abroad, or to some far-flung outpost of the British Isles, which meant he couldn't get back for a weekend or two, he would arrive home laden with presents. As he was pulling parcels out of his suitcase and handing them to us, Mum would begin to chide that he was spoiling us, but he'd reply with a wink, 'Oh, My, we can afford it.' Then he'd pull out some exquisite piece of jewellery for her which would leave her speechless.

Because of his long absences, when he was home he tried to do as many of the things that 'normal' fathers do. But normality went out of the window when Dad was around. Madness and hysteria were never far away.

As I've already mentioned, maths was a bit of a puzzle for me when I was young and so, to improve my sums, after school on a Thursday, I was sent for extra lessons to a maths tutor who lived nearby. This particular maths teacher was patient and kind, but I still learned virtually nothing. One of the problems was that his house smelled of an unappealing mixture of cats, pencil shavings and body odour, making it difficult to concentrate. At least, that was my excuse.

Usually it was Mum who collected me at the end of the lesson, but one winter's evening, Dad got back unexpectedly early from a trip away, and thought he'd surprise me by picking me up. Unfortunately, never having been to my tutor's house before, he called at the house next door. I can only imagine the look on the poor woman's face when she answered the door that dark winter's evening to find a beaming Harry Secombe standing on her doorstep, especially when he exclaimed, 'I am here to pick up the young Einstein!'

We giggled about it all the way home. And the thought of it still makes me laugh today.

Then there was the time he took Jennifer to school:

'One particular Monday morning…Roy, our chauffeur [who usually took us to school] was ill. Well, he used to drive us to school in Dad's Rolls-Royce, I'm ashamed to say. We used to tell him to park it round the corner, and we'd get out and slide into school.

'This particular Monday, Roy didn't turn up and we didn't know until it was a bit too late that he wasn't coming. So, Mum said, "Harry, you'll have to take them!" because Mum was obviously busy doing something else. So, he got up, still in his pyjamas, put his mac over the top of his pyjamas and drove the Rolls-Royce and, instead of parking in the place where you're supposed to park, he drove right outside the front of the school – the main entrance that nobody used except the headmistress.

'I was going, "Dad, this is the wrong place! You can't…" And he got out of the car – in his pyjamas – came round and opened the passenger door for me. I got out and looked to my left and there, in the staff room, were all the teachers – their faces pressed to the window…And in the other part of the school, all my mates going "Yeah!!"

'Then he bowed – I must have been blushing to the tips of my toes – and he got in the car and went off again. I think there were a few comments later in the day from my teachers: "Hmm, interesting new chauffeur you've got, Jennifer…"

'Yes, he knew how to embarrass.'

Jane Milligan was just too young to have caught the *Goons* first time round. Nevertheless, school life with a name like Milligan was never going to be straightforward:

'I don't think I was really aware [of *The Goons*] because when it's going on all around you, you don't pay it too much attention, because it's just there: funny silliness, that was just the general way of being in our lives…

'When I grew up it was the *Q* series that my father was successful with and, at the time, it was embarrassing for me because I found it very, very funny, having grown up with that sense of humour, but it was a little bit way-out for a lot of the kids I went to school with – a posh school in Highgate. They were all like – "There goes the girl with the crazy dad, folks!"

'The *Q* series was very eccentric and quite beyond its time. There was lots of stuff I didn't understand in it – there was lots of sexual stuff, Dad was quite…he loved his big-boobed women and all that, you know…knockers jokes and all that…and so I was a little bit embarrassed, a bit ashamed about all that.'

My sister Katy, being the youngest of us all, was used to battling for attention at home, and so was more than able to handle herself at school:

> 'I think I was treated differently at school from the other kids. Still to this day I have a real filter system with people. If I'm ever introduced as "Katy Secombe" rather than just "Katy", I know very quickly what they want from me. And that really stems from school, because I became more of a commodity than a person.
>
> 'There were a couple of teachers at school that took against me, but not massively because I was quite able to hold my own in class…I became class clown really. I didn't get bullied too badly, even in maths, which was my worst subject.
>
> 'I was actually quite a rebel, but I was seen as a goody-two-shoes because, at that time, Dad was just slipping into his cuddly family man/national treasure/sings on *Songs of Praise* persona, rather than being someone who was cutting edge, and I suppose they put that on to me. So if I got into trouble, I thought, "Oh God, what will Dad think of me…?"

I, too, remember feeling that pressure to be 'good' and not to upset Dad or let him down. As Katy says, having reached 'national treasure' status, and often referred to in the press as 'Britain's best-loved Goon', heaven forbid his children should ever do anything which might damage his reputation.

Like my brother David, I, too, was a shy, retiring child. Unlike him, I had an English master at my secondary school who liked me and wanted to bring me out of my bubble of introversion. The school I went to after attending that dismal prep in Epsom was City of London Freemen's, in the village of Ashtead, tucked away at the foot of Epsom Downs. The main house dated from the 18th century and stood in a large park, surrounded by hockey, rugby and cricket pitches. Compared to my grim prep school, this was a breath of fresh air and the best thing about it was that it was co-educational – it had girls!

The pupils were an interesting mix. As well as the usual public school types – the sons and daughters of lawyers, doctors, city bankers and civil servants – there were also quite a few scholarship pupils and a scattering of the children of British and foreign diplomats. It all seemed very exotic and exciting. Famous alumni from my time include Johnny Mellor, a.k.a. Joe Strummer (himself the son of a diplomat), Andy Ward (drummer with the band *Camel*) and Simon Cowell of *Wildlife SOS*. But I recently discovered my old mate Warwick Davis (of *Willow* and *Star Wars* fame, more recently seen as Professor Flitwick in the *Harry Potter* movies) also went there.

There were two teachers who would have big impacts on my life. The first was Mr Chasey, my music teacher and father of my best friend, Nick, who also happened to be first violin in the school orchestra. Mr Chasey taught me piano, or rather tried to. What he ended up teaching me was a great and universal truth: if at first you don't succeed, by all means try again, but if you're still not getting it by attempt number 53, you should probably give up.

It happened one day, halfway into a lesson in the small music study in the school's main building. While the sun beamed down on the school's manicured lawns and the sixth-form girls running up and down the hockey pitch in their blue gym-knickers, Mr Chasey and I were locked inside the dusty music room, struggling to come to terms with Beethoven's *Für Elise*. Although written by the great Teutonic maestro, this is quite a simple Grade One piece, but I'd been learning piano with Mr Chasey for about eighteen months now and for two years previously at my prep school, and I still hadn't got it. As usual, the lesson wasn't going well. Eventually, unable to contain himself any longer, he cried out, 'Stop, stop, stop!'

I stopped. 'Sir?'

He looked pained. Stubbing out his cigarette in the overflowing ashtray perched on the lowest notes of the piano keyboard, he exhaled a huge cloud of smoke and collapsed his head into his hands. I waited patiently for him to re-emerge.

Finally he looked up, reached for another cigarette, lit it and, taking a large drag on it, looked me seriously in the eye. 'Andy,' he said, then paused for a long moment. In the silence I could hear, far off, the sounds of lunch being prepared. Cutlery clattered and the smell of overcooked cabbage seeped under the music room door and swirled around our feet. 'Andy,' he repeated, 'you're a nice chap, so please don't take this the wrong way…' he hesitated, unsure how to proceed. In the small pause, he took another long drag on his Piccadilly. 'The thing is, if your talent is, shall we say, underdeveloped in one particular area, then it's probably worth thinking about transferring your energies and your innate creativity into other fields – areas in which you have a better chance to excel. Do you understand?'

I got the gist, although I wasn't altogether secure on the detail. 'I think so, sir.'

'What I'm trying to say is, you'll never make a piano player.'

This I already knew.

'Your father's a bit of a singer, isn't he?' Mr Chasey continued.

'A bit,' I agreed.

'So, as a musician, I'm sure he'll understand. Put your music away, lessons are over.'

'Shall I go then, sir?'

But Mr Chasey was a good sport. 'What have you been missing to come to see me?'

'Double economics.'

My erstwhile music teacher winced. From my expression he could tell that I, too, was not exactly a fan of the subject. 'Tell you what,' he said, 'it's only three weeks to the end of term. We don't have to tell anybody else that I'm not teaching you any more.' He winked at me.

For the next three weeks, I learned more about life from our little chats than I ever had from any formal lessons. I also learned about music. Not the playing of it, but its appreciation. He would play me snatches of famous pieces and explain what it was about them that made them so great. Whenever he heard footsteps passing outside, he would launch himself at the piano and play a piece of Chopin, or Mozart or Bach. Once, after one of these private concerts, I was caught leaving the music room by the headmaster, who remarked, 'Well done, Secombe – you're certainly coming on.'

I smiled and took the compliment. 'Thank you, sir.'

By the time I had been at Freemen's for a couple of years – I must have been around 14 – I was set on a career in journalism. Long gone was the bold pre-adolescent who thought nothing of clambering on to a Great Yarmouth stage to help a magician perk up his act. No, now public exposure was anathema and I sought anonymity. I had visions of myself sitting on hotel balconies in exotic locations, drinking coffee and smoking Gauloises, posting copy to my London-based newspaper about the current political situation. I had designed myself a future in which I was a lone wolf, an observer, isolated from people and their messy lives.

My English teacher, however, had other ideas. Mr Cairncross was a short, energetic Scot with a slight speech impediment and a passion for language I found inspirational. It was the second half of the summer term, that dead time when, exams over, everyone treads water until the holidays. At my school, to keep the pupils occupied and out of each other's arms down in the rhododendron bushes – bear in mind this was a mixed school and the heat of summer inflamed many an adolescent's loins – every class put on a play for the entertainment of the rest of the school. Form Upper IV(b) was to produce *The Man Who Wouldn't Go to Heaven*, a one-act play by F. Sladen-Smith.

'You, Thecombe,' lisped Mr Cairncross, pointing his blunt index finger at me, 'will play the part of the Lunatic.'

'N-no!' I stammered. 'I can't. Please, no.' But my protests fell on deaf ears. Mr Cairncross had made up his mind and that was that. The die was cast and the play was to be staged in three weeks' time, in the Italian garden at the back of the school's main building.

Three weeks later I found myself dressed in a pair of my father's pyjamas, crouched behind a rose bush waiting to make my entrance, shivering uncontrollably despite the brilliant summer sunshine. I'd wanted to wear a night shirt but Dad didn't possess one, so pyjamas seemed the next best option. As you might expect, they were about 15 sizes too big for me, so I looked pretty silly which, after all, was the object. But so that I'd be able to walk without tripping over, my mother – not what you might call an expert needlewoman – had turned up the bottoms with some large, untidy stitches.

As I waited for my cue that hazy summer afternoon, I could hear the sounds of cricket practice drifting up to me from the nets at the bottom of the games field and wished with all my heart that I was there, doing something I knew. Even taking guard against demon bowler Paul Buck would have been preferable to facing the unknown territory I was about to enter. Then, as I listened longingly to the distant crack of leather on willow, I became gradually aware of another sound closer to hand or, rather, a lack of sound. A silence had descended over the Italian garden and I realised with a start that I'd missed my cue.

Leaping up, I bounded out on to the main arena – a semi-circle of grass at the bottom of the wide stone steps which led up to the school building. In my haste to get on to the 'stage', however, I hadn't noticed that one of my turn-ups had caught on a thorn, ripping through my mother's inexpert stitching, causing the hem of the pyjama leg to unravel. I got as far as delivering my opening line, 'I'm here!' before falling flat on my face. I lay there, covered in embarrassment, too frightened to move, expecting disapproving mutterings from the audience. Instead, I heard laughter. I tried to get up and fell over again – another laugh. I fell over again, this time on purpose, and got an even bigger laugh. That was all it took – I was hooked. In that instant, all dreams of being a foreign correspondent evaporated – I was going on the stage.

I joined the school drama society, or 'Dram Soc' as it was known, of which Johnny Mellor was the leading light. Johnny was a lovely bloke and very, very funny. He was also responsible for dubbing me with a nickname which follows me around to this day: Scrotum. This was soon shortened to 'Scrote' but, on occasion, I could also be 'Scrotal sac' or 'Scrote's Porridge Oats!' depending on Johnny's mood.

Although I can't say I was ever a fan of his music, I suppose I was in part responsible for Johnny's rise to punk stardom. Towards the end of my time at Freemen's, I was the drummer in a school band but, fed up with playing Monkees' hits to groups of uninterested eight-year-olds in Scout huts, I had quit. If you play keyboards or guitar, you can happily while away the time playing riffs on your own to your heart's content, but a drummer needs other people to play with, otherwise it's all just rhythmic noise – and you can go deaf very quickly. Besides, after trying to emulate Robert Wyatt of Soft Machine or attempting, and failing miserably, to recreate Ginger Baker's epic 20-minute drum solo 'Toad' on the Cream album *Wheels of Fire*, I came to the conclusion I was never going to be that good anyway, and decided to take up another hobby – photography.

My father was a keen photographer and had a darkroom set up in the garage that he was too busy to use. It so happened that Johnny had a fairly decent camera he wanted to get rid of and was looking for instruments to form a band; the solution was obvious. Johnny got my drum kit and I took possession of an early Olympus SLR. But this was all in the future.

Back to school…

The Dram Soc was a bizarre collection of misfits of various ages and abilities who liked getting together after school on Thursdays to make each other laugh. We had great fun devising sketches and putting on shows for the boarders after tea and, for nine months of the year, our little society was a law unto itself. But come the Christmas term, a teacher was imposed upon us, whose job it was to choose and direct the major school production, which was performed at the end of the Christmas term.

Happily, the teachers who put themselves forward for this job were usually good sports and would choose something frothy and frivolous, such as *The Boyfriend* or *Free As Air*, both of which I appeared in. But one year it was the Dram Soc's misfortune to have Mr Conway, the maths teacher, forced upon it. We groaned collectively when we heard the news. Conway was a short, bad-tempered sphere of chalk-smeared tweed with not an ounce of humour in his being. Needless to say, he was no fan of mine either.

Apparently deciding that there had been far too much frivolity in the past, Conway had chosen *The Insect Play*, by Karel and Josef Capek. I had no idea then what it was about, and I'm not even sure I understand it now; all I knew was that there were no songs and precious few laughs.

The characters were all insects – I was to play a Parasite – and the play itself, I later discovered, was a commentary on post-First World War Czechoslovakia, the Parasite representing the opportunists who flourished in this period. Had I known this at the time, I doubt I would have felt quite so confident in assuming that I'd be able to slip in a few gags.

But I worked hard at it and, after the first night, when I'd had them 'rolling in the aisles' with my (secretly rehearsed) bits of business, a furious Mr Conway confronted me backstage.

'Secombe!' he said, 'That was a great deal of ham with an awful lot of mustard!'

'Thank you, sir,' I beamed.

He looked at me in disbelief for a few moments before walking away shaking his head.

'Was that on granary or white bread?' I shouted after him, then turned and ran out of the building as fast as I could.

But, apart from steering me into the arms of Thespis, school was generally not a happy time. Apart from the many good friends I met at Freemen's, I was not best served by the teaching staff. Sadly, as I approached my A-levels, the inspiring Mr Cairncross was replaced by a man with all the charisma of a dead slug.

To cut a long story short, this bearded, dreary man, not long out of university and already dead-eyed, did not like me, and took to using me as target practice to hone his board-rubber throwing skills. Thus, the animosity became mutual. He was also my form tutor in the lower sixth and in a position to make recommendations to the headmaster about who should proceed to the upper sixth after mock A-levels.

Although I did well in all my chosen subjects, he complained about my 'attitude' and recommended I stay in the lower sixth for another year. The headmaster, who also regarded me with suspicion, agreed. I was understandably upset at seeing my friends move up into the giddy heights of the upper sixth without me and thought it all hideously unfair.

Needless to say, I rebelled: I left my homework undone, refused to turn up for the detentions I was set and some days bunked off school altogether to drive out into the countryside in my green 850cc Mini. On days I did deign to come into school, I would occasionally leave at lunchtime, take off my blazer and tie and go down to the local pub, returning for the afternoon session reeking of beer and cigarettes. Looking back on it now, I suppose I was a bit of a handful and, in the end, my rebellious behaviour led to my being 'asked to leave' at the end of term, before my A-level year.

So that was the end of my less than glorious school career. I suppose I could have worked harder but, for the most part, the teachers, the teaching methods and the subject matter we were forced to study didn't exactly inspire. I found it hard to become enthused about such things as the birth of the Trades Union Congress or the development of the communications network after the Industrial Revolution. Thus two potentially fascinating subjects – history and geography – completely passed me by. I came away with a paltry four O-levels: English language, English lit, French and biology, and a strong commitment never to go anywhere near anything to do with education ever again. I auditioned for drama school instead.

My sister Katy, however, did extend her academic career, becoming the only one of the Secombe children to go to university. But then she went and spoilt it all by becoming an actress:

'I was at Manchester University, 1987–90. It was a real heady time – sit-ins in the library and protest marches. I was often caught walking down the street with an M&S carrier bag, and I'd always say, "Oh, right on, up the workers," and then go home and have lunch. I was a bit of spoilt girl.

'But I never felt any pressure at university, I think because people at my uni loved *The Goons*, and Dad was still seen as a rebel – so I was very proud. Everyone really thought I was cool…And then when I went to Bristol Old Vic there were people there like Toby Jones – Freddy Jones's son – and they all thought Dad was amazing.'

6

Home Life

Dad saw his house as his castle, a place where he could pull up the drawbridge, relax and be himself. So inviting friends home from school, although never actually forbidden, wasn't actively encouraged, either. I do have a vague memory of a birthday party – I must have been five or six – and of playing musical chairs in the living room, but that aside, I usually went to other kids' houses to play.

Jane Milligan remembers her childhood at home:

> 'I was quite a solitary child; I liked my own company, so if I invited anybody back home, it would be my best friend. She knew Dad very well. She was four when I met her and we were friends until we left school. I didn't bring many people back. But if there was a birthday or something, Spike was a "featured artist" that day. But if he wasn't in the mood, he'd just keep out the way. He was pretty up-front about whether or not he was "in" or "out".
>
> 'He was a very sociable man when he wanted to be...we used to have a lot of Sunday afternoon teas with local people, friends, artists, writers...Sunday afternoon tea was a big thing.'

By contrast, Harry was a hermit. It wasn't that he was antisocial, just that he liked to choose the when and where. He found it hard to relax and be himself when around people he didn't know very well, feeling that he had to perform. Home was a safe haven for him – a place where he could be himself, unseen by the rest of the world. The trouble was we lived on a main road and were therefore at the mercy of anyone who happened to be passing. Whenever there was a ring at the doorbell, my father would dive under the sofa and stay there until whoever it was had gone away.

I remember one Sunday, when Dad and I were dozing in front of the television after lunch, the doorbell rang. My father, immediately as awake and alert as if a 25-pound shell had exploded nearby, threw himself down on the carpet behind the sofa, so that he couldn't be seen from the big bay window at the front of the house. He looked up at me and whispered hoarsely, 'See who it is, Andy.'

Not being blessed with my father's powers of instant awareness, I got up blearily and went to the door. Opening it, I found a smiling Des O'Connor and his family standing on the doorstep. They'd 'just happened to be passing' and thought they'd drop in.

Now, I have a terrible memory for names, it's a sort of appellation dyslexia and has got me into trouble many times over the years with friends and colleagues. I knew who Des was, of course, and the previous Christmas had met him and his family in Barbados. We had chatted amiably over Planters' Punches on the beach and stood in line together at the barbecue, waiting for our steaks to cook. I was, nevertheless, stunned to see them on the doorstep, in Cheam, on an overcast Sunday afternoon. My surprise, allied to the after-effects of a large lunch, consequently pushed his name right out of my mind, along with the names of his wife and children.

I ushered them all in, searching desperately through the spaghetti of my mind for a name – just one name would have been helpful. I called out to Dad to warn him that we were no longer alone.

'Dad! Dad! It's…' But who the hell was it? It was no good, the harder I searched, the blanker my mind became – now I couldn't even remember my own name.

In the end, sweating, I opened the door of the living room – just as my father re-emerged from under the sofa, covered in

feathers – and announced our guests with the words, 'Dad, it's…
some of these.'

A cloud passed over Des's face and his famous grin became
fixed. After this less than welcoming reception, he didn't stay
long.

One thing that Dad insisted on when he was home at the
weekend was Sunday lunch. These lunches were long, leisurely
affairs featuring roast leg of lamb accompanied by copious
amounts of wine and *Two-Way Family Favourites*, a radio show
on the Light Programme, presented by Jean Metcalfe and Cliff
Michelmore. This was a request show designed to link families at
home in the UK with British Forces Posted Overseas. One
presenter was based in London, the other in a BFPO station in
Canada, West Germany, Singapore, Hong Kong or Australia,
each presenter taking it in turns to read a dedication and
announce the next record.

Dad used to have us in hysterics as he took off the singers of
the day and, as the wine flowed, he would feed us little snippets
of insider knowledge about their personalities. 'He's gay,' he
would announce, as the voice of some new teen heart-throb
came zinging out of the Roberts radio; or 'He wears a wig…'
about some established crooner. 'He likes wearing high heels in
private…'. 'She snorts drugs…' The revelations would come
thick and fast. Today, with models, pop stars and actors falling
over themselves to tell the public the truth about their obsessions,
drug habits, stints in rehab etc., all these things would be public
knowledge, but back in those more reserved times, had such
shocking disclosures become public knowledge, they would have
meant ruin for the celebrity in question, and we were all sworn
to secrecy.

Of course, these sessions would inevitably turn silly. Val
Doonican once came on the radio and Dad immediately said,
'He knits all his own jumpers.'

'Does he?' said Mum – all innocence – and we fell about
laughing.

Jen and I were always expected to be home on Sundays. But as we got older and started to develop interests outside the family, this became more and more difficult to organise. I remember one of the few arguments I had with Dad was about this very subject. I'd made arrangements for the weekend to go off and do something else with friends. I pleaded with him to be let off, but he wouldn't be moved, and I was furious.

'You always expect me to be here, and yet you're hardly ever here yourself!' I told him.

It was unfair of me because it wasn't strictly true; then at the height of his career, he no longer had to spend long periods away from home. But my remark hit him where he felt most guilty and he was deeply upset by it. Lunch that day was a subdued affair.

Ironically, after I'd left home, Sunday lunch gained an attraction it had not previously held for me. In those days, as I struggled to make a name for myself in the theatre, I spent a lot of time with various touring companies, getting to know the British motorway system rather too well. Living in a world of dingy dressing rooms, mould-stained digs and smoke-filled bars, existing on a diet of chips, beer and sandwiches, the prospect of a good meal was immensely appealing, as was the opportunity to have Mum do my laundry. The continuity Sunday lunch gave me with family life was also a comfort and helped to offset the dislocation caused by life on the road. Jen, by then living and working in London, would also try and get back as often as she could.

Dad had built a bar at the back of the house during his 'African phase', decorating it with many of the trophies he'd brought back from photographic safaris he'd made to Kenya: spears and shields, animal-skin drums, ritual masks and paintings of African landscapes. It was here, in the Africa Bar, that we'd assemble. I always seemed to be last to arrive, having got into the late-rising habit of actors on the road, and would walk through the door to shouts of 'Ah, here he is at last – the itinerant thespian!' Then I would have a drink thrust into my hand and the stories would start.

I would tell of my triumphs (or disasters) on the road. Jen, who

Early Goon performance in a room in Grafton's, circa 1949.

Grafton's pub in Strutton Ground, with a proud Jimmy standing outside (he's the one with the moustache).

Mike introduces Richard to a Bumblie.

On the set of the film, *Davy*, with Bill Owen, Mum and Dad and me, circa 1957.

Paddy and Spike with Jane at her christening in 1966.

Superman and the People-Lifter.

Peter and Michael.

The Bentine family take aim.

Spike being Daddy.

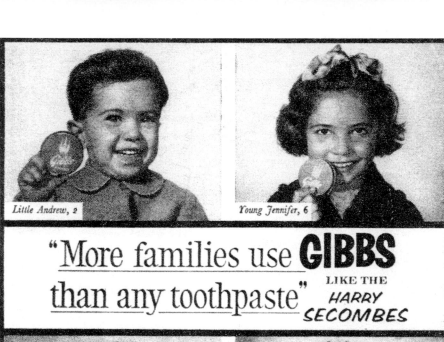

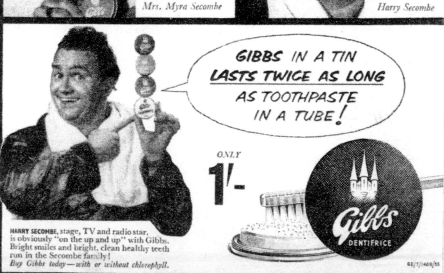

The finished Gibbs advert – the Secombe family's first and last foray into commercials.

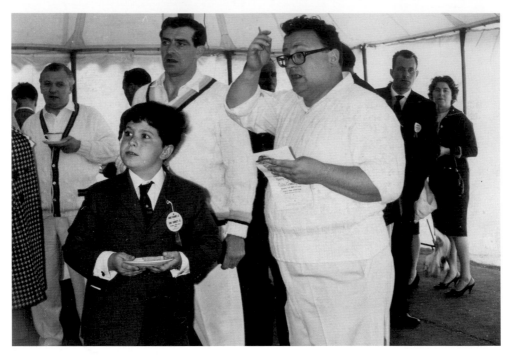

At a charity cricket match with 'Fiery' Fred Trueman and Dad. (Dad's driver, Roy Bexley, is visible over his left shoulder)

Me, Dad and Jen with the fabulous Daimler Dart (1961).

The Bentines watching Daddy on TV.

Paddy and all the Milligans.

Katy and the girls in the dressing room of Theatre Royal Drury Lane during a run of *The Four Musketeers*.

Britt Ekland – the second Mrs Sellers – baby Victoria and Peter. Peter's face says it all.

The Goons and Goon fan No.1: His Royal Highness, Prince Charles.

Katy's pre-school photo-call.

Jennifer Secombe

David Secombe

Richard with his dad, Michael Bentine

Moi

Jane Milligan

Sile Milligan

Sarah Sellers who never grew up

Katy Secombe

at the time worked for the publicist Theo Cowan, would give us all the latest celebrity gossip and then, if we were lucky, and he was in the mood, Dad would regale us with tales from his days in the army or Variety. These get-togethers were always the best of times, Dad happy to have his family around him, while we, a willing audience, laughed at his jokes and generally basked in his presence.

Mum, who was no mean storyteller herself, would inevitably excuse herself at some moment in proceedings and retreat to the kitchen. There, happy in her steamy domain, she would be kept refreshed by the odd gin and tonic, sent her way via the Secombe drinks delivery service (a role I played until my brother David became old enough to be trusted with the delicate art of spillage-free drinks conveyance).

Finally, she would summon us to the table and we'd all sit down to roast leg of Welsh lamb with mint sauce, roast potatoes, mashed parsnips, carrots, peas and jugs of thick, brown gravy. The menu never altered and we were glad of it.

Family mealtimes were equally important occasions in the Milligan household, as Sile Milligan remembers:

'We had a dinner party one year…and I think it was Dad's sixtieth, and he decided we were going to have dinner at home, which was his passion…if heaven was to be on earth, it was to have his whole family at the dinner table, at home, eating – he just loved it.

'So, anyway, we were all having dinner at home and…he used to like dressing up – he liked the whole thing of that elegance, and the manners. I always said he should have been born in Dickensian times…he was such a gentle man and a gentleman. So, normally we'd all be expecting to be told to dress up, but this particular time, he said, "Let's do something different. Everyone's got to come in fancy dress."

"Why?" I said, "are we having a party now?"

"No, it's just us for dinner, but let's all dress in fancy dress."

'So, we all turn up, Dad's dressed as Hitler, Shelagh [Spike's third wife] is dressed as Superwoman, I'm dressed up as a cat, Jane came in an Indian Gandhi outfit…Anyway, we were all having dinner and the doorbell goes. So, Jane goes and answers the door in her outfit – two policemen standing there. It's already a sketch, isn't it?

"Hello, is Mr Milligan in?"

"Hold on a minute," Jane replies, puts the door ajar, comes back into the room and says, "Dad, there are two policemen at the door who want to speak to you."

'Dad had a tremendous respect for the law, so he gets up really seriously, as if he's wearing a business suit, goes to the door, opens it, "Yes, officer, can I help you?"

'And they're standing there, staring at him, thinking, "My God, Spike Milligan has come to the door, dressed, at nine o'clock in the evening, as Hitler."

'It's not even as if he excuses the fact by explaining, "Sorry, officer, we're having a fancy dress party." It's like it's normal – you know, "We do this every Friday night!" So that was just one example of the ludicrous things that went on at home.'

The Bentines, too, enjoyed gathering around the table, as Richard remembers:

'That was another tradition – the children would do Sunday lunch. And it had to be three courses, with a starter, a main course and a proper pudding. You got put in charge of the kitchen and you ordered everyone else around.

'Dad was very into cooking – very into eating. When my wife and I moved to Beckenham, my parents came to live with us while their house was being gutted…and then, when we moved again, they moved with us. So we lived out of a frying pan for about a month before I fitted the kitchen and, to celebrate, my dad said, "I'll make pâté."

'And my wife said, "Oh, that'll be lovely…" because Dad was famous for his pâté. He would make vast terrines of the stuff, sealed with butter.

'What no one explained to my wife was, to make a pâté, he would start from scratch – with a pig. Dad was taught by one of the Belgian RAF people that he encountered and he would take all the inside bits out and grind them up and cook them. He was a very good cook, but for months afterwards we'd find little bits of chopped liver stuck on the kitchen ceiling or on top of a unit, because he was the messiest cook in the world – using every single pot and pan, with lots of South American arm movements, scattering raw ingredients from one side of the room to the other. I don't think my wife has eaten pâté since.'

Thankfully, none of the rest of us had to endure the complications of mealtimes in the Sellers' household.

In his book, *P.S. I Love You*, Michael Sellers describes a typical Christmas lunch:

'Family reunions are part of the Christmas tradition. But the atmosphere of goodwill hung uneasily over our household, because of the running feud between the two mothers-in-law, who had not even condescended to meet one another. Their differences, going back to Peg's disapproval of my parents' marriage, remained unhealed. Neither side was going to give way. Whenever it looked as though a truce had been reached, Peg would utter another remark and the wounds opened once more.

'So Christmas was always a delicate period. Christmas lunch, with all its trimmings, would be served at 1.00pm with my maternal grandparents in residence. But they would have to vacate the house at 5.00pm for the next 'sitting' when Peg and Bill would arrive for dinner with a fresh roast turkey and plum pudding cooked and served once more by my mother.

'This charade went on year after year until it was regarded as being normal routine; the only difference was that we could not talk of one set of grandparents in the presence of the other.'

One thing my father did share with Peter was a love of cars, although it never quite reached the heights of Sellers' obsession. Peter used to change his cars so often that Milligan described them as 'metal underwear'.

Dad in his time had many beautiful machines, including an Austin Atlantic, a pink 1950s Ford Thunderbird, a Jaguar Mk X, several Rolls-Royces, a 1960s Lancia Flavia, a gorgeous Alfa Romeo Giulia Spider and a Daimler SP250, otherwise known as the Dart: its looks were as brutal as the Alfa's were elegant.

The Dart occasioned one of Dad's few outbursts of rage at me. For those who don't know, the Daimler Dart was that rather staid company's attempt to get a share of the lucrative American sports car market. It was a low-slung two-seater with a 2.5-litre V8 engine under its long bonnet and, at the rear, some very sixties fins.

It has to be said, its looks weren't to everyone's taste. From the front it looked either like a grouper or a gargoyle with toothache, depending on your point of view. Dad's Dart was red, with a maroon leather interior, reminiscent of a fighter-plane's cockpit. In its day, it was one of the fastest production cars around and I loved it, despite its rather startling tendency to throw open its doors while cornering at speed – and this in the days when seatbelts were an optional extra.

My father, too, was extremely fond of the Dart and if ever he went missing at home, you could be sure to find him in the garage, sitting in his new toy, caressing its steering wheel or running his hand lovingly over the leather upholstery.

Driving to London one Saturday, where he was once again appearing at the Palladium, Jennifer was sitting in the front and I was perched on the bench seat in the back. He'd only had the car a week or so and was still very much in that heady fug of first love.

As we hit London, the traffic was bad and I, bored with our slow progress, lay down on my back and gazed up at the roof. I had recently seen Fred Astaire in a film where he appeared to dance up the wall and across the ceiling, and was still trying to work out how it was done. Absent-mindedly, I, too, now walked my feet up the interior of the car and on to the pristine, leather head-lining, where I did a sort of inverted tap dance. As I tapped away, Dad's voice broke into my reverie: 'What the bloody hell do you think you're doing!' he yelled.

At first I wasn't actually sure who he was shouting at. I thought perhaps someone had cut him up. I raised my head and looked out through the front windscreen, expecting to see a black cab or bus sitting diagonally across our path. Then I caught Dad's angry eyes in the rear-view mirror.

'Get your bloody feet off the roof NOW!'

I immediately did as I was told and sat still and silent for the rest of the journey. It was a while before I felt at ease in the Dart again.

Such incidents were rare in my sheltered existence and therefore all the more disturbing. But distressing as that incident was to me, it can't compare with what Michael Sellers went through:

'When I was four years old, I really ran into trouble – by touching a toy that was truly Dad's. Since marrying my mother, he had already bought and sold 40 cars. But now he acquired his first status symbol: a red Bentley Continental that cost £9,000. It had special coachwork and hand-finished interior fittings.

'Naturally after a succession of second-hand cars, Dad was immensely proud of it, carefully putting it through its paces on family drives around the neighbourhood. The day came when a hail of flying grit badly chipped the paintwork, and Dad was very upset. Feeling sorry for him, I set out to repair the car with a tin of touch-up paint I knew to be in his garage toolbox.

'Unfortunately, I couldn't actually see the chip marks, so to make sure every one of them was covered, I ran a stripe right around the car.

'Getting home from school that day, I expected to find Dad glowing with gratitude. Instead, he was waiting for me at the garden gate, his face crimson with rage.

"Do you know what you've done?" he yelled, grabbing me from the doorstep by the scruff of the neck. "You've ruined my car. What the hell made you do such a thing?"

"Daddy, I was only trying to make it look beautiful for you again," I sobbed.

'But Dad wasn't listening to my protests. Hauling me up to my bedroom, he yanked down my trousers and whipped me with his leather belt. Mum attempted to intervene as I screamed with pain, but she was thrown aside, my father's temper, once lost, being utterly uncontrollable.'

A lot has been written (mostly by outsiders) about what a monster Peter Sellers was, how self-obsessed, callous and uncaring. So I was relieved to hear from Sarah Sellers that home life wasn't a constant round of screaming fits and beatings:

'I wouldn't say he larked around at home like Clouseau, or whatever, but he would become other characters. When he did the film *What's New, Pussycat?* he had a long wig, and I can remember Britt [Ekland] introducing me to this person with long hair, and me not really being sure who it was…I mean, I must have been about five or six at the time…but he was a completely different character. I kind of had an instinct – it must have been the way she introduced him – and I thought, "Do I ask if it's Dad, because then I'll look really stupid if it isn't?" I didn't know quite what to do.

'I can also remember him ringing me up, putting on a voice, saying, "This is so-and-so…" and he just picked a name out of the air. It just so happened I knew somebody by that name, and I couldn't really understand why this person was ringing me. And then he burst out laughing – that was the thing with him, he would burst out laughing, so he couldn't always keep it up for very long if he was fooling around like that.'

But those famous powers of mimicry could also be put to a more sinister use:

'Dad used to impersonate people all the time, and quite often if he was irritated with somebody he might talk back to them in their own voice.

'I remember one occasion when he got irritated with his accountant. This accountant had a very particular nasal voice and I can remember Dad talking back to him in exactly his voice, complete with mannerisms and everything. I was cringing and I remember the accountant was sweating a lot. So, that could be a bit unnerving…'

I remember my father telling me that during the recordings of *The Goon Show* he used to watch Sellers in awe and admiration, saying, 'He used to stand at the microphone and morph from one character to another in front of your eyes. Whoever he was playing, he would become them – I swear he used to change shape.'

According to Sarah, whenever Peter was working on a film, he used to immerse himself completely in the character he was portraying, which must have made home life pretty interesting when he was playing multiple roles:

'Dad was always…characters, so it might have been Goon characters, it could have been anything, but he was always doing voices. In fact, it was quite a long time before I was really clear on which Goon parts he played, because he'd do all the voices at home.

'My first recollections of *The Goons* were the Telegoons, so I had an idea in my head what they all looked like. But then Dad would do doodles…little drawings and stuff, and so I had those as well…

'My mother said that *The Goon Show* days were the best days. She looked forward so much to the show on Sunday… the whole week revolved around it…'

'I think to do what he did, he really had to get inside people, so maybe he'd see somebody, or something would inspire him…I don't know. He was really interested in psychic things as well and I think that somehow he made connections with people and knew what went on inside their head, and I think that's how he did it…he really did become somebody else. It was more than just an outside observation, it was really getting inside somebody, so you would see, sometimes, personality changes…He wouldn't have been what he was if he hadn't had that ability.'

Here's what Michael says about his father's working methods:

'Playing a film role, searching for authenticity, would have an extraordinary, near schizophrenic effect on his own character and when he came home from the studios he could not switch off.

'Like the time he took on the role of a crook named Lionel Meadows, a ruthless underworld racketeer in *Never Let Go* in which he starred with Richard Todd and Adam Faith. Unable to shake off the character, he actually turned an 'evil eye' on his home and family – still playing the sinister Lionel Meadows. He was abusive and violent and we became terrified of him.'

Sarah adds:

'He was very sensitive to other people and picked up moods from them, so that if somebody was miserable, for example, he could get pulled down quite easily by it. If you didn't have the right expression on your face, he might pick up on it – that sounds very negative, but it was part of his make-up. He was very in-tune with moods, so I think it was probably quite hard for him – it is if you are sensitive to that sort of thing in others. But also then, because he was successful, I think the boundaries between reality and fantasy might have got a bit mixed up… because nobody contradicts you, you probably then think you're always right when perhaps you're not, so it's probably quite a hard place to be, to have those abilities. I think of him as an actor rather than a Goon. His job was an actor, but his personality was a Goon.'

And sometimes, for Peter, being a Goon on his own could be rather lonely, as my sister Jennifer observes:

'The saddest thing was…Dad and Peter have the same birthday – 8 September – although Peter was a few years younger. And I do remember, it was a Sunday and, you know, Dad used to like having all his chicks round the table at lunch on a Sunday. We'd sit there and have our lamb and wine and it was his birthday, so it was even more special – we'd all bought him presents and had a great day, and he got up and said, as he usually did on his birthday, "I must ring Peter."

'And he went off into another room. Peter was in Gstaad – it was at the time when he was estranged from his latest wife, Lynne Frederick, and had also alienated his children from two of his former marriages. Dad came off the phone in tears, and I said, "What's the matter?"

"I've just spoken to Peter," he said, "He's on his own, it's his birthday, I'm the only person who's phoned him. You know – he's got all the money and the fame and he's not happy."

'There couldn't have been more of a contrast in their two situations. Very sad.'

When Dad was home, he wasn't what you might call energetic – he would spend large portions of the day in bed, then get up and potter in his study or, if the weather was nice, lie in the garden with a book. He didn't have any hobbies, apart from reading and photography, and although he enjoyed the vista of a well-kept garden, gardening itself was a closed book to him. He once showed a visiting professional gardener around our patch in Cheam, proudly pointing out all the weeds.

Michael Bentine, on the other hand, sounds as if he never stopped and, as Richard remembers, home life could be occasionally explosive:

'Explosions were fundamental and occurred on an almost weekly basis in the Bentine household. Dad liked to use an explosive for just about everything. He enjoyed the bang, which is why I think he always had models on his shows that blew up. Some days in late summer, we had the ritual of potato digging, where children from far and wide would come and the youngest would be allowed to press the charge. Potatoes are grown in what I call "Toblerones", so Dad would crimp up charges in cigar tubes. He stopped smoking in the mid-sixties, but he never stopped buying cigars. He'd chew a cigar all day – never light it.

'So he had all these cigar tubes, which are ideal to crimp a charge into: just the right size and shape. So he taught all these children how to crimp a charge into a tube and then you'd poke a hole in the ground and push one of these in about half a metre apart, retire, charge up the wind-up box, and the youngest would get to pull the lever up and push the button – big Ka-Blam! – and everything would settle and you then simply had to remove the potatoes from the top. Fantastic. I thought that was how you dug up potatoes, I thought it was normal!'

People often ask me if Dad was as nice in person as he appeared to be on television. It's boring to have to say it, but he was. Dad at home was just like his on-screen persona, but with the volume turned down. I'm not saying that life with father was a constant assault of gags, raspberries and top Cs, but he was funny, in a way not many people saw; he was certainly much funnier in person that he ever was on television.

He was also good company. He could make an otherwise mundane trip to the local shops a joyous experience, offering a running commentary on things he saw, making jokes out of odd street names or advertising signs. I remember on one of the few occasions he drove me to school in Epsom, we passed a firm of solicitors named Gascoine-Pees, which happened to be right next door to a shop called Chambers.

'Have you heard?' he said as we drove past, 'Gascoine pees in Chambers!' which tickled my schoolboy sense of humour.

But best of all was watching television with him, especially if it was a bad film; he'd insert dialogue and off-screen noises and have you in hysterics.

Having said that, he had his off days like any normal person, and even – Shock! Horror! – occasionally got angry. However, one tried not to court his displeasure, not that he was verbally or physically violent, but he did have one weapon in his armoury that would stop us dead in our tracks. If we'd done something wrong, he would peer at us over the top of his glasses with his pale-blue eyes. Those eyes, normally so sparkling and alive, would be stripped of all humanity and warmth, and it was into a bleak, wintry landscape that we found ourselves gazing. The contrast was absolutely chilling; it was a look that hinted at unnamed terrors.

Five minutes later, after we'd slunk away and repaired whatever damage we'd done, apologised to Mum or the neighbours, or taken the cat down off the roof, Dad would be his old self again, the bogeyman lurking behind his eyes nowhere to be seen. He'd smile and ruffle our hair and say, 'Good kids,' and the sun would come out again. I think he was a better actor than most people gave him credit for.

Unlike Sellers, I don't remember Dad ever 'bringing his work home'. He might have wandered around the house singing snatches of new songs, but as far as he was concerned, there was a strict division between work and home. If he was in a new musical, for example, he would spend a day or so in bed, reading his lines, or sit in his office listening to a recording of the music, learning the songs – but that's as far as it went.

Neither was he keen on rehearsing too much. I always got the impression that he found the rehearsal period frustrating as it got in the way of the bit he enjoyed most: performing.

He could never understand why the actors he worked with loved rehearsing so much. Coming from a 'non-legit' background, he was always a bit in awe of 'proper' actors. And although he would inevitably refer to them using the old Variety term, 'La-di-dahs', he respected them and their craft.

He was, however, mystified by the reluctance of a number of them to get up and 'move' a scene until they knew exactly what motivated the actions of their character. This fondness for sitting and talking he found frustrating beyond endurance. While the 'La-di-dahs' sat around discussing the finer points of a dramatic exchange, mining the text for Stanislavskian gold, Dad, beneath a calm and polite exterior, would be seething, thinking to himself, 'Do we really have to go through all this bollocks?'

I tried to explain to him that this was the way most modern actors worked, trying to find the 'inner life' of the character. His reply was, 'You don't find the inner life of a character by sitting on your arse talking about it. You find it by getting up and looking for it!'

He has a point.

But returning to Michael Bentine's labour-saving method for unearthing potatoes, and the joyously dramatic effect it had on his family. Michael, having been trained by military intelligence, had also been schooled in the use of many different firearms, and was recognised as the best combat shot in the UK. He also held a Home Office licence, which meant unlimited gun ownership, and was occasionally asked to hold weekend shooting schools. It should, therefore, come as no surprise that the Bentine children were familiar from an early age with a whole range of weaponry, as Richard admits:

'We had a walk-in gun safe in Esher and, at any one time, we probably had anywhere between 30 and 70 guns in the house, ranging from standard military revolvers through light sub-machine-gun, heavy machine-gun, rifles, automatic rifles, sniper rifles…

'But more bizarre than that was that because of these guns in the house, Dad insisted we all learn about guns, to treat them with respect, but also how to use them, to strip and clean them…Sometimes, he used to hold weekend shooting schools.

'So, from the age of eight, I'd go with Dad to the shooting schools he held. We'd sometimes go to the Guards' range, near Bisley, where he'd give a talk about this combat firearm technique he'd developed called double-tap or shuffle-shoot, which is a method of moving through a building and being able to shoot in close proximity…and then he'd say, "I tell you what, it's much better if I get someone else to demonstrate it." And then he'd get either myself or my sister to walk down the range, demonstrating the techniques…and there was something impressive about a seven- or eight-year-old child walking down a shooting range chopping targets in half with an Uzi. And he'd say, "There you go, you see, fat, old, wheezy, asthmatic Peruvian and his eight-year-old children can do it… now it's your turn." He did that up until about 1978 or '79.'

And what of well-known wild man, Spike Milligan? Surely home life with that mad genius must have been unbearably chaotic?
Jane Milligan recalls:

'Everyone imagines that Spike's house must have been a house of chaos and madness, but it was so ordered and tidy and organised – he was an army man, he needed that organisation to be creative. So he ran a very tight ship.

'As Paddy [Jane's mum] became sicker, he began to take over her parental duties. He'd been living a lot at the office in London during the week, and when she died, he said, "I'm going to work from home now, I think I need to be with you." So he set up his office in his bedroom.

'We had big house in Barnet. He was very disciplined, and when he got up he'd do press-ups and his exercise bike. He played squash religiously; he swam – we had a pool in the garden and we swam in the summer. He was very fit – he didn't drink a lot. He took sleeping tablets because of the night-time dreams about the war. But he was a disciplined man during the day. He'd write until lunchtime – he never had lunch – he'd have a cup of tea and a piece of cake in the afternoon, then he'd write all afternoon and then stop about seven o'clock and come down for dinner.'

And of his famous bouts of depression Jane adds:

> 'He was a very sensitive man, a very intelligent man, and he suffered a lot in World War II. It left him mentally scarred and I think that was the root of his sadness. I've seen him when he was depressed, which he allowed himself to be. He'd get depressed and go to bed for a couple of days, take a lot of tablets, be out of it, and then he would relive the war – things that happened to him…
>
> 'When Spike was ill he was very creative in those times – he used those times to write. So he'd be in his room and be writing, sleeping, then writing poems and stuff, ramblings… He'd call down for food or tea or whatever, and I'd go up. He didn't really want to see any adults, so I'd take up his food. But that's just what my dad did.'

So, I suppose none of us could claim to have had a 'normal' home life, but then again, one's view of normality is defined by circumstance, and we didn't know any different. It was simply life as we knew it and, although we all enjoyed some fun moments and special holidays, none of us woke up in the morning and thought, 'Wow! My dad's a Goon…how special is that?'

For me, most of the time, life was fairly mundane: I'd go to school, come home, do my homework, watch television and go to bed. But then, from time to time, and for the weekends only, life really would become extraordinarily special.

7

The Palladium and Other Playgrounds

My very earliest memories of the Palladium are from when Dad was in a show called *Large as Life*, with a cast that included Terry-Thomas, Eric Sykes, Hattie Jacques, Adele Leigh and Harry Worth. Also appearing were John Puleo, The Dior Dancers, and Latona Graham & Chadel, whoever they were. The year was 1958 and the moment I walked through the stage door of that famous theatre I was hooked on showbusiness.

I loved the smell – a mixture of make-up, size and adrenaline (or was it sweat?). I loved theatre people, whom I have always found, almost without exception, to be friendly, generous and kind, so unlike the bitchy journalistic stereotype. I also loved the way they looked, their stage costumes and make-up giving them the appearance of beings from another, better reality.

Sadly, my memories of this show are patchy, but I do recall Hattie Jacques being very nice; Adele Leigh being very beautiful; Harry Worth bumbling around, strangely like his forgetful, on-stage persona; and Terry-Thomas making me laugh more than anyone I had ever met.

The Palladium show that has most memories for me, however, is a pantomime – *Humpty Dumpty*. With its all-star cast – Alfred Marks, Roy Castle, Gary Miller and Stephanie Voss – its colourful costumes and a chorus line of tall, glamorous girl dancers in fishnets, it was about as far removed from the dull, grey conformity of school life as you could get. There was even a scary ogre, a tall, black-robed villain with long, witch-like fingernails, upon whom Jennifer once opened the door of the loo, getting the fright of her life.

Saturdays would start early. I would wake up excitedly and, unlike school mornings, when pulling on my school uniform could take an age, I'd be dressed in seconds. Then I would run downstairs to ask, 'Is it time to go?' only to find that no one else was yet awake. The next few hours would be spent fretfully wandering around the kitchen, or playing with my dog, Jimmy, with occasional and excessively noisy trips back upstairs to Mum and Dad's room to see if there were any signs of movement.

Eventually, Mum would get up and prepare Dad's breakfast, which she would lay out on a tray and take back upstairs. Sometimes, I'd take his breakfast tray up to him. Mum would place the newspapers on the tray alongside his plate of toast and tell me not to spill the tea. So seriously did I take this instruction and so carefully and slowly did I mount the stairs, that by the time I actually reached the bedroom, the tea was cold and his toast a soggy, inedible mess. I would then lie on the bed next to him and try to get his attention, while he blearily came to his senses, ate his breakfast, turned on the radio and tried to catch up on what was happening in the world. I could never understand how he did it – I still can't – but he seemed to be able to read the newspaper, follow what was going on on the radio, eat breakfast and make conversation with me, all at the same time. How's that for multitasking?

Finally, after what seemed like years, Dad would eventually be up and dressed and, after an early lunch, we'd get into the Rolls and be on our way to London.

Jennifer remembers:

'It was like our second home, the Palladium. I think Dad's first Palladium show was around 1956, so he was still very much doing *The Goon Show*. And we used to go up in the morning and Dad would often make a big day of it and would take us for lunch at Verrey's, which was an Italian restaurant, I think it was in Regent Street, where they had the best Melba toast I've ever tasted. And we always had spaghetti and that lovely Italian fizzy water – San Pelligrino – that was the first time I'd had it and I thought it was very sophisticated, and Dad would speak to all the Italian waiters in his Neapolitan accent.

'And then we'd go to the theatre, and George, who was on the stage door, would welcome us in and we'd go to the dressing room. We knew all the stage hands and were great friends with lovely Jack Matthews, the stage manager. We were the only children who were ever allowed to stand side-stage at the Palladium because we knew when to get out of the way, and we were quite well behaved. I remember Gary Miller's sons weren't allowed, because the last time they'd been there, they'd climbed up onto the gantry and thrown things down on stage.

'It was like being in a magical world, especially shows like *Humpty Dumpty*, which had some wonderful costumes and scene changes, where an entire castle was transformed into a wreck. We'd be in the dressing room, or we'd be side-stage to watch the bits that we liked...

'One of my earliest recollections is standing side-stage, holding a brandy and ginger ale in one hand, and a chamois leather, soaked with 4711 cologne in the other, watching Dad, singing his heart out on stage, sweat pouring down him, with this glorious voice – top Cs ringing out – and then coming off, short-sightedly stumbling into the wings and saying, "Was I all right, Jen? Was I all right?" And me then patting his head with this cologne, and he'd take a great slurp from his brandy and ginger, and go back on for his encore.

'And that to me was just...I thought, "Coo, that's what my dad does for a living – it's got to be better than anything else."'

The Palladium No. 1 dressing room was split into two parts: one contained a make-up table, sink and hanging rail; the other was more of a reception room, larger, with a couch and chairs, and a wardrobe with sliding doors, which doubled as a drinks cabinet. This wardrobe held just about every drink you care to mention – Dad kept a very well-stocked bar. It also housed a huge chest containing a massive block of ice, on which beers and mixers were kept cool during the summer, and from which chunks were hacked off with an ice pick and placed in ice buckets, to be distributed around the dressing room for the use of guests after the show. I, too, used to enjoy attacking that block of ice, sticking the resultant chips in my Coca-Cola.

Dad's dresser was a canny East Ender called Billy de Haven. Billy was a real character and had once been in the business himself, in an act called de Haven and Page. He had a nose like a tomahawk and, in profile, looked like an image you might find carved on a Native American totem pole. He was also quite deaf, wearing hearing aids in both ears, which I'm almost certain he never turned on. This often led to confusion, as was the case with the affair of the nightgown.

It was coming up to Dad's birthday and his mother (Gladys) wanted to buy him something, but didn't know what to get him. Mum suggested a nightshirt, because, apparently, Dad wanted one – hard to believe that my father fancied himself as Wee Willie Winkie, but there it is.

'Don't worry,' Mum said to Gladys, 'I'm going up to see the show next week. I'll get Billy to get him a nice one from Simpson's or Liberty.'

Before the show, Mum explained the situation to Billy, gave him ten quid (this was the sixties) and Billy, nodding knowingly, went off shopping in the West End.

After the show, while Dad was getting changed in the other room, Mum took Billy aside and asked him how he'd done. Billy, tapping the side of his large nose, brought out a box he'd hidden behind the ice chest and proudly unveiled its contents: an extra large, sheer, pink, satin nightdress. 'She'll love it,' he said.

Billy was fiercely protective of Dad and, by extension, us – once he even saved me from being arrested.

Gary Miller, a good-looking singer, (famous for supplying the vocal to 'Aqua Marina' over the end credits of Gerry Anderson's *Stingray*) played Tommy Tucker in *Humpty Dumpty*, had three sons, all of them great fun and fabulously naughty. Jennifer and I were saints by comparison, five-card poker being probably the tamest thing we learnt from them. Jonty, the youngest, also taught me how to make paper water bombs.

Directly across the road from the Palladium stage door was a café called the Bon-Bon, which Billy would often take us to. Once, after taking tea there between shows – having smuggled a ready-made bomb out of the theatre in my pocket and desperate to try out my new-found skill – I surreptitiously filled it with vinegar from the Bon-Bon cruet while Billy went to pay. Coming out of the café, I lobbed it at a passing coach. Unfortunately I missed and ended up hitting a police car. Billy, horrified, immediately picked me up under one arm and belted back to the safety of the dressing room. Luckily, Dad was having a nap, otherwise I might have had to endure a severe finger-wagging.

When we arrived at the theatre before the matinée, Dad would take off his coat and settle down to the pile of mail delivered to the stage door that Billy had laid on his dressing table, and Jen and I would do the rounds, saying hello to our old friend Jack Matthews, and all the stage hands. Then we'd go and see if Roy (Castle) was in yet. Roy played Simple Simon in the show and was a lovely man, extremely fond of Dad and always pleased to see us. We probably overstayed our welcome on more than one occasion, but he never seemed to mind, allowing us try on his tap shoes and teaching us how to get a note out of his trumpet by blowing raspberries into the mouthpiece. Later on, he would teach me how to play the drums – Mum still hasn't forgiven him.

After this, while Jen went off to chat to some of the other acts, I might wander upstairs to the chorus room, where the girl dancers changed. They always invited me in and made a fuss of me – which was heaven. They were tall and gorgeous and wore next to nothing and, even though I couldn't have been more than six years old, I fell in love a thousand times.

When the half-hour was called, there'd be a definite change in energy. Dad would start to 'come alive', like a dynamo winding up to full pitch. By the time 'Beginners' was called, he would be raring to go; you could almost see sparks flying off him. We'd follow him and Billy to the side of the stage where he'd share a joke with Jack and various members of the cast, while the orchestra played the introduction and Roy went into the opening number. Then, when his cue came, he would explode on to the stage to be greeted by huge cheers.

Once the show was on, if we weren't watching from the wings, we might go through the 'pass door' which led from the side of the stage into a small corridor. To the right, through a red velvet curtain, lay the stalls, but to the left, a flight of stairs led up to the royal box, and many was the afternoon Jen and I watched the show from that exalted spot.

The theatre may have been a second home to us, but we learnt early on that it could be a treacherous place. Dad was constantly twisting his ankle and getting bruises from tumbling through trap doors, and you didn't want to get in the way of the stage crew during a scene change, as they hefted heavy bits of scenery and stage weights, especially at the end of the 'House of Cards' scene, when the entire set collapsed.

We stayed well out of the way at such moments and Jack appreciated that, so our appearance backstage was tolerated, unlike the Miller boys. In fact, as we became more accustomed to the ebb and flow of the show, we were sometimes allowed to help out. I, for one, was eager to get on stage – not in a performance capacity, I was far too shy back then – I just wanted to experience what it felt like to be in front of a Palladium full house.

There was one Palladium show – I think it was *London Laughs* – when, towards the end of the first half, there was a sketch with Thora Hird and Freddy Frinton as a pearly king and queen. During this, a miniature train came on stage, worked by a stage-hand who sat inside and pedalled like fury. The train was built to accommodate one man, and it was a tight enough squeeze for him, but so desperate was I to experience a Palladium audience, that I befriended the man who operated it and asked him to show me how it worked, which he obligingly did. A few nights later, I plucked up the courage to ask Jack Matthews if I could sit in the train as well, to help steer the thing. 'I know how it works,' I told him, hoping that my knowledge of the interior secrets of the mechanism might count in my favour. To my great surprise, he agreed, adding a warning that I should do everything the stage-hand told me.

'This is the professional theatre,' he said, 'If anything goes wrong, you'll get me in trouble.'

I liked Jack far too much to want to cause him any grief, so I said he could count on me. The train had to come on from the stage-left wings, describe a large, 180 degree parabola and stop, parallel to the orchestra pit, on a set of white marks. Then, after a short scene, move off into the wings again.

The stagehand and I both clambered into the train through a panel in the side which was held in place by a small ball-catch and had a painted gauze over it, which meant we could see out, but, under the lights, no one could see in. There was also a gauze at the front of the cabin, which allowed us to see where we were going. I waited nervously for our cue. The inside of the train was cramped and hot and smelt strongly of glue. Then, at a tap on the outside, we were off, the stagehand pedalling for all he was worth. I concentrated intently on where we had to go, determined not to knock anyone over and equally determined to hit the marks. The moment we crossed the threshold between the darkness of the wings and the brilliance of the stage, I could feel the heat from the several thousand lights concentrated on the apron – it was thrilling, I was on stage at the Palladium! Amply aided by the stagehand, who had been managing to accomplish the manoeuvre perfectly well on his own, twice-nightly, for several months, I managed to negotiate the train around the scenery and actors without mishap and hit our marks dead on. Feeling immensely pleased that, so far, nothing had gone wrong, I relaxed a little. While the scene went on around us, I gazed out through the gauze in the side of the train in awe to see 2,000 people staring back. The auditorium seemed to go on for ever, and it was full of shining, happy faces. I pressed my nose to the gauze to get a better view and felt the small catch give. Before I knew it, the door had fallen open and I had made my impromptu stage début. I have to say, it wasn't my best performance – I froze in open-mouthed astonishment, staring at the audience for a few moments, before the stagehand yanked me back inside and pulled the door shut.

I can't now remember the reaction of the audience, but luckily, neither Jack nor I got into trouble – in fact, everyone had a good laugh about it, but it was decided that it was probably best that I should not repeat the performance.

But the action at the Palladium wasn't only on stage, as Jennifer recalls:

'Dad's dressing room at the Palladium was like a gentleman's club. Dad always had an amazing display of drink for all the people who used to come in and, my God, the people came in! Huge stars: Zsa Zsa Gabor, Jean Simmonds, Paul McCartney and Jane Asher…loads of people came to his dressing room and we just watched it, it was like a moving kind of cinema.

'I do remember Frank Sinatra was once at the Palladium and my autograph book used to be in the dressing room permanently, so whoever was starring in *Sunday Night at the London Palladium* [a TV show that went out at the time] used to sign my book. Well, unfortunately, Frank Sinatra didn't sign my book, but what he did do was sign the dressing room mirror: "Thanks, Harry, love Frank!" But, of course, they couldn't leave it there, so Dad took a photograph of it – somewhere there's a photograph of the signed mirror. But, yeah, they were the days.'

James Grafton, too, was a Palladium regular:

'I was often at the Palladium when your dad was there – I was going out with one of the girls in the chorus line – and when

Harry's dresser was busy, I became unofficial drinks' monitor.

'I remember Tommy Cooper coming into your dad's dressing room one night and producing a bag and an egg, and he said, "I'm going to make this egg disappear out of this paper bag..." and he dropped the egg into the paper bag and it fell straight out of the bottom and smashed on the carpet. "There we are," he said, and walked out of the dressing room. I think I was left with the job of clearing up the mess.'

Jane Milligan remembers another Palladium story that sheds light on a side of Spike some might find surprising:

'I can remember the Palladium...I remember Spike meeting Bing Crosby at the stage door one night – we went to see Bing Crosby live – and it was interesting for me because Dad was already well known and a lot of people use to hang around and want his autograph, and there he was, desperate to shake the hand of the man who was his hero – my dad was a massive fan of Bing Crosby – he was almost on his knees shaking his hand. I found that very interesting.'

It has to be said that, despite its drawbacks, having a famous father is an undeniable advantage when it comes to entering the magical world behind the scenes, that closely guarded territory festooned with no-entry signs. Jane Milligan agrees:

'I spent a lot of time in the studio at the weekends with him. He used to take me to the BBC and I used to hang around, which was brilliant fun – absolutely great. Television Centre – I used to run wild, happily, on my own in that great, big circular building, going in props stores...I just had a brilliant time, it really was very exciting, and I was allowed to be there because I was his kid. You don't realise that at the time... mingling with the cameramen, hanging around watching things being filmed, watching your old man with all these other guys, creasing up, having the time of their lives.'

Sarah Sellers also enjoyed that privilege:

> 'I loved going to the film studios, I suppose because it's all make-believe…I often used to hang around the wardrobe and I found that all very interesting and also, the crew – they were always larking around, there were always practical jokes going on. It was great, although it's probably very different now…
>
> 'I went as well when Dad did a *Muppet Show*, and that was fascinating, to see behind the scenes.'

I remember visiting Dad on the set of *Oliver!* in which Dad played Mr Bumble. The day I went, they were filming the sequence where a trembling Oliver approaches Mr Bumble and says, 'Please, sir, I want some more.'

On that day, I also met Jack Wild, and found to my surprise that this cocksure, miniature adult was two years younger than me. Taking me under his wing for the day, he showed me around the studio as if he owned it, introducing me to the crew and the rest of 'the Orphans'. He was absolutely charming and it's very sad what happened to him later on.

On another occasion, Dad and Terry-Thomas were invited to appear on the *Tennessee Ernie Ford Show*. Tennessee was an American singer, famous for the song 'Sixteen Tons'. He'd come over to 'Little England' to record a 'typically English' episode of his show set in a golf club located somewhere among the green hills of Surrey – you can imagine. It was the middle of summer and so, of course, the weather was atrocious.

The day I went to visit the set, it rained persistently. All day, cast and crew were cooped up inside, in a dangerously well-stocked bar, waiting for a break in the clouds. I can't remember now whether or not any filming actually got done, but what I do recall is Terry keeping us all amused for hours with endless stories. He was a genuinely funny man and I don't think I've ever laughed so much in my life.

And it wasn't only theatres, film sets and television studios we had the privilege of visiting. In the sixties, Dad was made president of the Panda Club, the junior arm of the World Wildlife Fund, set up by Sir Peter Scott. In his capacity as president, he didn't seem to have to do much except attend the odd event and make the occasional speech.

Once, he was invited to London Zoo to meet a tiger cub they had just acquired, and he took us along with him. We had the most magical day; quite apart from the fun of getting to go 'backstage' and feed some of the animals, we were privileged enough to be allowed inside the cage with the baby tiger. Under current health and safety laws I doubt this would be allowed, but back then nobody minded if you were savaged to death, as long as you'd enjoyed yourself. About the size of a small dog, this young tiger was unbelievably cute and extremely playful but extraordinarily powerful. One gentle push from his oversize paws was like being hit by a train.

Jen and I became fairly blasé about meeting the rich and famous and, during the sixties, we met an awful lot of them. Charity golf matches always had a good celebrity count. Anything that involved golf would invariably attract people like Sean Connery, Stanley Baker, Bruce Forsyth and Ronnie Corbett. Then there was the cricket match that Dad held every year in the ground opposite our house in Cheam. The likes of Tommy Cooper, Graham Stark, Cardew Robinson and Eric Sykes would turn out to play, as well as some professional players, sporting heroes of the past such as Alec and Eric Bedser, Colin Cowdrey, Fred Trueman, Ted Dexter and Ken Barrington. I remember Shirley Bassey even turned up once – not to play, unfortunately.

Jennifer also remembers these matches:

'I do remember Dad used to have a cricket match every year, which was at Sutton Cricket Ground which was right opposite our house in Cheam.

'One year, Peter Sellers and Spike – I don't think Mike was there – they came and played cricket, and we had this big party afterwards, and it was the first time I'd seen lots of people drunk. It was absolutely amazing – I was walking round our house, which had turned into this extraordinary place. One actor, I think it was Mario Fabrizi, was sitting cross-legged on the floor eating peanuts, wrapped in one of our curtains. And my grandmother – Gran Atherton, my mother's mother – was absolutely furious. She was going back and forth into the kitchen, bringing out plates of food, and she was going, "He's on the floor! He's wrapped in the curtains!"

'And there's Dad behind the bar, dispensing largesse and large measures, fuelling all this mad behaviour…'

There were many such parties, which would usually go on all night. If Jen and I kept quiet and under Mum's radar, we could escape being put to bed early. Settling ourselves somewhere inconspicuous – under the piano was always a good place – we'd listen to the grown-ups' stories. Sometimes, Jen, being that bit older, had to explain some of what was being said. But occasionally even she was baffled by what the adults were talking about. Not that we really cared; to have the house full of these exciting, vibrant people was a pure joy. The storytelling, the jokes and the laughter are things I'll never forget.

But it was the time at the Palladium that shines brightest in my memory. Everything was heightened: the lights made everything clean and sharp; the costumes and make-up made everyone beautiful – it was a magical place and I wanted to stay there for ever. For one perfect day of the week, I was able to escape to a different world, where everyone had a happy ending. But, sadly, after Saturday came Sunday, and after Sunday, Monday, which could only mean one thing: school.

There was, however, one thing that got me through the long, dark days of the school year. One thought that kept me going as I shivered in goal in the pouring rain on a muddy football pitch, or faced ridicule from the Latin master because I couldn't tell my gerund from my dative, or once again suffered a beating from the florid-faced headmaster for some minor infringement of school rules. That thought was…Christmas in Barbados.

8

Barbados and Other Paradise Islands

The promise of Barbados shone like a jewel at the end of the long, dark tunnel of the autumn term. I endured pain and hardship with a smile because I knew that, in a few short months, I would be lying by an azure sea under a Wedgewood-blue sky, with ice clinking in the drink at my elbow, and not a care in the world.

These days, for the wealthy middle classes, trips to exotic destinations such as the Caribbean are the norm rather than the exception, but in the early sixties, air travel, especially transatlantic air travel, was only for the lucky few. My school friends would seethe with envy whenever I told them where I was going for Christmas.

Before being seduced by Barbados, the Secombe family had tried other tropical destinations – our first Caribbean trip, when I was about three, was to Jamaica, where we stayed in a hotel right on Montego Bay. Breakfast was served in the garden of our private chalet by white-gloved waiters. I remember, as an appetiser, they would peel an orange, stick it on a fork and present it to you. I've never tasted such fabulous oranges since. Unfortunately, the memory of this holiday is clouded somewhat by my father's insistence that I work.

I was due to start primary school the following year, and Dad thought, to give me a head start, I should be able to read before I got there. I wasn't keen and disliked intensely the half-hour I was made to spend in the company of Peter Rabbit every morning. I should point out, having laid down the law, it wasn't Dad who taught me, but Mum who was saddled with the task of trying to get an angry three-year-old to pay attention to the adventures of Peter Rabbit, Flopsy, Mopsy and Cotton-tail. I hated these sessions; as far as I could see, all they did was cut into valuable time that could have been much more profitably spent on the beach, and I have never been able to look at a Beatrix Potter book since.

Jennifer remembers:

'We first visited the West Indies when I was about seven and we stayed in Montego Bay in Jamaica. I learned to swim in the Caribbean. There was a fisherman who used to row his boat among the swimmers and brought me a different-sized conch shell every day. I thought he was a kind old man and only much later realised that my poor dad must have been paying for all those shells – half of which we had to leave behind because they were too heavy to carry home.

'I also remember an enormous black lady who used to sit at the entrance to the beach selling large bottles of coconut oil to promote a suntan. Mum used to rub this oil all over us before we went into the sea and we ended up with third-degree burns. I lost the top three layers of skin on my cheeks and shoulders – and to this day get freckles in those places – and Andy had burns right down both his arms as well. He was burning up in a fever with the after-effects of sunburn when the hotel's barman came to the rescue. He sent over a freshly mixed concoction that included white rum and lime juice and instructed Mum to bathe Andy from top to toe in the mixture. "The fever will leave through his feet," he said. And it did. I only wish I knew the full recipe.'

I've had a fondness for rum and lime juice ever since.

After Jamaica, we tried Trinidad and Tobago. I remember very little about these islands, save the endless, golden-sand beaches and the warm tropical nights. I do, however, have one memory of getting stuck in the hotel lift in Tobago. It was one of those old-fashioned gated lifts and on the inside above the buttons was a big sign which read, 'Do not attempt to open lift gate between floors'. This was like a red rag to a bull to me, and I burned with curiosity to discover what would happen if I disobeyed this notice. So, purely in the interests of scientific exploration, you understand, I yanked open the gate between floors two and three. What happened was that I got stuck and had to be rescued by the hotel manager. Dad was not amused and, after this incident, despite my protestations that I was only conducting an experiment, I was forbidden from riding the lift alone.

Jennifer, being that little bit older, remembers more about these trips than I:

'From Trinidad we flew to the little island of Tobago. We stayed at the Blue Haven Hotel, a place frequented by the likes of Robert Mitchum and Ava Gardner – sadly not during our stay. It was a wonderful holiday full of tropical beaches, new sights and sounds and dipping into a grown-up world. There would be a formal dinner served every evening, with the British in their black ties and the Americans in their white tuxedos. Andy and I had been brought up dining in restaurants and knew how to behave under those circumstances; consequently, we were allowed to accompany Mum and Dad to dinner.

'It was beyond glamorous. The velvety-black tropical nights, the rhythm of the steel band, the elegant guests foxtrotting on the dance floor, the exotic cocktails, the witty conversation. I couldn't wait to grow up.

'I remember going to a "Shipwreck" party one night with Dad – Andy wasn't very well so Mum stayed behind. The idea was to dress as if you had to abandon ship in a hurry. I wore one of Dad's shirts and Dad wore a vest and a pair of shorts. It was so much fun to have Dad to myself for a change – and he danced with me on the dance floor, too. He was the centre of attention, as usual, and I rather liked the feeling of being next in line.'

We once even took a cruise. Again, I have very sketchy memories of this, but I do remember playing the bagpipes in the shower. They were a present from Dad, but why he bought them for me, I have no idea – I don't remember being a *White Heather Club* fan – and the noise they made was unbelievable. Too embarrassed to play where anybody could hear me, I used to lock myself in the bathroom of our cabin. Needless to say, I never really got the hang of them and ended up using them as a multi-barrelled water pistol.

Jennifer remembers a little more:

'In 1956 we went on a cruise on board Cunard's new, luxury liner, the *Antilles*, from Southampton to Trinidad. We had a suite which had been full of vases of flowers sent from friends, including Eric Sykes, wishing us bon voyage.

'After a couple of days in the Bay of Biscay, the vases were regularly falling over. And for some reason we pointlessly kept picking them up and putting them straight again. The ship was enormous and there was a separate dining room for children, so that they could eat early and allow their parents to let their hair down later.

'All the ship's crew were French and I was very dubious about going into the dining room with my little brother and making myself understood. Dad had to sit on the steps outside the restaurant for nearly half-an-hour, reassuring me and teaching me the odd French word to help me get by. I think it was on this cruise that I realised that Dad was not as other men. Whenever we stepped out of our cabins, people stared at us and there always seemed to be an expectation from them for Dad to perform. He never usually disappointed, and it did sometimes seem as though he was being taken away from us against his will.

'But Barbados became our Christmas destination of choice

– we must have spent at least seven Christmases there when I was younger. We stayed at the Coral Reef Club, a colonial-style hotel with huge ceiling fans, wood panelling and cane furniture. The grounds of the Club sprawled over dozens of acres and enjoyed a frontage over one of the best bays in St James.

'I remember staying in cottages with names such as Frangipani and Bougainvillea, and smiling maids coming to cook our breakfast every morning. We ate paw-paw and ugli fruit followed by bacon and eggs and hash-fried potatoes and a fresh selection of home-baked breads and pastries.'

The Coral Reef Club was a sprawling, old-fashioned resort on the west side of the island, with individual chalets dotted around spacious grounds, and a clubhouse, open on three sides, with bars and dining areas, where one could eat lunch and watch the sea ripple lazily up and down the beach. The place was run by Budge and Cynthia O'Hara, an English couple who became great friends, inviting us on fishing trips and to parties and barbecues.

Days at the Coral Reef would be spent lounging on the beach reading, or chasing lizards in the surrounding palm groves. Sometimes Jen and I would go scuba diving with a man called Les Wooton, who ran a dive school next to the hotel. Les looked a bit like Lloyd Bridges, but walked like a penguin and spoke, as befits someone who spent long periods of time under the sea, with the adenoidal twang of a man with water up his nose.

He was a kind, patient man who loved his job and still, after years of teaching tourists how not to drown while under 30 feet of water, was not at all jaded. He excitedly revealed to us the wonders of the tropical reef that lay just a few hundred yards off-shore as if he'd just discovered them himself, leading us through clouds of tiny, silver-blue fish that parted before us like mist, pointing out huge, fearsome-looking conger eels slithering through the reef's nooks and crannies, and showing us delicate, filigree fan corals and squid that squirted sepia in our faces when we got too close.

Once or twice we got to go on the *Jolly Roger*, a four-masted schooner that sailed lazily up and down the sheltered coast of St James's with its cargo of tourists. The sole purpose of these jaunts seemed to be to teach adults how to drink a rum punch on a deck sloping at 45 degrees. Nevertheless, for a nine-year-old, such trips were packed with adventure. We'd drop anchor off a deserted beach and swim ashore to have lunch. And while the adults got stuck in to even more advanced rum-themed instruction, such as drinking in a horizontal posture, Jen would trawl the beach for shells and I would go looking for pirates. Or, if I was in reflective mood, I might sit under a palm tree and chat about life, the universe and everything with Quarrel, the gentle, leather-faced first mate, who was a natural philosopher.

Jennifer recalls:

'Dad always liked to take us out on a fishing trip every holiday. We would hire a small launch and skipper for the day, venture out into deep water and set up the fishing lines. Mum and I would find the best suntanning position on deck and soak up the rays. Dad would shout instructions at us periodically reminding us to apply sun cream. Meanwhile, he would be holding a rum punch in one hand and the fishing rod in the other, his face a picture of contentment. We rarely caught anything, but one trip we were escorted by a school of dolphins who played with the boat, diving underneath it and then leaping into the air in formation. It was a spectacular display.

'However, every year our fishing trip ended the same way - Dad as red as a lobster and nursing an almighty headache. We usually ate in our rooms after a day at sea.'

But when not nursing a 'fishing hangover' in our chalet, we would dress and wander along the moonlit beach to the dining room.

Dinner at the Coral Reef was a formal occasion and sometimes, beforehand, there would be a cocktail party at one of the chalets. I always loved these occasions, everyone looked so glamorous –

the ladies in their cocktail dresses and the men in their expensively tailored tuxedos. I would feel very grown up as I mingled in my very own white tux', sipping my 'Bentley', a non-alcoholic drink made with pineapple juice, grenadine, soda water and a dash of Angostura bitters, dressed with a dusting of nutmeg and a glacé cherry. The default drink for the adults at these affairs, as it was for most occasions on Barbados and for all I know still is, was the Planter's Punch, which was basically the same as a Bentley, with the cockle-warming addition of a generous slug of rum.

The traditional recipe for a Bajan Planter's Punch is one measure of lime juice, two of grenadine, three measures of dark rum, the whole topped up with soda water. A good way to remember this is by way of a short poem, taught me by a kindly Bajan barman: 'one sour, two sweet, three strong, four weak'.

Most of the time, people drank sensibly, if steadily, but just occasionally things could get a little out of hand. I remember one poolside party hosted by Johnny Johnston. Johnny was the man who wrote the 'Rael-Brook Toplin, the shirt you don't iron!' jingle, which was one of the first television commercials. He was also responsible for 'Beanz Meanz Heinz' and 'You can be sure of Shell!'

At this particular party, a bartender new to the Coral Reef had been employed and, obviously muddling his weak with his strong, made all the Planter's Punches double strength. After just a couple of drinks, the adults were all smashed. Some fell in the swimming pool, where they were soon joined by others, hooting with laughter. It was like the pool scene in *It's a Wonderful Life*, and that night a jolly mood prevailed in the dining room as the diners assembled in their soggy evening attire.

The food was pretty good, too. We would dine on freshly caught flying fish, barracuda and marlin, clam chowder, barbecued pork, fillet steak, or saddle of mutton. The whole event would be rounded off with a floor show while we tucked into baked Alaska or crème brulée. The cabaret – a troupe of fire-breathing limbo dancers accompanied by a steel band – never altered, and was probably incredibly naff, but to my young eyes it seemed wildly exotic and exciting.

After dinner, guests would wander out to take coffee on the terrace overlooking the moonlit Caribbean sea, accompanied by the chirruping of frogs. It was here, one magical evening, that John Cleese, whose knowledge seemed fathomless, taught me how to spot the constellations.

Jennifer continues:

'We spent many a New Year's Eve in Barbados in the presence of the great and the good. I remember the Centre Point millionaire Harry Hyams posing on the beach in full Red Indian headdress; Jimmy Tarbuck declaring in a stage whisper as he arrived unexpectedly in the dining room, "Harry Secombe's a poof!"; listening to the chimes of midnight with John Cleese, Michael York, Val Doonican, Des O'Connor, David Coleman, Nicky Henson, Wolf Mankowitz, et al.

'The writer, Wolf Mankowitz, had moved to Barbados to live with his family. That year, the *TV Times* printed a cover photo of Dad dressed in Dickensian costume to promote his TV variety show. It put the idea into Dad's head that he was the perfect fit to play Samuel Pickwick. He put the idea to Wolf over a few rum punches and, some months later, the first draft of the musical *Pickwick*, based on *The Pickwick Papers*, dropped through our letter box. It was a role that Dad would relish, that would take him to Broadway, win him awards and provide him with the hit song "If I Ruled the World".

David remembers:

'One thing I liked about seeing Dad at Barbados was that he was genuinely relaxed. He got to know the regulars so well it was like he felt he didn't have to perform. It was quite nice meeting people like Marty Feldman, because they were always pleased to see Dad. I remember meeting Eric Idle, and Dad just making him laugh continuously for about two hours over lunch. I don't remember Eric saying very much, just giggling.'

'But Barbados also had that dream-like quality…I remember once going back to school more or less the same day I got back and suddenly finding myself on a bleak January afternoon out in shorts on a fives court, going, "Why?"

We once even met the then Lord Mayor of London, whose name escapes me now. He was there with his family and was an extremely nice man with a very dry wit. Our two families got on well together. It just so happened that he was also chairman of the board of governors of the school I was then attending.

The following year, he visited the school on speech day, to hand out prizes to leavers and to pupils who had shown an aptitude for running fast, hitting balls or jumping over things. Needless to say, I hadn't won anything, but I did contrive to get a friend of mine who had to give the Mayor a message that I was in the audience and sent my love. The Mayor immediately looked for me in the crowd. I stood up and waved and, much to the annoyance of the headmaster, who already had a very low opinion of me, the Lord Mayor smiled warmly and waved back. I'll always remember my feeling of triumph as the headmaster twitched in impotent fury while the Mayor shouted out to me, 'Give my regards to your father!'

Another enjoyable facet of Christmas was, of course, the presents. As children we were spoilt rotten. On Christmas morning, we'd wake up in our beach-side villa to find the place covered in packages. How Mum managed to fit them all into our suitcases, I'll never know.

After opening our presents and leaving our rooms knee-deep in wrapping paper, we would go to church – something we never did at home. We were welcomed warmly at the local church but, as the only white family in the congregation, were at first regarded as a bit of a novelty. When, however, the singing started and the Secombe family let rip, any previous reservations the congregation might have had about us fell away. At home, Dad held back during community singing as, when he got going, his voice could easily overpower the lustiest of choirs but here, in holiday mood and completely anonymous, he was able to relax and sing out and, at the end, was applauded for it. It was wonderful to be in a congregation where singing was regarded as a joyful activity and not, as in most English churches, a chore to be endured.

After the service, back at the Coral Reef, there would be Christmas lunch, Bajan style. As a prelude to this, Father Christmas would arrive on water skis, complete with beard, red hat and coat, a huge sack of presents slung over his shoulder. To the accompaniment of a steel band, the guests (Planter's Punches in hand) would go down to the beach to meet him and be given a small gift – I lost count of the number of 'male grooming' sets I got year after year.

Then we'd all troop back to the clubhouse for lunch. Although there was traditional Christmas fare on offer – turkey with cranberry sauce and all the trimmings – most people opted for the barbecue: chicken, beef, pork, mutton, Spanish mackerel, marlin, shark, kingfish…whatever you wanted was thrown on the glowing coals and cooked to order by a phalanx of toqued chefs.

After lunch there would be more competitive drinking, much laughter and even more drinking. Most of the guests would eventually pass out on the beach, with only the hardiest carrying on partying through the heat of the afternoon. Then, around teatime, there would be a short amnesty while everyone slept it off or else ate toast and muffins on their verandas and prepared themselves for the evening's entertainment, when the party atmosphere would be ratcheted up even further and the drinking and dancing would go on into the early hours. Ah, happy days…

Jennifer also remembers these halcyon days:

'Every Thursday there was a barbecue night with entertainment from steel bands and limbo dancers. Part of the fun of these holidays was spending most of the day partially clad on the beach and then dressing up for the formal evenings.

'We were a magnet for other guests. People always warmed to Dad's personality – his sense of fun was infectious. As a family we were a self-contained unit, happy in our own company, laughing at in-jokes and generally radiating a feel-good atmosphere. We had our own pet names for people – "The waiter with the swept-back eyes" or "The woman with the very close legs" and we had our own codes. If Dad was being pestered by unwanted attention from over-enthusiastic fans, which happened only very occasionally in Barbados, that was the cue for the youngest of us at the time to feign tiredness so that we had the opportunity to make our excuses and leave.'

Our younger sister Katy remembers:

'Barbados in the seventies was the coolest place in the world – everybody who was anybody was there…I remember meeting Eric Idle at the Coral Reef Club and I remember John Cleese and his daughter being around…all these wonderful, glamorous people…

'I suppose because I was podgy and not very "glitterati", I felt a little bit out of place there. It was very glamorous: jet-set proper, very, very exclusive. I mean, anybody can go there now, but in those days it was quite rarefied with all these vastly wealthy people.'

But one of Katy's last memories of Barbados is not quite so glitzy, because it was here, after a 19-hour flight from Australia, Dad arrived with a perforated colon and raging peritonitis:

'We'd been there for about five days – we met Dad there. He came over from Australia and I so missed him: I hadn't seen him for a good 12 weeks, and when he arrived…he didn't look well. I remember meeting him at the airport and he was very grey, and even as a 12-year-old I knew something was very wrong.

'I was awoken in the middle of the night by some commotion; Mum had phoned for the ambulance and they were taking Dad away on a stretcher, and I remember him saying to me, "Look after your mother."

'I really honestly thought he was going to die then.

'I went and stayed in the next door chalet with my friend Katie; she tried to keep me occupied. That night he had to have life-saving surgery and was then in hospital for six weeks.

'We spent another two weeks out there, me and David, with Mum going back and forth to the hospital in Bridgetown every day. Thankfully, David and I were looked after by all sorts of people on the complex, but I felt very sad and confused and a bit lost. And then David and I flew back on our own, because we had to go back to school. That was a very lonely journey.

'But I didn't cry until I came back home. I didn't realise until I got home how much it had upset me. It was a horrible time. You're in this beautiful place, this paradise, and it kind of took the shine off it for me after that. I didn't really want to go out there any more.'

One year we shunned the Caribbean and went to the Seychelles, of which I remember little except the food. A mixture of French and Indian cuisine, I couldn't get enough of it and put on half-a-stone in the two weeks we were there.

Katy, however, remembers the Seychelles for an altogether different reason:

'People always ask me how I got into acting, and always expect the answer, "Well, because of my father…" But the real reason is that I went to a pantomime in the Seychelles with Dad, who pissed himself laughing all the way through it. But he had to leave at the interval. It was the worst pantomime ever – it was amateur, all ex-pats doing a turn for the natives, in this sweaty little tin hut. And I loved it so much, I decided there and then that that was what I was going to do it for a living.

'I remember saying, "This is the best thing ever!" I was absolutely entranced. Poor Mum had to sit with me for an hour. So that was my entrée into showbusiness. I didn't take any notice of what Dad was doing…'

I should probably explain why Dad left during the interval. Just before curtain up, David had tripped and hurt his ankle – not badly, but it was quite painful at the time. However, after being initially entertained by the atrocious performances in this truly appalling show, after an hour-and-a-half the joke was starting to wear thin and, at the interval, Dad said we should use David's twisted ankle as an excuse to leave early. But Katy would have none of it; she wanted to stay and threatened to scream the place down if we dragged her away. In the end, long-suffering Mum endured the torment of the second half with her, while Dad, David and I slunk back to the hotel. Dad and I put David to bed and stayed up chatting over a warming bottle of rum. Mum, arriving back much later, exhausted, with an over-excited and voluble Katy, was not amused.

Closer to home, in the years before Dad discovered the attractions of Mallorca, Italy was a favourite destination. Dad felt at home there and, from his army days, was familiar with the language and culture.

One summer holiday we spent on the Island of Ischia, in the Bay of Naples. The beach was covered in dark-grey volcanic sand, which was a novelty after the powdery, golden sands of the Caribbean. But there were a couple of other even more memorable things about this holiday: the ice cream, which was a revelation after what then passed for the stuff in England; and an equally eye-opening trip to Pompeii. It was still being uncovered back then, but to see the houses, shops, streets and squares, with their statues and vibrant wall paintings appearing out of the 2,000-year-old lava, took my breath away and fired an interest in Roman history which persists to this day.

We weren't the only Goon family to enjoy exotic holidays in exclusive locations. Mike Bentine favoured California, as Richard Bentine recalls:

'Dad bought the house out in Palm Springs in about 1978. He'd go out there every winter. He was asthmatic and, as you know, Britain is the perfect place for asthmatics – the perfect place to get it. So he used to go out whenever he could…

'Invariably, he was always trying to find work and then, at some point, he realised he didn't need to find work, he'd just go out to California where all his friends were – friends he'd made in America in the fifties and sixties – and he would write for them. So he would go out and write for people like Mel Brooks and Carl Reiner and Sid Caesar and Dick Van Dyke. He also wrote 18 books – some fiction, some autobiographies, some on the paranormal, short stories…he was an avid writer, in real longhand.

'He'd spend six months of the year in California, writing a book…He'd be sitting out in the sun, thinking, and Mum would go out to him and say, "Shouldn't you be doing something?"

'And he'd say, "I am doing something…"

The Sellers' holidays were, as you can imagine, not at all straightforward, as Michael Sellers confirms:

'My mother faced an embarrassing experience when spending a quiet holiday in the South of France with John and Jackie Boulting. By the second day, Dad was writing off the holiday as a disaster. He didn't like the hotel, he found the setting unsympathetic, and secretly protested to Mum that "he couldn't tolerate John at any price". This wasn't actually true, but Dad always felt threatened by John's intellect. He promptly walked out, taking his bag with him and checked into a hotel in nearby Nice.

'This left Mum in an extremely embarrassing position. She had to apologise on his behalf and try to account for his disappearance. She also had to explain why she was still there. Fortunately, John understood my father extremely well and didn't bear any malice.'

In the seventies, when work was slowing down for him at home, Dad found a whole new audience in Australia and began to spend more and more time out there. On one of his first trips, we all went with him and immediately fell in love with the place.

Sydney was our first port of call, I didn't know the city at all, obviously, but I remember one night, unable to sleep, wandering around Sydney on my own, getting happily lost, but feeling completely safe.

Katy felt the same way when she went out with Mum and Dad to film *Sunstruck*, a Jimmy Grafton-scripted film featuring Dad as a Welsh school teacher newly arrived in the outback:

'I loved Australia. I had a tutor. I didn't need one, but I demanded one – I was only about four – I can't remember what this person was like, but I do remember I was taught to read by them. David had the same teacher, although he was slightly older. I missed quite a few months of schooling during the filming.

'We stayed in Cairns and I remember having a crush on the make-up man, who I realise now was probably gay. I remember a succession of hotel rooms…We went to Sydney, we went to Adelaide, Melbourne, Perth. I remember going to New Zealand as well and climbing up glaciers.

'Maggie Fitzgibbon was the romantic lead, opposite Dad. She was lovely, very friendly and warm. Derek Nimmo was also in it, but I don't remember much about him. And there was that wonderful Australian actor, John Meillon.

'I remember we went to Dunk and to Malola Lyly, which is a little island off the Australian mainland. We had a tin boat each, because the hotel was based around a lagoon – it was extraordinary. I made friends with a maid called Rachel and she took me up into the rainforest, and her family lived in a tree – I'm not kidding. And I was given food on a banana leaf and I remember saying, "Oh, we have baked beans at home."'

Dunk is a tiny island off the Queensland coast, on the edge of the Barrier Reef and only accessible by air and, one year, we spent a memorable Christmas there.

Our first view of Dunk was from the window of a twin-engined Cessna which flew out of Cairns. It was a picture-book tropical island, its edges fringed with white coral sand and the interior covered in dense, emerald-green rainforest. Landing was a little hairy – on a beachside strip exposed to sudden gusts from the sea. But we got down safely and, after we'd disembarked, stood on the airstrip in dumb wonder, entranced by our surroundings.

The only accommodation was a small hotel, a homely place with, as you'd expect from a place run by Australians, no airs or graces. We had small but comfortable chalets and all the guests ate together in the bar. At night, flying foxes would appear; these are large, fruit-eating bats which have a fondness for coconuts and, in the evening, they used to raid the palm trees around the hotel. The bats' eating habits are not exactly refined, and at night they would crash noisily into the palms, causing most of the coconuts to tumble to the ground. Walking through the palm groves to dinner was like running the gauntlet, as coconuts thudded into the sand all around us.

There was a pool, but also a 'protected lagoon' in which to swim – an expanse of sea which, we were assured by the hotel owners, was absolutely safe and inaccessible to the many sharks that patrolled the reef. Nevertheless, we had never seen anyone actually swimming in it.

One day, enjoying a drink in the beachside bar, we understood why. We watched as a man, newly arrived on the island, stood up to his waist in the lagoon, fishing rod in hand, calmly waiting for a bite in this supposedly safe haven. Suddenly, Dad noticed something; there, at the very edge of the lagoon, was a sight familiar from a thousand Hollywood movies: a triangular fin slicing through the water, heading straight towards the place where the fisherman stood. Dad waved – the man smiled and waved back. But when we all started waving and shouting, he got the message and left the water hurriedly and, if I remember rightly, screaming in a rather unAustralian way – he must have been a Pom. We limited our bathing to the pool after that.

It turned out the hotel was rather sensitive on the subject of sharks. A few days later, I went fishing with one of the hotel workers and, for some reason, he insisted we walk half-a-mile up the beach before we got started. It seemed strange to me, but I soon discovered why he was so keen to be out of sight of the hotel.

In a deserted bay, we perched on some smooth, sea-worn rocks and cast our lines. After about an hour of casting, reeling in and casting again, I thought my hook had snagged a rock. Although I pulled with all my might, it wouldn't budge. Then, just as I was about to ask my fellow fisherman for a knife to cut the line, the rod jerked violently in my hand and whatever it was that had swallowed the hook, shot off towards the open sea, emptying the reel in seconds.

I stood on the shoreline for some minutes, having a tug of war with the unseen beast, while my companion shouted instructions as to what I should do.

'Get some slack in the line, mate!' he yelled. 'Pump the pole to give yourself some slack!' He should have saved his breath. I could do nothing; it was taking all my strength just to keep hold of the rod.

At last the fish turned and headed back towards the shore and the line fell slack. Winding like fury, pulling the rod upright and winding again, I gradually brought whatever it was to shore. As it neared the beach all became clear – it was a 5-foot, grey nurse shark.

'Ah, it's only a baby,' my Aussie friend said disparagingly when I'd eventually landed the thing.

'Thanks,' I said, dropping to the sand, breathless, feeling as if I'd been arm-wrestling with Arnold Schwarzenegger and his entire family.

Notwithstanding that my catch was only a youngster, the Aussie lost no time in finding a large rock and dropping it on the thrashing shark's head. It twitched for a few seconds then lay still. I had never seen a shark up close before and examined it minutely, absolutely fascinated. But as I studied it, feeling its rough skin, marvelling at its streamlined contours, staring in its black eye and at its wide, untidy mouth which was turned down at the edges, giving it a sad, gormless expression, I was overcome with compassion. There was something pure about this denizen of the deep. It had been patrolling the oceans, virtually unchanged, since before the dinosaurs walked the earth. A marvel of design, it was a simple, honest predator that mated when it got the opportunity and ate when it was hungry. And then some newcomer, a mere few thousand years old, had come along and, with all the artifice and trickery of his species, had dangled a bit of dead fish in front of it and deceived it. I felt dishonest and faintly ashamed. But it was too late now to repair what I'd done and put it back in the water; my Aussie friend had seen to that.

He mistook my dismay for disappointment, thinking he'd upset me by impugning the size of my catch. Trying to make it up, he thumped me on the back and said, 'Well done, mate, she's a beaut! But, er...' he looked suddenly shifty, then added, *sotto voce*, 'Don't tell anyone back at the hotel. Don't want to upset the guests, eh?'

I gave him my word I would not speak of it and we returned to the hotel, leaving the fish to be picked up later by a kitchen party.

That night, my catch appeared on the menu as Spanish mackerel. It proved very popular. I had the squid.

Such adventures aside, it's Barbados and the holidays spent on that Caribbean paradise I remember with most clarity. Sadly, we all have to grow up and, by the time I was in my late teens, family holidays were the exception rather than the rule. David and Katy still accompanied Mum and Dad on their annual Christmas trips abroad but, by this time, Jennifer and I had both left home and, although a free trip to Barbados could never be sniffed at, it was sometimes hard for us to work it in around our other commitments – in other words, girlfriends and boyfriends.

I do, however, remember Christmas 1973, when the prospect of a Caribbean holiday was just too tempting to resist. I was at drama school, living in a draughty, cold-water flat with a dodgy gas heater, longing for some sunshine. But there was a snag – spending Christmas with my family in the Caribbean would mean missing the first week of the spring term, and taking even a few days off was frowned upon.

I went to George Hall, the head of Central School and asked his permission. To my surprise, he refused, saying it wasn't fair on the other students (which was true) and that it was time I learnt to keep my commitments, just as I would have to in the real theatre. I thought seriously about what he said, completely saw his point, and decided to go anyway – the prospect of sea, sand, sun and rum punch was just too tempting. Using the fuel crisis as an excuse, the day before I was due back, I sent a telegram to George to explain my absence on the first day of term which read simply: 'No petrol – no planes'.

When I got back, I expected a severe reprimand from George, but he simply rolled his eyes at me and shook his head sadly. I think he'd been genuinely hurt by my actions, and it was only much later on that we were able to laugh about it.

That was the last time I went to Barbados and I still miss it. Not a Christmas goes by when I don't long to be lying once more on its pristine beaches, sipping an expertly made Planter's. I did take my family to Cuba a few years ago, but that was a miserable experience, with the exception of a trip to Havana, which was great fun. But the 'resort hotel' we stayed at was fenced off from the rest of the island to keep the guests 'safe from the natives'. It should have been the other way round – I would have much preferred to keep company with the friendly but dirt-poor locals than with most of the hotel guests.

One day I'd like to get back to the Coral Reef Club and let my kids experience the kind of Christmas I enjoyed when I was their age. But expecting it to be the same as it was when I was there is, perhaps, a fond hope. On second thoughts, it's possibly safer and potentially less upsetting to revisit my Caribbean in memory only.

9

Unwanted Attention

One of the problems facing any child of a celebrity parent is having a famous name – it's like a tag that marks you out from the crowd, especially if it's unusual, like Milligan, Bentine or Sellers, and a name like Secombe is a dead giveaway. When I was much younger, I approached parties with dread, as I knew that sometime between blind-man's-buff and jelly and ice cream, the father of the birthday boy or girl, usually after a surfeit of Bristol Cream, would get a certain look in his eye which always prefaced my being taken aside and treated to a welter of embarrassing *Goon Show* impressions. It was never meant maliciously, but it did get a little tedious.

Sometimes it was simplest to remain incognito, a technique Jennifer employed:

'I do remember as a teenager, going to parties…and I'd never give my surname. Madonna does it nowadays, I suppose, but then I was "Jenny – just Jenny". In fact, my family's never called me Jenny, it's always been Jen or Jennifer. Dad used to call me Frengible – but that's a whole other story…

'The biggest problem was that you were prejudged. People would either say, "Oh, have you got a lovely voice?" or "Can you tell me a joke?" or, "I'll bet you're not as funny as your dad!" and I'd think, well, no, I'm not, but, you know, I'm me. I was always so proud of him and loved him so much, but sometimes I'd think, "Hang on a minute, I'm a person as well."

David's strategy was to try and blend into the scenery:

> 'There are pictures of me at Jennifer's wedding where I am
> actually skulking…It's hard for a hesitant, insecure nature to
> have the klieg light of attention swivelled on to you just because
> you're sitting next to the celebrity who happens to be your
> father.'

Whenever I complained to my school friends about the attention
that having the surname Secombe occasionally attracted, I was
usually informed with a sneer that I could always change my
name. But that wasn't really a serious option for a 10-year-old. It
was, however, something I seriously considered when I became
an actor, not so that I wouldn't be buttonholed by drunks at
parties, but so that I wouldn't be compared professionally with
Dad.

In the end, I decided against it. The media would inevitably
have found out, and those in the business by whom I might want
to be viewed unconstrained by preconceptions – casting directors,
producers and the like – would know anyway, so there didn't
really seem to be much point. In the end, I'm glad I didn't,
especially after seeing how terribly affected some of my colleagues
at drama school had been by being forced to change their names
prior to joining Equity. It might sound daft, but for some of them,
taking on a new name was like taking on a whole new identity,
and one or two took a long time to come to terms with it.

Sarah Sellers had a similar love-hate relationship with the
family name:

> 'Sometimes people ask me and then look at me and say, "Oh
> yes, I can tell by looking at you." Sometimes people say in an
> offhand way, "Any relation?" And when I say, "Yes," they
> almost fall over because they can't believe it. I mean, sometimes
> people who I've known for years say, "Oh, I never knew that
> your father was Peter Sellers," and they're really surprised.
>
> 'But I suppose I like it that way, because I feel that if people

know your background they make judgements about you without knowing you and that's the thing I don't really like. Other times, people just don't put two and two together and that's fine…'

'I mean, that's always been my life, so you kind of get used to it, but sometimes people find it intimidating or something like that – they think you're going to be…whatever. I don't know what they think…but when they get to talk to you and get to know you, they say, "Oh, you're not at all like what I thought you'd be."

'I've gone through various phases, but having said that, I do use Sellers for business and it just seemed a bit silly to change it. As I'm an antique dealer, I think probably the connection isn't that obvious, whereas if I was working in the media there probably would be more reason to.

'It's mattered to me to be successful in my own right and so, I think, doing anything in film or related areas would have been hard for me because I'd have been always wondering – if I had been successful at all – whether it was the name…I mean, other people might not feel that way, but it does matter to me.

'I suppose for the years the kids were at school, I used my married name, so it was quite easy – I suppose from a woman's point of view, it's easier to do that. But nowadays, I don't really feel that I should have to pretend to be someone else. I've kind of done all right. Most people think I've done quite well in life, just from the point of view that I've got nice children and my business is OK. I think I'm fairly stable, so I don't feel a need to be anybody other than myself.'

Meeting all the Goonchildren, it struck me as odd that so few of them had followed their fathers into the business. Paddy – Jane Milligan's mother and Spike's second wife – was a singer, so Jane had two parents in the business. Although the tragedy of losing her mother quite early on certainly played a part, perhaps – even though she finally ended up following in her father's footsteps –

her experience gives a more general insight as to why so many of us shunned the limelight:

'I find it very interesting, fame…you feel quite special sometimes, because you're with this amazing person who's getting all this attention and you're on the periphery of it and sometimes life is nicer for it – and then sometimes it's not.

'I loved the theatre, I felt really good in that environment and I think that was my calling, to be a singer and a performer… I was very sad about losing my mother and I think she would probably have been a shining light and a guide to me – I'd have gone to drama school and all that, but having lost her young I then spent quite a lot of time trying to recover. It was such a tragedy for our family – it blew our world apart. She died when I was three months short of my twelfth birthday. It's never a good time, but it was a bad time for a young girl – my confidence was really shattered and I spent a few years trying to build it back up and then drama school was looming and I really wanted to go and I used to get the prospectuses every year, and then I'd look at all the information and stuff…I had the talent, I could have done it, but I thought, "No, they're going to destroy me – they're going to break me down!" – you know how they do? They kind of break you down, then rebuild you, and I thought, "I can't put myself through that."

'Plus, having Spike as a father, I found that troublesome at school sometimes, with the teachers – they just assumed that I had an attitude that I didn't have. I remember in the drama group and in the English group, they would always leave me out…But even now, people assume you have a certain attitude, because you have this famous dad.

'You couldn't find anyone more insecure about their talents than me. And so I crept into theatre through the back door. I started out taking tickets at the Duke of York's Theatre, then I became a runner for Cameron Mackintosh, then I was a dresser, then an acting ASM [Assistant Stage Manager], then I was a sound no. 2, then I was a sound no. 1 – I climbed up the backstage ladder.

'I was quite successful at sound, I was running the sound department on *Phantom of the Opera* when I was 21, so I really achieved a lot. And then I got fed up with all these actors with terrible egos, so I left theatre and became an aromatherapist for a while. By then I had a flat and, of course, being an aromatherapist didn't pay the mortgage, so that's when I joined *Forbidden Planet* – I auditioned for Bob Carlton and I became a part of Bob's troupe.

'I toured with *Planet* for two years, and then I did 'Jack to a King'…I was an actor/musician really. I play a lot of instruments and I got that from Dad. His attitude to instruments was, "Have a go!" There were pianos everywhere at home, so there was a lot of music in our house.

'Theatre is my real love, musical theatre. Not mad keen on telly, there's a lot of waiting around and a lot of idiots involved. I love films and I love radio – I love all that.'

Richard Bentine never contemplated following in his dad's footsteps, but I suspect this was only because he was already deeply involved in the Michael Bentine creative industry:

'I was never tempted into the business…from when I was very young up until Dad died, if he did a show, I'd go along and see it. Or I'd go along and drive him – even though I had my own businesses to run – just for the opportunity of spending time with Dad.

'I'd do front of house for him – get his props sorted…I'd do all of that because he was the best person in the world to travel with – everything was funny. He would do this endless stream of consciousness rant about drivers, pedestrians, vans, signs on shops: 'Have a nice cup of…CLOSED'…'One of the finest buffets on…CLOSED'…'All-day breakfast, served… CLOSED'.

'And he'd comment all the way through films, too. Dad was

a brilliant person to sit and watch films with…I was brought up with black-and-white cowboy films, black-and-white war films and black-and-white science-fiction films. And, of course, Buster Keaton, Harry Langdon, W.C. Fields – he used to adore visual gags.

'We went through a spate of about four years where we'd make movies in the garden – like Peter. Unlike Peter, who used 16mm film, Dad used Super 8 and stop-frame animation, sand pits, toy soldiers, aeroplanes…We made quite a lot of war films. There's one shot I've still got of a Stuka with one wing tied to a ruler and I'm running behind it down the garden, holding the camera on this Stuka coming in on a bombing raid. It was great, and we had a little editing suite…editing the film with sticky tape and razor blades.

'I also used to do some of the voices [on *Potty Time*], especially if they had to sing, because Dad was tone-stupid. Dad was convinced he sounded like Howard Keel; I can only assume that it was Howard Keel at the bottom of a mine-shaft…

'From a very young age, my earliest memory is of Dad walking in with a script saying, "Tell me if this is funny." Then sitting us down and telling us the whole story and seeing if we would laugh…He was convinced that all comedy was fairly universal in age and it was how you dressed it up…A lot of the sketches from *Square World* were used as stories on *Potty Time*…

'When he started doing *Potty Time*…I think there were 130 episodes…for each of those episodes he would design all the characters, all the sets, all the costumes and any props that were required and he'd do those as A2 or A3 drawings. A model, for instance, was an A2 or an A1 drawing which had footprints put on and labels saying: 'This explodes' or 'Tree bends as giant passes by…', 'Well handle turns, bucket drops…', 'Invisible Man falls in well, spume of water…' all that sort of thing…And we'd stick the labels on or colour them in…

'For a normal storyline for a *Potty Time* there might be between 20–30 drawings…so there were thousands of them, of which I have quite a large collection on my walls at home. Basically, everything Dad did was normally a family activity.'

Peter, it seems, was keen on his kids following him into the business, but Sarah Sellers wasn't lured by the bright lights and knew from an early age that showbusiness wasn't for her, saying, 'I wasn't remotely tempted. I think there are just so many insincere people…Because Dad was so successful, you kind of saw the worst of it, the worst of the hangers-on, and I just can't bear people like that – the insincerity.'

Her brother Michael, however, did dip his toes in the water:

'Having left school, it was time to think about my own future. Dad would have been happy if I had chosen to go into the theatre and did his best to persuade me into it. I was actually given a small part in *The Magic Christian* as a young hippie in an Afghan coat and I was paid £30 for five days' work…

'Dad was very patient with me. Blake Edwards invited me to work on the video equipment of *The Return of the Pink Panther*. My initial enthusiasm, however, quickly waned. For three months, I just hung around the set, with less to do than the clapper-board boy.'

Michael actually ended up as a sound engineer in the studios run by George Martin, who, apart from being the Beatles' record producer, also produced several of Peter's comedy records. There, he worked with many of the day's top bands, and even got to play bass guitar on various albums. But, finally, fed up with the pop/drug scene, Michael decided on a career as far removed from showbusiness as possible – he became a carpenter.

In the Secombe family, however, there were two of us mad enough to follow Dad on to the boards: me and sister Katy, who occasionally wished she'd chosen a more sensible career, like mountaineering:

'In my first term at Bristol Old Vic, in 1990…the first term at drama school is always a bit wobbly, because you're being taken apart…I did a concert for the World Wildlife Fund, I think at the Avon Gorge Hotel…I used to get terribly nervous when I sang. And I found out that someone had leaked to the press who I was and I remember flipping out, getting into an awful state, thinking the audience would be full of journalists. I remember feeling this awful pressure…what if it all goes wrong? What if my throat closes up? In the end, it turned out to be one man from the local paper.'

Katy went one stage further than me and actually appeared on stage with Dad, in the revival of *Pickwick*. She got the job purely on merit, but there were some people who were not convinced:

'The only time I had it really badly thrust in my face was at Gillian Lynne's party [Gillian Lynne who choreographed *Cats*, and also worked on *Pickwick*]. Bryan Forbes, who used his wife, Nanette Newman, in all his films, came up to me and said, "So, nepotism's great, isn't it?" And it was like a real slap in the face. Because I was worried enough about doing *Pickwick* as it was.

'I was also taken out by a journalist to The Ivy – I can't remember her name, but she was a particularly nasty piece of work. I was naïve – I wouldn't do it now – and she was trying to get the dirt on me and find out what it was like and why I got the job. And she ended up saying in the article, "Of course, she wouldn't have got the job unless she was Harry Secombe's daughter."

'And then, when I was playing Madame Thénardier [in *Les Misérables*] I did an interview for a late-night show on LBC, and the interviewer said, "Well, basically, you're Harry Secombe with tits, aren't you?" I didn't know what to say to that.'

As this remark demonstrates, one of the tiresome misconceptions some people have is that any offspring of a celebrity is a miniature version of their famous parent. When I was younger, I was always being asked to tell a joke or sing 'If I Ruled the World'. I usually got round this by learning to blow as fruity a raspberry as Dad to cover a hasty exit.

Here's David's perspective:

'Because you come with all this pre-existing stuff, people have preconceptions about you...I think people are always looking for a way of trying to work out who you are and what you're about and so, if you're the offspring of a famous person, there's a ready-made template they can attempt to apply to you.

'I had a twerp of a housemaster who thought that I would be happy to play Mr Bumble in the school production of *Oliver!* and I said no. I was 14 or 15, very shy and had no theatrical inclinations whatsoever. The trouble was, he had seen me at my previous school – the only time I took part in any school theatrical event – and from then on was constantly trying to get me into everything...and he gave me a really hard time. I remember his deputy – a nasty little Rottweiler – gave me a dressing down because my refusal was seen as a betrayal to the House.

'For me, photography was a much more seductive way of being...it was something you could do on your own. I don't think for me there was any attraction for the stage. When I made my one and only foray onto the stage, I promised myself afterwards that I would never do anything like it again. Maybe if I'd got laughs, things would have been different...but the reaction I got was more, "He'll be gone in a minute, don't worry..." So I don't think I was a great undiscovered talent, I just found the whole thing a bit of an embarrassment.'

Sile Milligan, on the other hand, although she had no stage ambitions, seems to have quite enjoyed the attention she got:

'I was very young [during *The Goon Show* years]. But then,

right up until my 40s, *The Goons* was still prevalent in peoples' minds, so they'd always ask you about it. There were still loads of *Goon Shows* on the radio and stuff like that…and I used to mimic…Eccles and sketches… you know, and people would say, "Come on, come on, do it, do it! Go on, please, Sile do it!" And I'd be pushed against a wall at school and made to do it. I actually enjoyed doing it, but I didn't really know what I was doing…'

I think a low point for me was after a performance of *Hamlet* at the Young Vic, in which I played Horatio, Hamlet's friend and one of the few left alive at the end of the play. Just after the Prince dies in his arms, Horatio has that wonderful line, 'Goodnight, sweet prince…And flights of angels sing thee to thy rest…'

I thought I was rather good, giving 'a warm and affecting performance', to quote one reviewer. But after the show one night, in the pub next door, someone came up to me and said, in all seriousness, 'You're not as funny as your father.'

It was to avoid remarks such as this that I sometimes denied the family connection. But such a course of action could occasionally backfire.

In the sixties, Mum and Dad fell in love with Mallorca and bought a house there. We would spend the long, lazy days of summer swimming and basking in the Mediterranean heat. It's a beautiful island; Mum still has the house, and the family visit whenever we get the opportunity.

On one trip, when Dad was still alive, I needed to hire a car and went to a garage in the local town. After I'd filled in the rental agreement form and handed it back to the (English) man behind the desk, he looked up at me and said, 'Oh, any relation?'

I was hot and in a hurry and the last thing I wanted was to get involved in a discussion with a stranger about what a lovely man my Dad was, and how patient and kind he'd been that day, when he'd seen him lay the foundation stone for Barnsley Youth Centre, or opened the paediatric ward at Macclesfield General.

So I said, 'No.'

'Oh,' he replied. 'That's a coincidence – because he's got a place near here.'

'Really?' I said, feigning surprise.

Then he looked at what I'd written as my local address. 'Funny you didn't know that, because you seem to be staying in his house.' He looked at me and smiled in a knowing and not altogether friendly way.

I wanted the floor to open up and swallow me. I went bright red, paid hurriedly and ran out, a contending mixture of guilt, embarrassment and shame. I brought the car back under cover of darkness and pushed the keys through the letterbox.

Jennifer recalls:

'I was once waiting for a flight to London from Palma Airport at the height of the summer. Dad was trying to hide behind a newspaper and I was on guard. From the corner of my eye, I saw a large lady in a polka dot dress and a straw sunhat who was approaching us rapidly from across the far side of the departure lounge. She bore down upon us like a galleon in full sail, put her face close to Dad's and then stepped back in shock. "Oh, I'm so sorry," she said, suddenly remembering her manners, "I thought you were Harry Secombe." She disappeared as quickly as she had appeared. Dad and I looked at each other, open-mouthed for a beat. Then Dad said, "I thought I was, too."

'On another Palma to London flight, Dad and I were sitting on aisle seats next to each other. The couple on my left started digging each other in the ribs and whispering to each other. This behaviour was well known to us. We used to call these people the "'Tisitisn'ts" – "It is Harry Secombe…no it isn't…" A few moments later, the woman touched my arm. Dad was quietly dozing on my right. "Excuse me, but am I right in thinking that that's Harry Secombe?"

'"Yes," I replied.

'"I told you so," she said to her husband. "We always meet

somebody famous when we go on holiday," she confided to me. "We were in the same nightclub as Frank Sinatra in Las Vegas once. He wasn't very friendly though. And last year we went to Rome and saw the Pope."

Visiting restaurants with Dad was always an occasion. He loved Italian food – a habit he picked up during the war – and would take us to the best Italian restaurants. The waiters always loved him because he spoke fluent Italian with a Neapolitan accent – something else he picked up during the war – and they would fuss around him, laughing at his jokes and pandering to his every whim.

Around halfway through the second bottle of Barolo, he would inevitably burst into song, typically 'Torna a Surriento', or 'Santa Lucia'. The waiters would join in, but drop out one by one, unable to keep up as Dad neared the 'big finish' and hit the final extended top note. He would end to riotous applause and cries of 'Bravo!'

When we were young, Jennifer and I used to love these times and would beam with pride and pleasure as we soaked up, at one remove, all that adulation. Unfortunately, David and Katy found such experiences excruciatingly embarrassing – David most of all. I remember on one occasion he crawled under the table and stuffed his napkin in his ears.

I recently visited an Italian restaurant in Soho and, when one of the waiters glanced at my name on the booking, he looked up at me and said, 'Any relation?'

I sighed, smiled wanly and nodded, and his face lit up.

'Oh, your father used to come in here all the time. He was such a lovely man. I'll never forget, I sang a duet with him – we sang 'Torna a Surriento'. It was very special – special memory for me!'

I didn't have the heart to tell him that Dad had sung that song with every Italian waiter in London.

Jennifer continues:

'Because Dad was such an unmistakable figure and quite

difficult to conceal, he was always being spotted by fans when he was out and about. Taxi drivers in London would beep their horns and shout hello, fellow diners would come over to our table to ask for autographs…some pushy ones would insist Dad accompany them to their tables to have a photograph taken with their wives/mothers/daughters.

'Most of them were polite and charming but there were exceptions. Dad used to tell the story of when he popped into a pub one Saturday night for a pint after doing two shows. A man recognised him and started shouting, "Sing us a song, Harry!" To which Dad volleyed his usual response, "I can't, I've got a bad leg!"

'Unfortunately, this particular bloke didn't get the message and continued the barracking. Eventually, Dad turned to him and asked, "What do you do for a living?"

"I'm a miner," he replied.

"OK, then," said Dad. "You dig a hole and I'll stand in it and sing."

Occasionally, we would get dragged out to a big, dressy occasion such as a Royal Command Performance or a film première. These, depending on one's mood and temperament, could be either heaven or hell.

Katy remembers:

'I remember going to things like Army Benevolent evenings, being trotted out in my ballgown. I once danced with Eric Morecambe. But I'm very shy, so part of me didn't really like it, being dragged out as this…'thing', and also because I'm not very beautiful, I always felt a bit lumpen, and always thought, "I'm sure they expected someone prettier."

Sarah Sellers, too, found it all a bit intimidating:

'Well, I was shy, I didn't like all the camera flashing and all the rest of it, and you kind of had to play a part and Mum always wanted me to wear my best clothes and all that kind of stuff, and so the whole thing was a bit excruciating, quite honestly, but that's my personality – I'm quite a private person so I didn't particularly like it.'

Jennifer adds:

'We went to dozens of charity balls, cricket matches, golf tournaments, bazaars, fairs and auctions. Dad was always working for his favourite charities. He particularly had a soft spot for the Army Benevolent Fund – he loved the fact that Lance Bombardier Secombe HD924378 was rubbing shoulders with Field Marshalls and Generals and helping the troops to boot.

'He used to organise a biennial concert, "Fall In the Stars", for the charity. There was a fantastic army marching routine that he used to do with Eric Sykes and Norman Vaughan (two other ex-servicemen) in which the trio marched in time to a brass band. It was a perfect comedy vignette.'

When I was young, I used to rather enjoy these big events, but then, as I grew older and more self-conscious, they became something to be avoided. And I remember one occasion when I definitely should have stayed at home.

As Jennifer has already said, Dad was a great supporter of the Army Benevolent Fund, a charity which helps support ex-servicemen. One Sunday, when I was in my early twenties and newly started at drama school, he asked if I'd like to go and help him out at a concert the ABF were organising at the Drury Lane Theatre.

I wasn't keen – I knew what it would be like. I would hang around backstage like a spare part, making sure every hanger-on who visited the dressing room had enough to drink. I felt too old to still be playing the part of Harry Secombe's kid and was heartily fed up with being introduced as 'son of...'

My father, however, was incredibly persuasive when he wanted something, and promised that, apart from all the celebrities who would be performing, there would be all sorts of directors and producers there – people who could help my career in the future. I reluctantly agreed to go.

When we arrived, it was as I had suspected: Dad had bent the truth to suit his own ends. The only director I met was the director of the show – Billy Chappell – who was far too busy to pay me any attention. I consoled myself by laying into Dad's Courvoisier.

But just before curtain up, one of the celebrities – I forget who, but I think he was a sportsman – cried off. He was due to play a homesick squaddie in a short sketch and hadn't turned up. His non-appearance prompted a flurry of activity backstage; in such unwieldy shows as this, things can change at the last minute and the obvious option in this case was simply to cut the sketch. But Dad, fed up with me moodily stalking the dressing room, had an idea. As I'd just started at drama school, he 'volunteered' me to take this celebrity's place.

I can't say I was exactly thrilled at the prospect but, after much persuasion, in the shape of brimming tumblers of fine cognac, I was hustled into a squaddie's battledress, my long hair was stuffed under a beret, and I found myself, after no rehearsal, sitting on a camp bed behind the closed curtains of the vast Drury Lane stage.

As I waited nervously for the curtains to open, I went through the scenario Billy Chappell had given me. As I was replacing a sports star, the sketch had been tailored to his acting skills – all I had to do was sit there.

'You're a young soldier far from home, writing a letter to his mother, telling her how much you miss her,' Billy had told me, handing me a pad and pencil.

The voice-over had already been recorded by the actor Tony Selby and, while 'my' thoughts were relayed to the audience via the theatre sound system, I was supposed to scribble them down on the pad, looking up from time to react appropriately to what was being said – hardly a difficult task. Even so, as I hadn't even heard the pre-recorded tape, I was more than a little apprehensive.

My mouth was dry, the blood pounded in my ears, I felt faint and slightly sick and wished I hadn't consumed quite so much brandy.

The previous act finished and I heard the applause die down as my skit was announced by an unseen Master of Ceremonies. Then the curtains opened and I was momentarily blinded by the lights. As my eyes adjusted to the glare, I looked out at the magnificent auditorium and was filled with terror. The stage of the Drury Lane is one of the largest in London and I suddenly felt very small and alone. I was isolated in a pool of bright light, as if marooned on a vast ocean. The distance from where I was sitting to the orchestra pit must only have been about 20 feet, but it felt more like 20 miles. I was alone on the stage which Edmund Kean had made his own; the stage across which he'd strutted, bellowed and wept, changing the face of acting for ever. What did I think I was doing here? I was not worthy. The only thing I had in common with Kean was a fondness for brandy.

With such thoughts swimming through my head, I became dimly aware that I was standing centre stage and the audience was applauding. Standing? I hadn't even been aware of getting up off the bed.

It took me a while before I realised the audience's applause meant that the sketch was over. I bowed and retreated hurriedly to the wings to be greeted with a 'Well done, Jim!' by my proud father (for some reason the Goons always called each other and everyone else 'Jim'). To this day, I have no idea what exactly it was I did – it was a miracle I hadn't fled the stage screaming – but whatever it was sufficiently impressed Billy Chappell for him to offer me a job in a revue with Beryl Reid, some years later. Maybe the brandy helped after all?

Another bane of my young life was golf. Sundays, which, as I've described, were usually fairly relaxed, homely affairs, were occasionally ruined by my father having to go off and show his face at some charity Pro-Am tournament. He never liked turning up at these occasions alone and would therefore use all his powers of persuasion on either me or Jennifer to get us to go with him.

I never enjoyed accompanying my father on these jaunts and,

as I got older, became more and more uncomfortable; self-consciously aware that I had no role to play.

Dad's secret weapon when all else failed was his 'hurt' face. He somehow managed to make himself look like the last puppy in the shop. This was almost impossible to resist and, once he knew he had won you over, he would immediately do a very good impression of a spaniel with a stick.

The one thing worse than actually having to turn up at golf tournaments was caddying. I've never understood golf's appeal and lugging a heavy golf bag around an 18-hole course is certainly not my idea of fun. I've no real objection to sitting in a warm clubhouse listening to amusing anecdotes from interesting people, but traipsing round in the cold and rain watching men in Pringle sweaters try and hit a little white ball into a hole is not really my thing.

Just occasionally, however, an otherwise tedious afternoon could be enlivened by an unexpected event. I remember one well-attended Pro-Am celebrity golf tournament, at Effingham, in Surrey. The afternoon kicked off in the clubhouse with a merry and mainly liquid lunch with some old mates – Ronnie Corbett, Norman Vaughan, Bruce Forsyth and Sean Connery. The fans, waiting outside and anxious to get a glimpse of the celebrities, would crowd round the first tee any time one of them emerged to start their round.

When Dad's turn came, he joked with the spectators that he hadn't played for a while, so warned them to stand back, saying he hoped they all had health insurance. Everyone laughed and pressed in even closer, little suspecting he was in earnest. While I stood at the edge of the tee, golf bag in hand, doing my best to be invisible, Dad posed for photographs for the fans and local press.

There was a distinct format to these photographic shoots. He would start, hand on hip, in 'starlet' pose, then pull his cap down low over his eyes in 'idiot' mode then, finally, wander around like a gorilla. On this occasion, after the gorilla episode, he picked me up and slung me over his shoulder, as he was wont to do.

(There was a time when anyone standing too close to him could find themselves, without preamble, lifted into the air. During this phase we used to refer to him as 'the People Lifter'.)

Much to my relief, after loudly announcing to all and sundry, 'He's my son, you know!' he put me down, chose a club from the bag and, after a rousing chorus of raspberries and a couple of practice swings, stepped up to the ball and gave it an almighty swipe. Unfortunately, due to the combined effects of lack of practice and a surfeit of Pernod, he sliced the ball. It came zinging off the face of his 4-wood, curved viciously to the right and hit a lady spectator smack between the eyes. She keeled over like a felled tree. There was a sharp intake of breath from the crowd, followed by a stunned silence.

Dad went white and immediately rushed over to where the woman lay on the damp ground, groaning faintly, a lump as big as an egg already swelling on her forehead. A doctor was soon on hand and reassured my father that she was fine, that an ambulance was on its way and that he should continue his round.

But Dad, being a sensitive soul and worrying about that unfortunate woman, couldn't concentrate on his game and, after a few more holes, hooking, slicing and gouging divots as big as houses out of the fairway, gave up and retreated to the clubhouse, allowing me, with relief, to dump his golf bag in the car. He didn't, however, want to upset the fans by his early departure, so said he would stay to the end and distribute the prizes.

While waiting for news of her condition, Dad found out which hospital the woman had been taken to and sent his apologies and a huge bunch of flowers. When, finally, the news came that she had regained consciousness and was going to be fine, Dad relaxed and became his old self again. The drink flowed and so did the stories as, one by one, the various celebrities finished their rounds and returned to the clubhouse to take up their positions at the bar.

I'm sorry that woman had to suffer to make my afternoon but, in my view, sitting at a bar listening to comedians tell stories beats the hell out of dragging round a golf course any day.

My brother David, even more shy and retiring than me, found the exposure of being the son of a celebrity to be damaging in a very direct and immediate way:

'I remember when Dad was the host of a Royal Command around 1978 – I think, televised live – and there was Dad in front of the royal family and he did this link, something to do with being classified as a middle-of-the-road artist:

"I asked my 16-year-old-son, what does 'MOR' mean?"

"Middle of the road", he replied, pausing to squeeze a pimple…"

'Then he followed this up with a joke that went:

"He's just come back from a Bob Dylan concert and he's got a T-shirt that says "NALYD" on the front. I haven't got the heart to tell him he's wearing it inside out."

'And this was Sunday night and I was thinking – I'm going to school tomorrow…I can't say I liked that very much. He also went on the *Russell Harty* show and said how he used to fake sick notes for me. That actually became an issue for me at school.'

But by far the most disturbing aspect of being related to someone famous or powerful is never being entirely sure whether the person talking to you is relating to you for who you are, or because of what they think they can get out of you. This can induce a kind of paranoia that leaves you trusting no one.

Sarah Sellers observes:

'I can remember as a little girl – I think I was quite a sweet little girl – people being particularly nice to me and feeling somehow it wasn't quite right, that it wasn't genuine, and I really don't like that. I think I've always been my own person – I don't really like being part of something, I like doing my own thing.'

These days I'm fairly well adjusted and know who my friends are, but when I was younger and starting out in the business, I was deeply insecure and constantly on the alert to being used. It rarely happened, but when it did it was upsetting, doubly so when perpetrated by someone who should have known better.

In the early eighties, my uncle Fred, who was a prebendary of the Church of England, split up with his wife of 20 years and set up home with another woman. This incident caused a considerable amount of upset within the family and stirred up interest in certain quarters of the press. Dad was very close to Fred, but also felt for Connie, his wife, not to mention their five children. It was a very painful time for everyone involved.

Jennifer, who was then working as Dad's publicity agent, put out a press release along the lines of it being a private matter, that we were trying to work things out as a family, out of the glare of the media spotlight, and would appreciate the press's co-operation in this. For the most part, this request was respected.

At the time, I was appearing in a programme on Channel 4 called *Chips' Comic*, written by David Wood and designed by Jan Pienkowski, of *Meg and Mog* fame. The programme was a series for children with learning difficulties, and I played a dog called Rover, who used to hurtle around on a motorised trike, finding out things like how ice cream is made, or how a fire engine works, or demonstrating that a visit to the dentist is nothing to fear.

Because it took a slightly different approach from the norm – a comic was produced during the making of each programme that went on sale the week it was broadcast – it provoked quite a bit of interest and I did a number of interviews with various newspapers, most of which seemed more interested in the programme than my lineage. This was very refreshing, and no one even mentioned my uncle – after all, what place could there be for a story about a marriage breakdown in a piece about a programme for special needs children? So when a reporter from a certain red-topped Sunday newspaper strolled into my dressing room at the recording studio, my guard was down.

After a gentle start with a few questions about children's

television in general and my role in *Chips' Comic* in particular, the man of the press got down to the real reason for his visit by asking a question about my uncle's sexual proclivities. I could see immediately where this was going – in his mind it was the classic 'randy vicar' story. I told him I couldn't comment.

So then he changed tack slightly and asked me about *my* sex life. I caught sight of myself in the mirror: I was in full dog make-up – big brown eyes, shiny black nose, and wearing a headpiece complete with big floppy ears. I laughed, but he wouldn't be dissuaded. I rebuffed a stream of questions about girlfriends, boyfriends, soft fruit…Even as I was showing him out, he persisted, trying desperately to unearth some shocking revelation about the hitherto squeaky-clean Secombes.

'Well, if not sex, how about drugs?' he asked from the other side of the closed door.

The interview never appeared; it was obviously far too tame for that prurient Sunday rag.

Some days after this encounter, an old mate phoned out of the blue to ask if I was free for lunch. This was a man I hadn't seen for some years, and when he told me that he was now working for the *Sun*, alarm bells should have started ringing, but they didn't.

He was the son of a famous father himself, so understood my situation entirely. 'At least he won't want the technicolour details of my family's sex life,' I thought.

'Where do you want to eat?' he'd said. 'Anywhere you like – the *Sun's* paying.'

At the time I lived in Child's Hill, north of Swiss Cottage, an area in those days not exactly blessed with a profusion of good restaurants, but as central London was only a short tube ride away, I could have chosen Sheekey's, The Caprice or even The Ivy. As it was, I suggested the Cosmo, on Northways Parade, Swiss Cottage.

Anyone who remembers the Cosmo, a restaurant with a faded grandeur which had catered to the Eastern European Jewish community ever since the end of the last war, will probably wonder why that particular name sprang to my lips – I'm afraid I can't tell you. Perhaps it was nostalgia: I went to the Central School of Speech and Drama, which is just around the corner in Eton Avenue, and often ate at the Cosmo as a student. Or perhaps it was some kind of inverted snobbery – I was going through a rather unconvincing, left-wing rebel phase at the time – I don't know, I still wonder about it now. But as it turned out, it was a lucky choice.

There we were, eating borscht amongst the ageing clientele – the men in their dark suits, the ladies dressed in their furs and faded finery, smelling faintly of mothballs – talking about old times. It wasn't until the veal arrived that the reason behind his asking me to lunch became clear – he was angling for the dirt on Uncle Fred's affair, so that he could get an 'exclusive'.

As soon as he broached the subject, I was glad we'd come to the Cosmo. If we'd gone to Sheekey's or The Ivy, I might have felt obliged to come up with the goods. As it was, he could hardly use the circumstances of our lunch as a lever to prise the story out of me.

We finished our meal in silence.

I suppose it was naïve of me to think he'd looked me up just to reminisce – after all, he was a journalist – but I was saddened that he'd abused our friendship in this way.

I have no idea where my erstwhile friend is now, but the last I heard he had become involved with a page-three model and was being prosecuted for passing off an ordinary green tea as a slimming aid.

But the irritations I occasionally endured at the hands of the press fade into insignificance beside the journalistic intrusions the Bentine family had to suffer after a family tragedy, as Richard Bentine recalls:

'My elder brother Gus died in a plane crash when I was about 12, and the thing that was very public about it was that they were missing for about eight-and-a-half weeks before the plane was found.

'The aeroplane hadn't been maintained correctly and there

was evidence that the log book had been tampered with: the hours had been taken down incorrectly…but they didn't know that.

'It crashed in woodland in autumn only about 50 or 60 feet from a railway line in Hampshire, and because it was so close to a railway line, people didn't walk through the area, and because it was far enough from the railway line, no one saw it. They weren't discovered until the leaves started falling – that's when somebody spotted the wreckage.

'Originally, the inquest recorded the cause of the accident as pilot error. The pilot was not my brother, but his friend. But Dad said, "No, this is not how it happened," and he got the investigation reopened. Eventually, they found it was a cracked manifold underneath the exhaust and, basically, they succumbed to carbon monoxide poisoning. They passed out and the plane just went into the ground.

'For eight-and-a-half weeks, Dad carried on doing shows, because that's what you do. He was doing various clubs, etc. …I can't now remember what exactly he was doing, but I remember talking to him later and there were times when he was standing in the wings and thinking, "Are they here to see me crack up?"

'I don't think my sister twigged what was going on – she was a year younger, but I was 11 when he disappeared and 12 when he was found.

'We had a wonderful children's nanny called Nursie who came to look after my elder brother and sister when they were one and two, and never left. By that stage, she had been with us for 15 years, I suppose. She took Suki and I away to go and stay with her sister in Norfolk – in Diss – just to get away, because by that stage we had newspapers camped on our doorstep.

'There was one incident where two reporters climbed over into the garden to try and take photographs of Mum playing with Suki and me, and Dad just wandered out and said, "I've got 40 guns in the house. I give you 30 seconds to get out of my garden, because I'm going upstairs to load one of them now and, if you're still here when I get back, I'm going to shoot you."

'So these two reporters, visibly shaken, got in their car and drove straight up to Esher Police Station and reported Dad. And they were taken into an interview room and the superintendent in charge said, "What's the nature of the complaint?" And when they told him he said, "Well, that is very serious, because I know Michael – he's a bloody good shot, so if I was you I wouldn't do that again."

Thankfully, I've never had to suffer the death of a sibling, so I can't possibly imagine what it must have been like for Richard to lose not one, but three:

'Dad was married in 1942, to a French lady. As a marriage it only lasted about a year, and they had a daughter called Elaine, who we didn't meet 'til I was around 18 or 19. She was spirited away to France and we just didn't know about her. Mum knew about her, but we didn't. And this rather elegant, beautiful woman arrived on the doorstep one day and said, "Hello, I'm Elaine, I think I'm your sister."

'Elaine was very much part of the family from day one when we met her. Dad hadn't seen her for 32 years…She sadly died of cancer when she was 38 or 39. My elder sister Fusty – the eldest of us four children – was ten years older than me, Gus was nine years older than me. When Gus died, Fusty went to pieces, my mother had a nervous breakdown, Dad went into a sort of automatic flight mode, because he was trying to get hold of anybody he could to help with the investigation into the crash and Nursie was there to hold us all together. Suki was too young to really take an active part, so I decided I was going to do "things".

'I redecorated my brother's room, packed up all his things and moved up there. It was a major move – right up at the top of the house, no lights…The spooky corridor bit before you got to the light switch, where monsters hid. And that was it – I was the man of the house, I would do the washing up, clear the table…"Don't worry, Mummy, I'll look after you…"

'It's not so wonderful and lovely as it sounds looking back on it, because it was a very difficult, grim period. And then Elaine died from cancer, then Fusty died from cancer, and Dad died in 1996 and so we've had this relentless wave of decades where we've always had to deal with some terminal illness. It's got to the stage now where, when I see my mother, I normally yell out, "Good heavens, it's the widow Bentine!" and she'll turn round and say, "Good heavens, one of the surviving children!"

10

Friends in high places

The Goon Show's popularity, like all the best comedy, was universal, crossing class boundaries. Indeed, Prince Philip was an avid *Goon Show* afficionado, but its most famous fan has to be the Prince of Wales, who developed genuine friendships with Harry, Peter, Spike and Mike, even joining them for mad, Goon-themed afternoons.

Sarah Sellers remembers:

'I do recall an event that took place at Elstead [Sellers' pile in Surrey] because Prince Charles wanted to meet them all. And so they had a sort of Goon afternoon and I was allowed to have the day off school, but I hid because I was too embarrassed to meet Prince Charles.'

I first met Prince Charles after a charity concert at the Palladium and he greeted me with the words, 'I hear they're sending up a rocket to try and photograph the dark side of your father.'

Dad was extremely proud of his relationship with the royal family and very fond of telling the story of a reception he once attended at Buckingham Palace. I can't now remember all the circumstances, but I do know that it was a rather dreary affair, with a large number of self-important dignitaries present.

Dad, happily circulating, finding amusement where he could, was suddenly seized by the Queen's equerry, who told him, 'Her Majesty needs rescuing.'

My father, thinking that perhaps there was a plot against the Queen's life, was for a moment surprised that he had been chosen at the sovereign's saviour. Nevertheless, if fate had laid this duty at his door, who was he to argue? He downed his champagne, laid a hand on the pommel of his imaginary rapier and said, 'She's in danger?'

'Yes,' said the equerry, 'in danger of being bored to death.'

'Oh,' Dad replied, slightly crestfallen.

He was led to a small group, where the Queen was being forced to listen to the deadly conversation of some dry aristo who purported to know everything about ballet. Dad, standing on the periphery of the gathering, listened intently for some moments while the man, who obviously regarded ballet as a mathematical rather than an artistic exercise, was in the process of draining all emotional content from the art by expounding his theory that the height of a male dancer's leap has an exact correlation to the distance from knee to waist and that the two increase in the same ratio.

Dad, probably having downed more than a few glasses of wine, shook his head, muttering, 'Oh no, no, no.'

The man, furious at being contradicted, turned to him and asked imperiously what he knew about it.

'Well,' Dad said, 'that theory may hold true with the Royal Ballet, or even the Paris Opera, but if you're talking about Nureyev, it's a totally different matter.'

The man, wrong-footed, fell for it. 'How so?'

Dad smiled, 'It's a well-known fact that the Russian ballet dancer's foot is a good inch-and-a-half longer than the norm.'

The aristo was aghast. 'An inch-and-a-half…Really?'

'Oh yes,' Dad continued. 'And it's because of the extra leverage this gives them that they can leap so high. It's why the Russians are so highly sought after. With your knowledge of the ballet' he added confidentially, 'I would have expected you to know that.'

The man, dumbfounded, wandered away, shaking his head, his theory in ruins.

The Queen, meanwhile, did her best to keep a straight face and Dad, having performed his allotted task with alacrity, was rewarded with a royal wink.

Although Dad, revelling in his association with royalty, was forever deferential to the upper classes, deference was something that Spike never had any time for.

I once went with Dad to see one of Spike's shows in the West End. It was a night when Prince Charles was also in the audience and, after the performance, there was to be a small reception in the Prince's honour.

During the interval, Dad and I were invited to a private room behind the royal box where we chatted to the young Prince and enjoyed foaming glasses of bubbly. Then, after the curtain came down, we joined the royal party on stage, where tables had been set up laden with smoked salmon and bottles of Bollinger, Charles's favourite tipple. Royal protocol demands that a party cannot start until the royal personage has arrived, and also dictates that no one must leave until the royal guest has departed. This, however, did not sit well with Spike's republican sentiments and, besides, he wasn't drinking at the time and was eager to get home.

After 20 minutes, he started muttering, 'Hasn't he gone yet?'

Charles, enjoying himself and in no mood to leave, laughed it off. But Spike wouldn't leave it alone, prowling the backstage area, complaining about 'free-booting royals' and asking, 'Hasn't he got a palace to go to?'

It was just a bit of a joke but, as ever with Spike, one could never be entirely sure he wasn't in earnest. Charles's equerry was definitely not amused.

Eventually, the Prince, charming as ever, took the hint and left, joking, 'I'd better go before he throws me out.'

But the future King of England isn't the *Goon Show*'s only upper-class devotee. Princess Margaret and Lord Snowdon were also fans and became very close to Peter, to the extent that they even made home movies together.

I visited Lord Snowdon in his Knightsbridge office one morning and was shown into the kitchen by his assistant, Lynne.

Snowdon was sitting at a table with a glass of wine in front of him. He waved the bottle at me, but I declined – ten-thirty in the morning is a little early for me these days. But the lord would hear nothing of it and insisted. Who was I to contradict the great man? He handed me a glass of delightful white Burgundy and, I have to say, after a few sips I began to appreciate the efficacy of a mid-morning sherbet, becoming remarkably relaxed and expansive. I also discovered two things about Snowdon that not many people know – he has a great sense of humour and can do a wicked impression of Spike Milligan.

'Was I a fan of the Go-Ons?' he said. 'Oh yes, tremendous, but I knew Peter best of all. I went down to photograph them somewhere, I can't remember where. And then we became great friends. Peter was incredibly generous – I bought his car off him; a pale-blue Aston Martin. It had only done 5,000 miles and I paid about £3,000 for it. I adored it. But then I gave it to my son who promptly went and sold it.'

He sipped his wine in silence for a few moments – the memory of the lost Aston still obviously causing him a degree of anguish. But his sombre mood didn't last for long.

'Have you seen "Snowdonioh-Doh"?' He asked, brightly.

I was forced to admit I hadn't.

'Oh, you must, it's very funny. I can't remember where we made it…I think it was at Jocelyn's house on the Test.'

Lynne was summoned then despatched to find the movie.

'We used to go a lot to San Lorenzo's – that's where Peter liked going. Then Peter's…what was the grand wife called?… Miranda [Miranda Quarry – Peter's third wife]. She was very grand, and I went over and stayed with them in Ireland – Peter sent for me – and at dinner, she said to Peter, "Don't you know that port goes round to the left?"

'And Peter said, "No I fucking don't. I'm a fucking Jewish fucking actor!" And Miranda had all these birds in cages and Peter let them all out. And so we left and went and stayed with my sister. But he'd never stay anywhere for long – he'd want to leave immediately. It was quite irritating.

'He used to get so depressed. I remember he had once been very, very depressed the last time I'd seen him, and so I called him up on the telephone to find out how he was and Spike answered, 'Hello! Hello! Wha'! Ho, ho! How are you?'

'I said, "Can I speak to Peter?"'

'And he said, "No, we're having a party!"'

'Peter had forgotten he was very depressed and was enjoying a party.

'He used to have some amazing things that went on inside his brain. He thought he'd had an affair with Gina Lollobrigida, but I don't think he'd ever met her. It was the same with Princess Margaret – he thought he'd had an affair with her, but he just made it up. But I do remember when he was married to Britt Ekland and the marriage was breaking up, he said he'd "Britt off more than he could screw."

As well as an appreciation of fast cars and beautiful women, Peter and Lord Snowdon also shared a love of photography, but on Peter's prowess with a camera, Snowdon was less than flattering: 'He was awful! I managed to get him a page in *Vogue* – because he wasn't very good – and he got more pleasure from that than out of making some film. He was really quite difficult on-set, you know, because he'd suddenly walk off, leaving the crew standing around, and go and have lunch.'

Lynne reappeared, a VHS cassette in hand, and we all settled down to watch the home movie Peter made with Lord Snowdon, which turned out to be called *I Say, I Say, I Say!* being a Snowdonioh-Doh Production.

This rag-bag of a movie is a series of skits featuring Princess Margaret, Peter, Snowdon, Jocelyn Stevens (Sir Jocelyn was managing director of both the *Evening Standard* and *Daily Express* in the sixties, and was also one of the backers of pirate radio station Caroline), Janie (Sir Jocelyn's wife, Janie Sheffield – lady-in-waiting to Princess Margaret) and Sir Evelyn Rothschild – quite a cast.

The film opens with a sequence about Rivtec, 'Get him now!' A humble river warden wades through a river (presumably the

Test) charged with policing the grounds of a grand house (Sir Jocelyn's). Peter sets the scene with an Edgar Lustgarden-style voice-over, and then appears as the river warden himself.

This is followed by Sellers as quick-change artist, The Great Berko, who, fresh from his recent triumph at the Workmen's Institute, Penge, announces that he is going to perform his world-famous impersonation of Princess Margaret. He disappears behind a screen and, to the frantic accompaniment of 'The Devil's Gallop', clothes fly out from behind it in every direction. After a few seconds, Princess Margaret herself steps out from behind the screen, graciously takes the cheers and applause and then withdraws. Immediately, a dishevelled Sellers reappears from behind the other end of the screen and takes a bow.

It carries on in this vein, with short improvised scenes, one featuring Lord Snowdon himself as camp gangster to Peter's underworld boss, and ends with an improbable chorus line: Princess Margaret, Sir Jocelyn Stevens, Janie Sheffield, Sir Evelyn Rothschild and Sellers, singing that *Gang Show* staple, 'We're Rolling Along on the Crest of a Wave'. It's surreal to say the least.

And from bona fide royals to the upper echelons of the church Establishment, in an incident which I include because it demonstrates how Dad's anarchic attitude to life could surface in the unlikeliest of places…but mostly because it makes me laugh. The occasion was my brother David's confirmation at St John's School, Leatherhead.

David takes up the story:

'It was 1975 or possibly '76, Dad and Fred [Harry's brother] came along to witness the great event, which took place in the school chapel. The service was presided over by the Bishop of Guildford – a strangely ascetic figure – and after the service there was a reception in the main hall, a red-brick, gothic affair, a bit like the one they used in the film *If*.

'The headmaster and the chaplain were very keen to introduce the Bishop of Guildford to their one celebrity whose son attended the school – after Cliff Michelmore's son left, I was the only game in town.

'So, they brought over the Bishop, this thin, bald man, and he said to Dad, "What's the name?"

'Dad, always slightly embarrassed by his own fame was, nevertheless, quite thrown to be presented to somebody who didn't automatically know who he was. The headmaster and chaplain were also slightly taken aback and didn't immediately rush to his aid. So Dad shook the man's hand and self-consciously muttered his own name, "Harr'Scombe…"

'The Bishop, being slightly hard of hearing, and having spent the best part of his life in Africa on missionary service, had no idea who this short, well-built man was. He leaned forward and said, "Excuse me?"

'Dad, now feeling extremely awkward, repeated his name, but in an even more garbled fashion, "Ha'Scom…"

'Again the Bishop shook his head, "Sorry, I didn't quite catch that."

'Dad, his embarrassment building and surrounded by the trappings of history and privilege, suddenly flipped into madness. He grasped the Bishop's hand firmly and, with a wild gleam, looked him straight in the eye and said, loudly and clearly, "Hattersley…" and then, so that there could be no mistake, "Roy Hattersley. And this is my brother, Fred Secombe."

'The headmaster and chaplain, sticky, nervous smiles fixed on their faces, stood frozen in disbelief either side of the now confused Bishop, who asked, "How can a man called Hattersley have a brother called Secombe?"

"Ah, we're a very old family," Dad replied with a broad smile.'

11

That's All, Folks!

Like my childhood, *The Goon Show* also had to end and, in 1960, it did just that. Starting out, in 1951, as *Crazy People*, it had spanned the decade and taken the airwaves by storm. But it was not the end of the four protagonists. Those once wild men went on to bigger, although not always better things.

After leaving *The Goons*, Michael Bentine slid sideways into television with, in 1954, the innovative children's series *The Bumblies* on the BBC. Later, he teamed up with Sellers on *Yes, It's the Cathode Ray Tube Show* for ITV, then, in 1959, presided over a show which mixed animation, news stories, sketches and celebrity guests called *After Hours*, on which he collaborated with Richard Lester (who would later go on to work with Sellers and Milligan on *The Running, Jumping, Standing Still Film*, and, later still, the Beatles' movies, *A Hard Day's Night* and *Help*).

In 1960, Mike went back to the BBC and struck television gold with *It's a Square World*. This groundbreaking show had a terrific cast: Dick Emery, Frank Thornton, Clive Dunn, Deryck Guyler, John Bluthal and Ronnie Barker, and mixed slapstick, satire and animation, featuring everything from a beautifully realised flea circus, to a 40-foot whale attempting to get inside the British Natural History Museum. He also sent Television Centre into orbit and famously sank the Houses of Parliament, thereby fulfilling a lot of people's dreams.

After several years away from television, in 1974 he found a whole new audience with *Michael Bentine's Potty Time*, where the blob-like Potty People (who bore more than a passing resemblance to the Bumblies) retold classic works of fiction or re-enacted great historical events, such as the Armada and the mystery of the Mary Celeste. The episodes had names such as *The Invisible Potty*, *The Potty in the Iron Mask*, and *The Great Potty Escape*.

In 1995, Michael received a CBE for services to entertainment, but entertaining was not the end of Michael's talents. An accomplished pilot, yachtsman and archer, in the 1960s he took part in the first hovercraft expedition up the River Amazon. He also had an interest in parapsychology and wrote two books on the subject: *The Door Marked Summer* and *The Doors of the Mind*. Later, he became president of the Association for the Scientific Study of Anomalous Phenomena.

Richard Bentine explains:

'Dad's interest in the paranormal encompassed everything from healing through to ley-lines – anything and everything. He wanted to have a look at it, and he wanted to have a look at it in the most empiric way he could. A lot of things he decided were just not worth the money and other things were genuine shockers for him.

'One of the difficulties is that if you have a family that's prone to cancer, you do come across an awful lot of faith-healers and healers and whatever, and you encounter people who just have no right to be alive but are in remission and doing really quite well. What achieves it? I don't know…

'After Dad died, I helped start a charity called Everyman and I sat on the board of trustees for Cancer Research for nearly three years…in those three years, we raised £17.5 million and built the first male oncology research centre at the Marston in Sutton…And I got to talk to an awful lot of people, including people doing the human genome project, and the one question no one could answer was: why does cancer start and why does cancer stop?

'That in itself is paranormal – it's a normal cell one day and then becomes abnormal for no apparent reason. Obviously, there are the trauma-based cancers: if you smoke you get lung cancer; if you sit out in the sun without sun cream you get melanomas; but they're aggravated assaults on the cellular system, but the other stuff is…one day it's normal, the next it's not.

'For some unknown reason, I always think of cancer as a B-movie Mexican bandit. I think Dad was also of the opinion that it was a Mexican invention…either Mexican or Eastern Bloc: sinister, and probably wearing a trenchcoat.'

Michael's interest in the paranormal sometimes caught out my extremely sceptical father. One December in 1978 or '79, Dad and David went to Mike's for Sunday lunch. I'll let David tell the story:

'I can't remember now why it was just Dad and me, but we went to Mike's house in, I think it must have been Esher. Mike had been on fairly good form during lunch – he was a fascinating man and very, very funny. Then, after lunch, the conversation started to take a more mystical turn and he started talking about the paranormal. I think it was fairly soon after his eldest daughter had died.

'After lunch, we somehow found ourselves in an upstairs bedroom, and Mike started talking about the power of the mind. He said that the power of the mind could disperse clouds – apparently it was a property of a certain part of the brain.

'It was a strange scenario – there were Dad and I, looking out of a double-glazed window at a leaden sky, with Mike standing between us, muttering, "Disperse…disperse…" I made the mistake of catching Dad's eye and both of us had to bite our tongues. On the way home, we cried with laughter. But I have to admit, the cloud did thin a bit…'

I can imagine the look on my father's face.

Post *Goons*, Milligan went on to become the nation's favourite lunatic, with the inspired madness of the *Q* series on the BBC. After the ill-starred *Curry and Chips*, in which Spike played an Asian immigrant looking for work, *Q5*, a surreal sketch show and the first in Spike's *Q* series, appeared in 1969. There was a six-year gap to *Q6*, which was broadcast in 1975. *Q7* followed in 1978, *Q8* in 1979 and *Q9* in 1980. In 1982 came *There's a Lot of It About*, which was *Q10* in all but name, and was to be Milligan's last television series.

He also made numerous appearances in films: as country postman Harold Petts in *Postman's Knock*, in 1962; *The Bed-Sitting Room* (1969), a post-apocalyptic comedy based on the stage play he wrote with John Antrobus; *The Magic Christian* (1969); *Alice's Adventures in Wonderland* (1972); *Adolf Hitler: My Part in his Downfall* (1972), based on the first volume of his war memoirs, starring Jim Dale as Spike, with Spike himself playing his own father; *The Adventures of Barry McKenzie* (1972); *The Three Musketeers* (1973); *The Great McGonagall* (1974); *The Last Remake of Beau Geste* (1977); *The Life of Brian* (1979); *History of the World, Part I* (1981) and *Yellowbeard*, in 1983.

He also appeared on stage, most notably in *Treasure Island* at Bernard Miles's Mermaid Theatre and *Son of Oblomov* at the Comedy Theatre. This started out at the Lyric, Hammersmith, as a straight play, *Oblomov*, based on the novel by Russian writer Ivan Goncharov. But during a sticky first night, Spike started ad-libbing, which did not go down well with his fellow cast members, nor the critics. However, during the next few weeks, his ad-libbing completely transformed the show, turning it into a hit comedy, which was retitled and transferred to the West End, where it enjoyed a long and very successful run.

He published a steady stream of books, including his seven-part war memoirs: *Adolf Hitler: My Part in His Downfall*; *'Rommel?' 'Gunner Who?'*; *Monty: His Part in My Victory*; *Mussolini: His Part in My Downfall*; *Where Have All the Bullets Gone?*; *Goodbye Soldier*; and *Peace Work*.

He also wrote children's books, including *Silly Verse for Kids* and *Badjelly the Witch*; several novels, including the very funny *Puckoon*; and even a guide to depression: *Depression and How to Survive It*, with psychiatrist Anthony Clare.

Sadly, towards the end of his life, feeling frustrated and let down by the industry to which he had contributed so much, he would refer to himself as 'the leper of the light entertainment industry'.

Sellers, after making a number of wonderful British films, such as *Only Two Can Play*, *The Ladykillers*, *Two-Way Stretch* and *I'm All Right, Jack*, went on to became an international movie star. His greatest hits include: *Dr Strangelove*; *The Millionairess*; *Lolita*; and, of course, Blake Edwards's *The Pink Panther* (1963), in which a certain Inspector Clouseau makes his first appearance. *A Shot in the Dark*, released the following year, was the second of the *Pink Panther* series. In 1969 came *The Magic Christian* and, in 1970, *There's a Girl in My Soup*. Then, in 1975, after a hiatus of more than a decade, Sellers returned triumphantly to the role of Clouseau in *The Return of the Pink Panther*, which was almost immediately followed by *The Pink Panther Strikes Again*. Peter's final, conscious, outing as Clouseau was *The Revenge of the Pink Panther*, released in 1978, shortly before his death.

In 1982, however, utilising unused material from *The Pink Panther Strikes Again*, Blake Edwards released *The Trail of the Pink Panther*. It was not a great success and neither was the 1993 *Son of the Pink Panther* with Roberto Benigni as Clouseau's son. This box-office flop was Blake Edwards's final attempt to keep the franchise going.

More recently, Steve Martin has taken over the Clouseau role, in films such as *The Pink Panther* (2006) and *The Pink Panther 2* (2009), but to anyone who is a fan of the original series, these dire offerings are an affront to Sellers' comic genius.

Sellers' last great film, *Being There*, was released in 1979. His performance as the empty vessel, Chance, was, according to my father, as close as he ever got to playing himself.

During the seventies, Jennifer came across both Spike and Peter from time to time in a professional capacity:

'I had more dealings with Peter Sellers and a bit with Spike, later on, when I was working with Theo Cowan, the publicity company. Peter Sellers was one of the clients and lived in the same road the company was in: Clarges Street, Piccadilly.

'As soon as Peter knew I was working there, whenever he was in town, he used to phone to talk to me. I remember he once wanted half-a-dozen pink grapefruit delivered to the Playboy Club at twelve o'clock…I mean, you immediately call your publicist, don't you? So, I'd do that, and then, another time, he wanted a new coffee pot, and I said, "What kind of coffee pot do you want, Peter?"

'And he said, "Tell you what, I'll do a sketch."

'So, we were, like, four doors away, and he did a sketch of this plunger-type coffee pot, then got a messenger to pick it up, to walk four doors down to the office to give to me…I mean, I could have gone and got it.

'And so I looked at this sketch and thought, "Mmhmm, OK." I gave it to our office boy, who went out, bought it, brought it back and took it to him.'

But of the four, it was my father's career that took the most improbable turn, leading him to become the face of Sunday religious broadcasting.

Mitch Benn continues:

'Harry didn't seem to do much in the way of comedy later…I remember him being around in my youth – I remember him being knighted and referring to himself as Sir Cumference – ultimately loveable.

'Later generations probably know him best for his Sunday hymn shows…That's one of the weird things – you get this contrast between him doing something as completely anarchic as *The Goon Show* and then doing something as un-anarchic as *Highway*, the least anarchic thing on British television…it's as surreal as *The Goons*. In many respects, he's the one who had the broadest appeal because everybody knew him – he was very much a fixture on TV.'

Actually, and to his great surprise, he enjoyed doing *Highway*, although he used to affectionately send it up in private. 'Thank God I don't wear a wig,' he once said to me, 'Otherwise, how could I walk though a howling gale on a Welsh hilltop singing "Nearer My God to Thee"?'

He insisted that the ordinary people he met were the real stars of the show – ordinary people who had done extraordinary things. It was, he said, a humbling experience and one, I suspect, although he never talked about his faith in any depth to any of us, which brought him to some broad understanding of, for want of a better word, God. I don't think he was drawn to Sunday religious television because of his religion – if anything, I suspect it was the other way round; doing the 'God slot' made him, if not exactly religious, then at least more aware of his spirituality.

Katy observes:

'I worked as a PA on *Highway* for a bit during my gap year, and I remember Dad saying he was spiritual rather than religious. I felt he didn't want to mislead people; I think he was quite hot on that.

'Because Dad liked to keep an open mind. I think he took all sorts of things on board, and he encouraged all of us to be like that. I remember at 13 saying I didn't want to be confirmed, because I didn't know whether I wanted to commit to that… Mum was beside herself, but Dad was like, "No, that's fine, you've made your decision."

David adds:

'I think, in some respects, all the Sunday night stuff was almost like him opening up a separate franchise…as far as he was concerned, it was just something else he did.

'I remember he did a charity concert at Cranleigh School in

what must have been the late eighties, and he was on really good form that night – it was a big crowd and people were really thrilled. I remember overhearing someone say, "He's much funnier than I thought he was going to be."

'You would occasionally get him at full force, like when he did *Pickwick*, but when he was doing all the *Highway* stuff, essentially what you were getting was a character he'd created that was called Harry Secombe that was…like spreadable butter as opposed to the real thing.'

Dad wasn't exactly a fan of the musical, but, in the early sixties, he launched himself into a big-budget, musical spectacular called *Pickwick*. The *Pickwick* that David mentioned earlier was the revival, which also featured sister Katy and played the Chichester Festival Theatre in 1993. But *Pickwick*'s first outing was at the Saville Theatre (now the Odeon Covent Garden). It ran for 694 performances from July 1963 to February 1965. With music by Cyril Ornadel, lyrics by Leslie Bricusse and a book by Wolf Mankowitz, it was directed by Peter Coe and choreographed by Gillian Lynne. H.S. played Pickwick, and the original cast featured Teddy Green, Hilda Braid, Jessie Evans, Gerald James, Julian Orchard, Oscar Quitak, Anton Rodgers, Dilys Watling and Peter Bull.

After its West End triumph, it went to America and, starting in San Francisco, toured right across the States before opening on Broadway in October 1965. At the beginning of the tour, the part of Sam Weller – Pickwick's faithful manservant – was played by the then little-known Davy Jones.

Davy was only scheduled to be with the show until Detroit, where Roy Castle was to take over and go with it all the way to Broadway. Detroit was then the 'Automobile Capital of America'. Everybody in town, in one way or another, was involved in making, buying or selling cars.

In the first week in that grim, industrial town, Roy was swiftly rehearsed in and, during the second week, played the matinées on Wednesday and Saturday before taking over full-time when the show moved to the next town. On Davy's last Saturday, during the matinée, I was hanging around backstage as usual, watching the show from the wings, wanting to see how my old mate Roy was getting on, when Davy appeared out of the backstage darkness, grabbed hold of me and said, 'Come out front.'

I followed him through the pass door out into the half-full auditorium, where an audience of arc-welders and mechanics sat, glumly trying to come to grips with the on-stage English accents, and we made our way to the back of the stalls. On stage, Samuel Pickwick had just been thrown into debtor's prison because of a colossal misunderstanding with his housekeeper, Mrs Bardell, who had successfully sued him for breach of promise. It's a rather poignant moment in the show, where Pickwick, friendless and alone, ponders his future. All he has with him is a basket of food, hastily prepared for him by his manservant, Sam. At a certain point in the proceedings, Pickwick shares the contents of his picnic hamper with the other poor wretches who share his prison cell. But as Dad picked up the wicker hamper and began to undo its straps, Davy elbowed me in the ribs, and said, 'You'll like this, Andy.'

When Dad threw open the lid of the basket, a live chicken flew out and squawked noisily all over the stage, much to Dad's consternation.

As the on-stage cast chased the frantic chicken, Davy hooted with laughter while the matinée audience sat in silent bewilderment. Dad, never fazed for long, looked out into the auditorium and, seeing Davy convulsed at the back of the stalls, guessed immediately who was to blame. He fixed him with a stern gaze and delivered the immortal line, 'What a fowl trick!'

I liked Davy, apart from the fact that he was fun to be around, he was also one of the few adults I knew, apart from my mother, who was near my height. It wasn't long after *Pickwick* that he went off to join the Monkees, America's answer to the Beatles, and the rest is history.

When *Pickwick* hit Broadway, it was an instant critical success, leading Dad to be nominated for a Tony, for best performance in a musical. Unfortunately, after only a few weeks, he was struck down by mumps and the understudy had to go on. Sadly, despite a strong cast, Dad was the core of the show and, without his energy and personality, not to mention his voice, there was a big hole at its heart. The audiences stayed away and, after a run of only six weeks, the producer, David Merrick, fed up with losing money, closed it down.

Dad read the announcement that the show was coming off in the newspapers, lying in his sickbed in his penthouse apartment. It was a sad end to a great show, and also the end of Dad's dream of 'capturing' America.

Back in England, Dad had other notable theatrical successes: *The Four Musketeers*, which was a reworking of Alexandre Dumas' *The Three Musketeers*, was one. With a cast that included Jeremy Lloyd, John Junkin, Kenneth Connor, Aubrey Woods and Elizabeth Larner, it enjoyed a long run at the Drury Lane Theatre, despite the fact that Dad mimed his way through most of it.

He played D'Artagnan and, part-way through the run, developed a severe throat infection. But rather than take time off, in all probability allowing the show to die and putting a large number of people out of work, he decided to carry on, miming the big numbers to a track pre-recorded for just such an eventuality.

During the first of these 'taped' shows, he started off with the best intentions, miming in perfect synchronisation with the tape. But then the bizarre nature of what he was doing struck him and the madness took hold. As his recorded voice continued to fill the theatre, he stuffed a handkerchief in his mouth. Then he proceeded to slowly drink a glass of water, like a ventriloquist. This got huge laughs and he decided to keep it in for the rest of the run – it must rank as the longest sore throat in history.

The final scene of *The Four Musketeers* required him to ride a horse on stage. Dad wasn't particularly 'horsey' and, initially, both horse and rider regarded each other with deep suspicion. One night the animal became so frisky, he reared up the moment he'd left the wings, nearly unseating Dad and depositing a steaming brown pile on Kenneth Connor's feet. But once Dad discovered that carrots were the way to his mount's heart, they became firm friends. Indeed, so attached did he become to this animal – a dapple-grey, 18 hands high – that he bought it, rechristening it D'Arty.

For a few years, Sundays were disrupted by early starts, as Dad would wake the whole household in his eagerness to get down to Chobham where D'Arty was stabled. Dad, never one for doing anything by halves, kitted himself out in the full gear: hacking jacket, jodphurs and knee-high boots. But he never reached the standard of the National Hunt jockey he imagined himself to be, achieving, at best, a slow trot. In the end, and with regret, Dad sold D'Arty, as the stabling costs far outweighed the use he was getting out of him.

Plumber's Progress was Dad's next big theatre show. This was adapted by C.P. Taylor from a play by Carl Sternheim called *Schippel*. Set in Germany in 1913, it's basically a play about class; because of the death of their tenor, a quartet of snobbish Meistersingers are forced to recruit the local plumber to take his place.

Dad, of course, played the plumber, the working-class idiot with the golden voice, looked down upon, and yet so desperately needed by the upper-middle-class Meistersingers.

Plumber's Progress was a bit of a departure for Dad; although there were a few musical numbers, it was a play with music rather than a musical. And under the direction of Mike Ockrent, he played it straight. That's not to say he didn't get laughs – getting far more humour out of the part, I'm sure, than ever Sternheim or C.P. Taylor thought possible – but he stuck to the script.

The show opened in Manchester in 1975 and, sadly, things started to go wrong from the start. Bernard Delfont, who produced the show, thought the title, *Schippel*, too difficult for Dad's audience demographic – the blue-rinsed coach-party – hence its change to the uninspired and distinctly downmarket, *Plumber's Progress*. Another concern was the inclusion of 'Deutschland

Über Alles' in the finale. There to make a serious point about the
resurgence of German militarism, it was thought the singing of
this anthem might offend certain sections of the audience and it
was therefore changed to 'Stille Nacht', totally emasculating the
effect that Sternheim had intended.

Delfont was also worried that Harry Secombe's fans might take
offence to him swearing. At the end of the second act, Schippel
leaves the stage after uttering the word, 'Bollocks!' A tame enough
curse, you might think, but this was the early seventies and people
were more easily offended by bad language back then, especially
when used by safe, roly-poly entertainers such as my father.

To circumvent criticism, several different but less contentious
oaths were tried instead, but none of them had the same satisfying
ring as the roundly delivered 'Bollocks!'

One matinée, Dad, fed up with what he saw as pointless
tinkering, exited the stage with the line 'Blood orange!' which
elicited puzzlement from the audience and widespread corpsing
from the cast.

Plumber's Progress opened later that year at the Prince of Wales
Theatre in London and, although critically well received and
despite a terrific cast – Simon Callow, Roy Marsden, Roger Kemp,
Gordon Clyde and Priscilla Morgan – it was never a huge
commercial success, for a number of reasons. Admittedly, it was
probably too great a leap for Dad's many fans to make but, at the
time, the West End was not in great shape, with many theatres
'dark', and in a smaller theatre it might have been able to struggle
on for longer than it did. But when Dad was forced to leave the
show with a nasty bout of viral pneumonia, the writing was on the
wall. Roy Marsden took over the title role for a short time, but then
he too succumbed to illness and the management pulled the plug.

Katy was the only one of us who actually worked with Dad on
stage, playing in the chorus in the revival of *Pickwick*, and
understudying the part of Mrs Bardell:

'On stage he was very naughty – he always went off the script and did his own schtick. I remember how much it cost him to sing every night, because the top C was always a bit of a worry… and for someone who sings, he was absolutely awful at coming in on cue. I don't read music very well…but I've learned to blag it through doing a lot of session singing. I'm also very quick at picking things up. Dad was very good at that, but he wasn't very good at taking his conductor's cues, because he didn't have his glasses on and couldn't see the monitor.

'There was one song called "Do As You Would be Done By" and it had quite a tricky rhythm, which Dad couldn't get at all and he used to get into a state about it.

'So I piped up and said, "Why don't I stand behind you and tap you on the shoulder when it's your turn to come in?" And that's what I used to do every night.'

This reminds me of a story Dad used to tell about the filming of *Song of Norway*, a movie about Norway's best-loved composer, Grieg.

Dad did make a couple of decent films: *Jet Storm*, a drama set on board a transatlantic airliner, directed by Cy Endfield, with Richard Attenborough and Stanley Baker; and *Davy*, about a Variety artiste who tries to make it big in opera. But, in the main, Dad seemed to have a nose for bad films and, notwithstanding his earlier disasters – *Penny Points to Paradise* and *Down Among the Z Men* – *Song of Norway* was one of the worst. One American critic declared it, unequivocally, 'A total bomb!'

Dad described it as, 'The kind of film you can take your children to see…and leave them there.'

With a cast that included Robert Morley, Oscar Homolka and Florence Henderson, it also featured one of the last performances of the great Hollywood star, Edward G. Robinson. Edward G. was one of my Dad's heroes and he was thrilled to have several scenes with him. Dad was also delighted to discover that the great man was kind and courteous and possessed of a wicked sense of humour and, although well past his prime, his mind was as sharp as ever. His hearing, however, was not what it had once been.

In one scene, Dad, Florence Henderson, Edward G. and a German actress were seated around a table. The German actress had rather a soft voice and, during rehearsals, Eddie found her difficult to hear, which made him late with his own lines. Just before the take, the screen legend turned to Dad and said, 'Harry, when it's my turn to speak, just tap me on the leg under the table.' And that's exactly what he did. In the finished film, Edward G. Robinson, of course, steals the scene.

But Dad wasn't always quite so accommodating, as Katy remembers:

'One night, [during the run of *Pickwick*] Dad and David Cardy [playing Sam Weller] tied me to a lamp-post at the end of the skating scene and left me on stage – he was very naughty.

'Working with Dad is one the saddest memories actually, and I've never told anyone before, but we were doing *Pickwick* at the Birmingham Hippodrome and there was man called John Curtain…His wife, I kid you not, was called Annette… He was something to do with the management and he was arrested on charges of fraud – he was embezzling funds from the Hippodrome.

'But before he came to trial he disappeared and we'd just opened in *Pickwick*, we were about to embark on a tour and the show had to close because there was no money…Eventually we were bailed out by Ernst and Young and the show continued after a gap of six weeks.

'The day it happened, we'd just done a matinée and were about to get ready for the second show when we were told the news. The management said, "Put your civvies on and go and find somewhere for a coffee while we work out what's going to happen."

'Mum was usually with Dad, but for some reason she wasn't there, and he was at a loose end and he asked if he could come with me.

'I was 23 or 24 at the time and, apart from being worried about losing my job, I'd also just split up with someone I'd been going out with in the cast. I was behaving like a complete idiot, saying things like,"I haven't got a job, I haven't got a relationship, my life's over!"

'But although he was completely and utterly flabbergasted by what had happened, Dad was very calm and just said, "Oh well, that's showbusiness." He was very wise about things like that.

'We went to this burger joint with all the kids from the chorus and he sat and had burger and fries with us. I remember that so well. He took it all very calmly.'

Dad's star waned through the seventies. I'm rather hazy about this period as, from 1971 through to 1977, I was away from home almost constantly, first at drama school and then on tour with various companies. Apart from seeing him briefly for the odd, extremely enjoyable Sunday lunch, we had little contact during this time.

I know he toured Australia several times, as *The Goons* had a huge following down under, and it was there he made another terrible film, *Sunstruck*, with Maggie Fitzgibbon, John Meillon and Donald Houston, written by Jimmy Grafton and directed by James Gilbert.

David was still at school during the seventies and so was around more than I was at that time:

'I was born in 1962 and didn't really discover *The Goons* until I was about 11 or 12, so it took a little while to get to grips with the fact that my father had done this wonderfully mad thing, because it was so different from what he was doing at the time.

'I think we kind of split into two families: you and Jennifer and me and Katy. You and Jen saw someone who was on this upward, exciting slope – unquestioningly brilliant, a lot of energy, not around a lot, etc.…

'But by the time I was growing up, his career had settled down, he was at home more; his career had plateaued; certain career choices had been made and it meant that maybe expectations were lower.

'One of the things I came across in the trunk in Mum's house was a script for a pilot he recorded in America called *Lampoon*. It was a sketch show, but didn't go anywhere because *National Lampoon* [the satirical magazine] sued over the use of the name, so killed it before it was even aired. But for a while...I think it was 1975 or '76, he was over in Hollywood and he was quite excited about it. He certainly had the idea that it could be something big, but it never happened.

'He also wanted to do more acting but never had the opportunity. I remember him playing these dingy clubs in the north of England. I suppose, to be fair, the early to mid-seventies was a fairly depressed period in Britain and the entertainment world in general. I think one of the reasons that he liked Australia so much was that he was a big deal when he went over there. Even though he was playing these funny little desert towns, he said the audiences were fantastic and it felt great.

'It's difficult to separate out the different strands of disillusionment – either with the kind of stuff he ended up doing, or with getting older and losing his gifts. You get a sense looking at the cuttings around the end of *The Goon Show*...it's a bit like when a famous band breaks up...there's this huge expectation about what each of the protagonists is going to do next...

'I think part of the trouble was his variety of interests...He did say to me once, and I don't know how true it was, but... after *The Goons* finished there was an opportunity to do more straight singing work in Europe. I wondered why he hadn't jumped at the chance and he said, "Ah, but if I'd gone you'd have had a very different life."

'I think also, he didn't take up the offer because of insecurity. Because the straight musical world is *so* straight. He didn't read music and he didn't play an instrument and I think he found it a bit daunting. It's a pity...

'Not long before he died, he was thrilled when someone sent him a cutting from an American music magazine about an album he made with the Vienna Concert Orchestra, and it said, "Excellent voice…who is/was he?" That made his day.'

Katy was also still at home during the seventies:

'He wasn't on television too much around that time. But I do have a very dim and distant memory of sitting in a control room in a TV studio and I had to clap with my two fingers, because the producer's assistant told me I wasn't allowed to clap with my hands, because it was too loud, but I could clap with my fingertips.

'I also remember sitting in a studio, watching Dad do a Laurel and Hardy sketch with Roy Castle. I remember the Nolans, too – they were in green, velvet dresses, covered in shamrocks. I also remember Olivia Newton-John doing a guest spot on one of Dad's shows.'

One of the many people who used to appear regularly in his Australian shows was an Aussie singer called Jim Pegler. Jim was as nice a man as you could hope to meet, but wore the worst wig ever seen outside of Madame Tussaud's. It sat on his head like a dead rat, immovable and lifeless. Every time he looked down, this conglomeration of acrylic fibres stuck stiffly out at the back, glinting in the sun like the spun nylon it was, and exposing six inches of bare scalp.

Dad was an avid 'wig-watcher' – he could never understand what it was that compelled an otherwise sensible chap to clamp something that looked like road-kill to his scalp the moment he became a little thin on top. Although, in his latter years, his once-lustrous hair may not have been quite as thick as in his youth, he still had an awful lot of it and so never had to face the awful question, 'Toupee or no Toupee?' He was, therefore, perhaps less than sympathetic to the plight of the tonsorially challenged.

Dad was fond of Jim but he couldn't help himself making fun of him and his 'syrup' at every opportunity, the more so because Jim would never own up to wearing it. When they were touring

Australia, staying in various hotels, Dad would amuse himself by diving into the pool and urging Jim – lying sedately on a sun-lounger in the shade of his rug – to jump in and cool off, an invitation he always politely declined.

But once, on getting off a plane in a high wind, Jim was forced to clamp his hand over his hairpiece to stop it from flying away. Jim had been visibly distressed at being forced, by this act, to own up to his shortcomings in the follicle department, and from then on Dad took pity on him and laid off.

And while we're on the subject of wigs, Dad also had a story told him by a make-up lady about Charlton Heston – famous bad wig wearer and obviously as determined as Jim Pegler that no one must know. But as the deep ginger of his wigs seemed to darken as what was left of his own hair got lighter, this was a vain hope.

The story goes that Charles 'call me Chuck' Heston was shooting a film at Pinewood in which he had to wear a long wig. Knowing how touchy some stars are about their personal hairpieces, the make-up lady placed the wig he was to wear in the film on the dressing table in front of him, saying, 'I'll just leave you to sort yourself out and come back in a minute,' before discreetly withdrawing, expecting Chuck to swap wigs and leave his own toupee on the wig stand. But when, after five minutes or so, the make-up lady came back to apply the rest of his make-up, the wig stand was bare. In his absolute determination to keep his 'secret', he had pulled the heavy-bottomed wig down over his own ginger job. I wish I knew what film it was, but if ever you see a movie in which Charlton Heston wears a long wig, in all likelihood there's something resembling a small furry rodent sitting underneath it.

A good deal, although by no means all, of my father's work after *The Goons* didn't show him at his best. A lot of bad career decisions were made, for which Dad has to take some of the blame, but then he was not always best served by those who were supposed to be advising him. The television spectaculars he made during the sixties and seventies were, for the most part, pretty dire, but having said that, television could not hope to capture his 'essence'. The stage was his arena; the confines of a television studio and a carefully timed script cramped his style. On stage, he was in his element; there he could fly and, on form, was a sight to behold. He would come on like a train with a full head of steam, a high-octane mix of raspberries, top Cs and giggles, and the audience loved him.

I'll leave it to David to add a slightly sad postscript to Dad's career:

'I heard Larry Gelbart on the radio talking about A *Funny Thing Happened on the Way to the Forum*, and he was saying that when he brought the show into the West End, apparently they'd decided that there were only two people who could play the part of Pseudolus, the slave [played on Broadway by Zero Mostel]; one was Harry Secombe, the other was Frankie Howerd. "I don't know why," he said, "but we couldn't get hold of Harry Secombe, but we saw Frankie and he agreed to do it…"

Ah, what might have been.

There were many attempts to translate 'Goon humour' into pictures. The first was the truly awful – *Penny Points to Paradise* in 1951 – which Peter Sellers called 'a terrifyingly bad film'.

Writing credit goes to John Ormonde, although it's really a succession of 'turns', held together by an incredibly thin plot. The story of two idiots (Secombe and Milligan) who have had a win on the football pools and the efforts of a succession of people intent on stealing those winnings is the excuse for the cast to show off their various acts.

Dad performs a mime I subsequently saw him do many times – a nervous surgeon carrying out an operation; Paddy O'Neil does her Bette Davis and Gloria Swanson impersonations; and she and Harry do a hypnotist music-hall act together. Milligan seems a bit lost and spends most of the time mugging at the camera. Sellers is the only one who gets close to getting away with it, playing various characters, including a dodgy Major (shades of Bloodnok) and a Canadian salesman.

My sister, Jennifer, also makes her one and only screen appearance in this epoch-making film. In the final scene, as the Secombe and Milligan characters get married to their on-screen sweethearts, they are surrounded by a host of cheering extras, two of whom are my mother and young Jennifer. During the first take, when Dad appeared, Jennifer raised her arms to him and screamed, 'Daaaadeeee!'

Apart from the three Secombes, Milligan and Sellers, the cast includes Freddie Frinton, Bill Kerr, Sam Kydd, Joe Linnane, Paddie O'Neal, Alfred Marks and Vicki Page.

Unsurprisingly, the film lost money and was quietly forgotten about, until a 16mm print was found in 2006. Using this as a reference, and with funding from an American Sellers' fan, a careful restoration was made from the extant, but incomplete, 35mm stock. In 2009, it was given a showing at the BFI in London and has subsequently been re-released on DVD. It is by this same process that bits of discarded rubbish, like old lavatories, if left buried in the ground for long enough, become precious antiques.

The film, *Let's Go Crazy*, was next, and only came about because they'd used just three of the four weeks' studio time already paid for to film *Penny Points to Paradise* (and it looks like it). *Let's Go Crazy* is an even more hurriedly thrown-together series of musical and variety acts, with Milligan and Sellers in various guises as waiters and customers.

During the fifties, more films followed: *Down Among the Z Men* (1952), written by Jimmy Grafton and Francis Charles and, next to *Penny Points to Paradise*, about as bad as it gets; *The Mukkinese Battle-Horn* (1956), with Dick Emery taking my father's role (where Dad was I have no idea – probably behind the wheel on one of England's A roads). But this, too, is hardly what one might call distinguished.

The most successful attempt to put Goon humour on screen must be *The Running, Jumping & Standing Still Film* (1960). Shot in a field over two Sundays in 1959, it was directed by the then unknown Richard Lester and featured Sellers, Milligan and Mario Fabrizi. It's only 11 minutes long and is a succession of sight gags. Nevertheless, it was nominated for an Academy Award.

Although, more often than not, it proved difficult to translate the mad flights of Milligan's mind to the big screen, Goon humour had a more successful transition to television. *The Idiot Weekly, price 2d* was a sketch show for ITV with Sellers and Milligan. Using the set-up of a tatty Victorian tabloid run by Sellers, the sketches were linked by the eponymous newspaper's improbable headlines. Milligan wrote most of the scripts, Eric Sykes was script editor and Dick Lester produced. The cast included Sykes, Valentine Dyall, Kenneth Connor, Graham Stark, June Whitfield, Patti Lewis and Max Geldray. Five episodes were broadcast, on Associated-Rediffusion in 1956, in the London area only – presumably the provinces had to be protected from such lunacy.

A Show Called Fred followed later that same year, with basically the same cast, and then, in September, *Son of Fred* appeared. These two seemingly chaotic shows really did challenge the established comedy format. The shows used minimal scenery, and what little there was was likely to be dismantled during a sketch to reveal the rest of the studio. There was no audience, but off-screen laughter came courtesy of the watching actors and technicians, who, along with assorted studio equipment, were often in shot.

Milligan also introduced surreal concepts such as completely inappropriate back-projection. Sketches had no punchlines and simply merged into one another (in some instances, the cast of one sketch would simply walk across the studio into another set-up and start again) or were separated by animation sequences. Both of these techniques would be used, with much success, by the Monty Python team in the 1960s.

Astonishingly, apart from the wonderfully insane *Ying Tong Song* signature tune, there were also 'straight' musical interludes supplied by Max Geldray and singer Patti Lewis which, in the midst of all the madness, appear doubly conventional. To get an idea of their incongruity, think Val Doonican turning up to do a spot at the Brit Awards. Whether these musical breaks were Milligan's idea or imposed upon him, I have no idea and, despite attempts to leaven their conventionality (in one of them – Max Geldray's rendition of 'Lady be Good' – Sellers appears during the middle eight and 'plays' the soda syphon) they do now seem incredibly out of place.

I'm sure the bosses of ITV enjoyed these musical interludes enormously but, back in 1956, they deemed the rest of *Son of Fred* too way out and, after eight shows (of a scheduled sixteen), it was cancelled.

Much later, of course, the *Fred* shows were hailed as 'brilliant, ground-breaking comedy' and, in 1963, ITV screened a 30-minute compilation of the two shows entitled *Best of Fred*. It would be another 13 years before such lunacy was again seen on television, with Milligan's *Q* series.

There was also a puppet show – *The Telegoons*, in the 1960s – which was supposed to bring *The Goons* to a whole new generation. But I don't think Spike, Harry or Peter were overly impressed with the results and it didn't last long.

The Goons reformed for one last hoorah in 1972 with *The Last Goon Show of All*. This was recorded at the Camden Theatre in front of an audience which included Princess Margaret and Lord Snowdon. Unfortunately, due to official commitments, Prince Charles couldn't make it.

Sarah Sellers, however, was there:

'That was really exciting. I don't exactly know whether they rehearsed it and did the show on one day, or whether there was a rehearsal the day before, but anyway, Michael and I, and Victoria were there for the whole thing, and sitting in on the rehearsals was really interesting, because you could see how the whole thing evolved, and how they all worked together and…what the script was and what they actually did were two different things altogether! So, it was fascinating seeing that, I mean, I'd been used to film sets and stuff, but this was radio,

and seeing all the people up on stage doing the sound effects
– that was fascinating…

'It was kind of like taking a step back in time…it had a real
excitement and it was so well received. Quite often when
people have reunions or whatever, they're not that great, but I
think that even the biggest *Goon* fans in the world really liked
that show and it's one that's still very popular…'

I was there too, as were quite a few of the Goonchildren. Sadly, I
don't remember much about the show, aside from enjoying the
spectacle of my dad, Spike and Peter messing around, having
fun. But I do recall ending up in the early hours of the morning
at a hotel off Piccadilly, having scrambled eggs and bacon with
Snowdon and Princess Margaret.

Jennifer also remembers that royal scrambled egg experience:

'One of the most memorable experiences happened after the
recording of *The Last Goon Show of All* when Peter Sellers
instructed me to get Dad and the rest of us to go out to dinner
afterwards.

'We went to the Berkeley Hotel for what Princess Margaret
described as "scrambled eggs and a sing song" – which is just
what we had. I remember Peter giving a rousing version of
"Any Old Iron" accompanying himself on the spoons and
Princess Margaret commanding Dad to sing a particular
Welsh hymn.'

Her Royal Highness also told me to get my then fashionably long
hair cut. Needless to say, I didn't.

Looking back at *The Goon Show* now, one is inevitably tempted
to ask, is it still funny? Or should it be consigned to the discard
pile of history, along with Jimmy Edwards' mortar board, Archie
Andrews's blazer and the Home Service?

Barry Cryer observes:

'I did listen to one about a week ago and, I have to say, with great admiration and affection, some of it did sound dated, because that's the penalty of being a pioneer…it is a period piece now – a wonderful period piece – but it did sound of its time, very much so…'

Steve Punt adds:

'I think *The Goon Show* tends to be revered by people who are already radio comedy fans, because they tend to seek it out – they know their history and know this was a really important show. So, if you talk to comedy fans, they will have gone and bought some CDs, or bought the scripts, but I think you can't really get a flavour of it from reading the scripts.

'I suppose, if I'm really honest, it's probably true to say… because it was such a thing of its time…it probably hasn't maintained its appeal like some other shows. For example, Tony Hancock – contemporary with *The Goons* in terms of radio – is almost more accessible, because Hancock is a universal character.'

But *The Goon Show* is not dead – it lives on. I'm glad to say that a whole generation is now awakening to the world that the Goons created. BBC Radio 7 runs regular *Goon Show* repeats, which I listen to with my boys whenever I can, and it always brings a smile to my face.

Sarah Sellers agrees:

'I find it very hard to be objective about anything that my father was in so I think I'm a kind of fan by default. I couldn't not be a fan, but I wouldn't say I sit and listen to *The Goons* a lot.

'When I listen and they make me laugh…it's more because I can visualise my dad doing the voices…so I can't really separate out from it enough to really appreciate it for what it is.

'As I say, it's hard to be objective…But you see people being interviewed on telly – you see the Pythons being interviewed, and all the rest, and they talk about the relevance and everything, and I do often think about that side of things – what part they did play in English comedy – and I do think it was an important part.

'And you see those boundaries being pushed further and further, though I don't think there's much further they can go because you really can get away with anything now…Perhaps it was just a particular moment in time. When you see comedians being really crude, I don't really find it very funny. It's almost like they're saying, "I can say rude words now and I can get away with it." It just doesn't seem that funny to me. It was the innuendo and the fact they had to be inventive to say something without really saying it. That was part of the humour, but now those boundaries are gone.'

It's true to say that *The Goon Show* conjures a distant, more innocent age, when we knew who the baddies were and you could tell the heroes by the Union Jack sewn into their long johns; those long-lost days when jokes about 'Hugh Jampton', or the 'pink oboe', or the 'last turkey in the shop' flew straight over the heads of the BBC management to make thousands of ex-servicemen all over the country hoot with joy.

But I don't think *The Goon Show*'s lasting appeal can be put down entirely to nostalgia, and listening again to many of the shows for the purposes of this book (many for the umpteenth time), I was impressed all over again by the skill of the performers and the brilliance of the writing. It may be true that some of the jokes haven't weathered well, but the freshness and energy of the performances is all too apparent – great comedy timing has no sell-by date.

12

The Goons' Legacy

In later years, Harry, Spike and Peter would occasionally meet up for lunch. Dad looked forward to these occasions as they were usually one long laughter-fest, allowing the old mates to catch up, share stories and generally reminisce about the old days.

One such lunch was scheduled for the 23 July 1980. But that morning, as Dad was getting dressed, he received a phone call telling him that Peter had had a heart attack. This was just another incident in a succession of heart troubles Peter had suffered over the years and, although worried for him, Dad expected him to recover – Peter seemed indestructible. As it turned out, he wasn't. Peter never recovered consciousness and was pronounced dead at the Middlesex Hospital at lunchtime the next day. He was the first of the Goons to go.

Mike Bentine was next, falling prey to prostate cancer on 26 November 1996. He was followed by my father who, after a series of debilitating strokes, eventually also succumbed to prostate cancer in April 2001. Last of all was Spike, who died of liver failure on 27 February 2002.

Sile Milligan recalls:

'Dad actually didn't want to be reminded about *The Goons*, which I find really strange. If you've achieved something so great, which actually elevated him into the position he was in, it's very, very strange.

'I was very young but, of course, in my early years, right up until I was about 14, it was still very prevalent in people's minds – they'd always ask you about it, and there were still loads of *Goon Shows* on the radio. Whenever I talk to anyone about my dad, I get the same thing, even now, it's always straight to *The Goons*, I find it really difficult. I can talk about Dad far more in other areas than I can about *The Goons*.'

I suppose it's understandable that Spike should feel a certain reluctance to talk about *The Goon Show*. After all, not only had it pushed him to the limits of his sanity, but he had also done so much more. Both Dad and Peter, however, remained loyal to the show's memory, remembering it as being the best of times. Indeed, Dad never tired of telling stories about the wonderful times he had during those days and still, even at the very end, wasn't averse to slipping into a Goon voice to raise a laugh.

After suffering a second stroke at home, Dad was found by the housekeeper's husband lying, incapable of movement, on the landing. Bending over to help him up, the man was addressed in Bluebottle's voice with the line, 'I can see right up your nose!'

Notwithstanding Spike's later feelings about *The Goons*, he couldn't deny the show's influence on a whole generation of comedians, as Barry Cryer affirms:

'In the *Goon Shows*, there weren't a lot of punchlines… Milligan, he was a great pioneer in that – you don't have to have the orthodox format: da, da, da, da, da – last line – punchline – end of sketch. He would just wander off into something else, and that fascinated us.

'We did student shows at the old Empire Theatre in Leeds, Rag Revue and all that sort of stuff…I did stand-up, although we didn't call it that then, and I told jokes, but I was more freewheeling in the way I talked to the audience, young as I was, than I would have been had I not heard *The Goon Show*. Because we thought, no, you can just be silly now – digress and be stupid.

'Spike was ambivalent [about *Monty Python*]. When *Python* came along, one day Spike would be saying, "Those gallant lads are flying the flag!" and the next he'd say, "Those bastards have ripped me off!"

The show had enormous appeal to people at all levels of society. Well-known *Goon* fans include The Beatles (Yoko Ono gave John Lennon a collection of *Goon Show* tapes for his 37th birthday), Peter Cook, Elton John, Eddie Izzard, Paul Merton and, of course, its most famous and highest-ranking fan, Prince Charles.

There are several *Goon Show* fan clubs, but probably the best known is the Goon Show Preservation Society. It produces a yearly newsletter and puts fans from all over the world in contact with each other. Gill Nicholas is the society's archivist and, needless to say, an avid *Goon* fan. She lives not far from me, in Penzance, and has dedicated one room of her, it has to be said not overly large house, to *The Goons*.

When I went to visit her I was amazed by the amount of stuff she'd accumulated over the years. Apart from every available *Goon* recording going, including DVDs of the awful *Penny Points to Paradise* and *Down Among the Z Men*, there were theatre programmes, boxes of photographs, shelves full of *Goon*-related books and paraphernalia, and even a small, stuffed representation of my dog, Jimmy (although I must say, I found that slightly creepy). She showed me around:

'I call this "The Goon Room"; my friends call it other things quite often, and they all think I'm mad, but I've always been a fan of *The Goons* and, particularly since I've retired, I've been collecting *Goon* memorabilia. And this is where I display it.

'I've got a wall per person, really. Bentine along the top; the rest of it is Goon collectively as opposed to Goons individually. I've got a couple of autographed photographs, one which your mum sent me – I've also got one that Shelagh Milligan sent me. Obviously, the rest have come from various places, some are LP sleeves, some are from the Goon Show Preservation Society...

' I've got a shelf of Eric Sykes: books, tapes...you name it... Peter Sellers books, videos, tapes...These are more *Goon* LPs, I've got about 130 of the Goon Show Preservation Society newsletters, press cuttings...

'That wall is pretty well your dad, from his big days to his little days – fat dad and slim dad. There's even one of him in drag. And there's your Uncle Fred's book and yours are over there. That section is Mr Milligan, and all his tapes and things are in that case; your dad's LPs are down there, umpteen of them. And a carousel with more Milligan stuff – a revolving Milligan section. I've got press photos...the whole collection is catalogued.'

It is an extraordinary collection with some very rare photographs, many I've never seen before. There is even one with Dad, Anthony Newly, David Dimbleby, Bruce Forsyth and Peter Finch, although what they were all doing together I have no idea. There's also a picture of my brother's christening, with David in his christening robes, looking slightly nervous in the midst of Bruce Forsyth, Jimmy Edwards, Roy Castle and Eric Morcambe.

Gill continues:

'Some people think I've taken my obsession a little too far – my friends think I'm totally nuts. But I didn't join the society until about seven years ago and since then I've gained a whole load by swapping things with other members, and I'm still collecting stuff.

'I've also allowed myself to be talked into looking after the Goon Show Preservation Society video library. When it arrived, it came in four packing cases with about 600 videos. About 100 are commercial ones and the rest are what people have taped off the telly – bits of this, bits of that. And we are currently in the process of transferring the whole lot to DVD.

'Soon, I'm either going to have to move house or throw my husband out to make room for it all.'

But the fans aren't just in this country, Gill picked up a fair amount of her collection in Australia, a country in which both Harry and Spike worked a great deal and which still has a huge *Goon* following today. In fact, Gill picked up so much stuff the last time she went out there, she couldn't lift the suitcase to come home.

The madness has even reached the U.S. Because I had a small part as an alien called Watto in the *Star Wars* saga, I occasionally get invited to conventions where large numbers of fans gather to dress up as Wookies and Jedi Knights, meet the stars and collect autographs. A couple of years ago, I was at one of these celebrations in a vast concrete and steel convention centre in Los Angeles when, off in the distance, I heard a vaguely familiar voice.

Finally pinpointing where it was coming from, I saw him, walking towards me through a sea of C3POs, Princess Leias and Darth Vaders – the hair, the beard, the glasses, he was the image of Mike Bentine in full Osric Pureheart mode. The *Star Wars* fans parted nervously before him and he stood in front of me and delivered a five-minute monologue. He was about to go into Bentine's chairback routine when he was dragged away by an Intergalactic Bounty Hunter I took to be his wife. It turns out there's a huge American *Goon Show* fan club – is there no end to the insanity?

But, closer to home, it still seems to be garnering fans today. Steve Punt wasn't even born when *The Goon Show* was first broadcast, but he, too, now counts himself among the faithful:

'I suppose my interest stems from the fact that, as a child, I was conscious that, for example, when we were on holiday and at the beach, my father, for no apparent reason, would suddenly go, "He's fallen in the water!" Or, if anyone broke wind in our family, he would inevitably say something like, "No more curried eggs for me!" My parents were in their teens in the fifties and my dad was a classic *Goon Show* listener.

'I also started to notice, when I got interested in comedy in my teens, if you read an interview or a biography of any of the next generation of comics – whether it's Cleese, whether it's Peter Cook, whether it's Palin…any of those people – the first thing they always said was, "The thing that changed my life was *The Goon Show* because my parents didn't understand it." I think Michael Palin says, quite specifically that his father didn't get it at all, so he used to listen to it on his own.

'It's a bit like what happened with music a few years later – *The Goons* was the new rock 'n' roll, except it was first, because it was a youth cult several years before rock 'n' roll was a youth cult. And I know from talking to my dad, it had this enormous appeal, just as *Python* did, just as *The Fast Show* did later on, this enormous appeal to teenagers: "This is something that belongs to us, and we can do these voices in the playground." It wasn't the first of those cult shows, but I think it was the first to have a fan base that was that much younger.

'In its own comic way, *The Goon Show* was very much part of the initial pushing against government, against the church, against what's now called The Establishment, and it was part of the feeling that these institutions were not untouchable that would eventually culminate in *Beyond the Fringe*. Peter Cook was a great fan of *The Goon Show*.

'If you'd been in the army, you'd have seen first hand that the people at the top were sometimes idiots. And, certainly for Milligan, the people at the BBC were the same. There's a very gentle, British, anti-Establishment feeling about the Goons, which again teenagers would love, because, of course, they had their own authority figures: teachers and parents. So they absolutely understand comedy that's coming from the point of view of knocking the people upstairs.'

It has to be said, if it was made today, *The Goon Show* would be very different. It's wildly politically incorrect – regular references are made to Max Geldray's Jewishness and Ray Ellington endures constant jokes about his colour; Bluebottle's cry of, 'Don't touch me, you'll rub off on me!' being one of the least offensive. Indeed, some of the shows have actually been re-edited to make them more palatable to a modern audience.

Barry Cryer says of this aspect of the shows:

'It was of the time and, yes, it makes you cringe. I did a series called *Hello, Cheeky* with John Junkin and Tim Brooke-Taylor and I heard one of those on Radio 7 recently and you really cringe. I played a funny black guy who used to ring up and pretend to be other people, and the audience used to think this was hilarious. I used to say things like, "Hello, dis am de Archbishop of Canterbury..." and, honestly, there was no sort of malice at the time, we just thought, "Well, that's a funny character voice...it's a black guy pretending to be the Archbishop of Canterbury." Which, funnily, would be topical now, what with the Archbishop of York.

'But *The Goon Show* had – if there is such a thing – "jolly racism" – though that's an awful thing to say. Subsequently, Spike blacked up for *Curry and Chips*; Peter, too, in *The Millionairess* and *The Party*...Now, of course, we've got *Little Britain*, who do gays, black people, fat people...but it's ironic now, they're winking at the audience as if to say, "This isn't serious" – that's the licence to do it.'

Spike wasn't a racist. As Sile says, he saw everyone as equal and, therefore, fair game – even disabled people. But his mockery was never malicious and was more often than not used to make a point. Even the ill-starred *Curry and Chips*, in which Spike played a half-Pakistani, half-Irish immigrant called Kevin O'Grady, was an attempt to highlight prejudice and ridicule racism.

One of the funniest of Milligan's sketches was sent to me by Jane. Called 'Laugh at the Cripple' it's a send-up of reality TV. The point Spike's making, of course, is that television exploits people for its own ends, especially weak or disadvantaged people.

One need look no further than the execrable *Jeremy Kyle Show* for an example of this.

Jane Milligan says:

> 'I remember working with P.P. Arnold quite a few years ago on a show called *Once On This Island* – I was doing the sound – and I remember Spike had made quite a controversial statement about black people on television and P.P. just smiled and shook her head and went, "Your dad…"
>
> 'She was wise enough to see he wasn't being racist – thank God; I was working with a whole black cast. He was a realist, he wasn't a racist. He was brought up in India – he spoke fluent Hindi.'

And, although *The Goon Show* does have its fair share of women fans, having grown out of robust, male, barrack-room humour, it's hardly surprising that some of the jokes are not exactly what you might call feminist-friendly. Even Sile Milligan calls it 'a very male sort of thing'.

Looking back through the distorting lens of our modern mores and preoccupations, it's tempting to condemn the show for these reasons, but I think it's naïve rather than malicious. I'm not for one minute suggesting that we should excuse casual racism or sexism, but that we should rather view *The Goon Show* in its cultural and historical context – we can't impose our morality on the past. If I may invoke the oft-quoted L.P. Hartley, 'The past is a foreign country; they do things differently there.'

Even in death, Spike courted controversy. He had wanted 'I told you I was ill!' on his tombstone, but the powers that be at St Thomas's Church, Winchelsea, where he was buried, wouldn't allow it. Eventually, a compromise was reached, with the Chichester Diocese approving the phrase only once it was translated into Gaelic. Which is, I think Spike would have agreed, Irish logic – appropriately enough. The headstone now bears the legend *'Duirt me leat go raibh me breoite'*, and below this, the phrase that Spike used to sign off all his missives – 'Love, light, peace'.

Spike's death was truly the end of the Goons, and left some people with a sense of something unfinished.

Barry Cryer remembers:

'Spike and I knew each other for many years, we did chat shows and all sorts of things together and, not long before he died, he rang up.

"Cryer!" he said – by then he was getting so bitter about the BBC not wanting to know him; he was the angry old man in the corner shouting at the world – and he said, "I've dusted off a script I found in a drawer. Me and Eric Sykes wrote it years ago, but it's not right. Eric and I were going to work it up and submit it to the BBC, but Eric's got busy…Are you up for it?"

"Yes!" I said, "Sorry to be evasive, Spike, but I'm up for it."

'But it never happened. I was quite excited; I thought, "I'm going to write with Milligan – that's wonderful." I could see it on my CV: "Has written with Spike Milligan." Then he died.

'I never even found out what it was.'

But the recordings, films, books, television programmes and memories they left their fans aside, what did those four hairy men leave their children? It certainly wasn't a large financial inheritance as, apart from Peter, who cut his children out of his will, none of them died a millionaire, having just missed out on the television era that rewarded its stars with eye-wateringly large fees. In fact, most of them left behind nothing but a tangled financial mess. But money isn't everything, as Sile Milligan observes:

'Being the child of a Goon is like being a member of a private club…I saw Stella McCartney on television one day, and I thought, "Christ, she's one of the Beatles' kids – that's huge!" Then I thought, "Hold on a minute…" Since Dad died, I've realised that it's humungous to be the child of a Goon. I mean, *The Goons* did for comedy what the Beatles did for music.

'I'd like, really, to have known more about *The Goons*. I still think I'd like to get my head around it and listen to it more.

But the nice thing is, I have three teenage sons, and they do listen to *The Goons* sometimes. It's obviously not widely available, you'd have to be a *Goon* fan and research when it was on…but they do and have also listened to the CDs…

'For all of us and, more importantly for our fathers, I'd hate to see it die away into insignificance. That would make me really sad…'

Jane Milligan adds:

'I really haven't listened to all *The Goon Shows*…The ones that I'm knowledgeable about, I absolutely adore and it's something I still think needs to live – it's still got breath in it. Dad's imagination was quite something, and I put that down to his mum and dad being born in India, which must have been mind-stretching in a wonderful way, both religiously and environmentally, being brought up in different surroundings, and then moving to Burma – another very interesting place – where Desmond, his brother was born, so a very exotic upbringing, which stimulated him, I think. And then this terrible journey to England, arriving on the frosty, frozen shores…so all these amazing experiences…

'Then in the army – it was survival, his humour was survival. And I think he cheered up a nation at the end of a most terrible, depressing time in our history. He kind of went, "Fuck it! Look at us, how funny is this?"

'I was too young to have been around to listen at the time, but the love I get as his child from people – guys in their seventies, who hung by that radio whenever *The Goon Show* was on – they got so much joy from it. I feel so privileged. And how brilliant that such an anarchic show was on the BBC!'

Richard Bentine says one of the greatest things he got from his father is the ability to pick himself up and carry on:

'The last show he did was for the RAF, because he'd always do a big charity show for them once a year. It was going to be in Bristol this year, but they were worried about his health. And I asked if they couldn't lay something on to make it all a bit easier for him.

'And they said, "OK, how big's your garden?"

"It's quite big," I said, "and it backs on to a golf course."

"A golf course we can work with," they said.

'They sent a Sea King helicopter to pick him up from his garden and then took him down to Bristol where he did the show.

'By that stage he was wearing a catheter – peeing into a bag strapped to his leg. In what other profession would you stagger on stage in that state, do an hour-and-a-half show and then stagger off? What other profession in the world requires you to do that? If there is one abiding thing we all share because our parents were Goons, it's, "The show must go on!" I've dragged myself up from my deathbed to go to a meeting where other people I know would have taken the week off with just a bad cold.

'He also left me the gifts of a sense of humour and observation. Humour gives you the ability to laugh at just about anything life can shove at you. Observation allows you to understand that, no matter how bad it gets, you can still function and still find a way through. And, honestly, I think those are the two best lessons you can learn in life.'

For me, one of the nice things is the knowledge that *The Goon Show* is still making people laugh today, even those cynical sophisticates on Radio 4, as Steve Punt attests:

'I always find Eccles inherently funny – whenever Eccles comes in, I just start laughing. To me, that is a Goon, and he's probably my favourite of the characters. Maybe because I have a memory of my dad doing that voice and it reminds me of childhood, but it is just such a funny voice.

'There's such a feelgood factor about *The Goon Show* as a

whole, partly because of the way it was recorded...but also partly because you know these voices are clearly tried and tested in the pub. You just know this is a group of friends who make each other laugh and now they're going to make you laugh as well. It's also the joy of knowing that voice is something Milligan was making people laugh with on basic training.'

My father's death was both a tragedy and a release, and not just in the sense that it released him from the terrible pain he was in. In my younger days, he seemed to me like a god and, despite the love, affection and laughter he gave me, I can't deny he cast a long shadow. While he was alive, I struggled to assert myself in my own right – indeed, my first novel wasn't published until after he died. Not that he ever deliberately stifled my creativity, on the contrary, he was always very supportive of whatever I happened to be doing. So perhaps a good deal of the creative constriction I felt was of my own imagining. But, although it was hard to lose him – and I still miss him to this day – his death was like a vast tree falling over in a forest and me, the weedy sapling who'd grown up in its shadow, feeling the sunlight on its leaves for the first time.

Sarah Sellers also recalls what life was like after Peter's death:

'Life certainly changed after Peter died and probably that's true, I was more able to explore my creative side. I went to art college originally, but I didn't get on very well there...I mean there's always been a creative side, and I suppose nowadays I'm following that more than I was and I'm not afraid about it...

'I look at my daughter who wants to be a stylist and she has issues and she's a grandchild! I know for a fact that she's worked at *Vogue* because she's good at what she does, rather than because of family connections, but she's also got a part-time job in a shop and they've been quite difficult with her – a bit "Well, it's all right for you!" But actually she's worked damned hard to get where she is. And that's one generation further down the line, so there are problems and issues but, I don't know, maybe it makes us more interesting people?'

I suppose I was lucky in that Mum and Dad had one of the happiest and most stable relationships in showbusiness and therefore I had a comparatively secure, if not entirely conventional, upbringing. I was also lucky in that I grew closer to Dad in his later years and was able to talk to him about subjects I would have found it hard to approach in my younger days.

Sile Milligan says:

'So much of the history is told to us through newspapers, interviews, the *Michael Parkinson Show* and this, that and the other – you're being given that information all the time and receiving it and you don't actually go out of your way to find it out yourself, from your dad, because it's been given to you on a plate. But then you start asking yourself…what was the truth? And now he's not here, I can't ask him.'

It's easy to become complacent and accept the public history and the folklore that adheres to a famous person, even if one is part of the family. And with the passing of time, it becomes harder and harder to separate fact from fiction.

When Dad was alive, I talked to many people who had recently lost their fathers and who complained bitterly about the unfinished business left between them. 'If there's anything you want to ask, ask it while he's still around,' they urged me. 'When he's gone, it's too late.' I'm glad to say, I took their advice.

As I've already said, we Secombes were lucky in that our folks stayed together. But things weren't quite so straightforward for the other Goonchildren: Peter's philandering was legendary, and Spike married three times, his first marriage breaking up when Sile was only 18 months old. But she was wary of discussing Spike's relationship with him:

'I never wanted to edge into that area…starting to ask Dad,

"Why did you leave our mother? What happened?"…I had all these questions…

'But then if I had asked him, he would have ended up in bed for three days, depressed, and would it have been worth it? No!

'That's the life I led. I wanted to ask questions, but then thought, no, it's rude, and I love him and everybody makes mistakes…but when he died, I thought, hang on a minute…'

Recently, details of Spike's many affairs have come to light, as has the news that he fathered two illegitimate children. Sile's sister Jane wasn't quite so afraid of facing up to her father, possibly because, as the youngest daughter, she was allowed to get away with more:

'Spike was old-fashioned in his attitudes to women. He liked someone to make his dinner. We all know now that he had a lot of affairs…I don't think they were big love affairs, I think he was quite happy to have a wife at home, who would always be there. It didn't mean a lot to him, I think, people's hearts being broken.

'The main person I would have been protective of and upset about was my mum, but she'd already died when I found out, so she was safe in a way. But I think I did go through a bit of anxiety when I found out that he was "playing away" while she was very ill with cancer. I had it out with him and he apologised. I had a very honest relationship with Spike. Yes, he was selfish, but it might have been self-protection. Spike didn't like being on his own – he was a mummy's boy. Grandma made sure of that – she really spoilt her sons.

'I feel terribly sad for my brothers and sisters, because they had two mums: their mum and dad divorced, and then they got another mum, whom they called "Mum" – Paddy was Mum to them because they were quite little when she came along and, in fact, I didn't know they were my half-brother and sisters for a long time, we were just like a unit. And then she died, so they lost two mums.

'I had the joy of knowing my mum loved me very much – I was very loved by Paddy, like a waterfall of love, incredible love. And Spike was very good at that as well. But in their minds, they were abandoned by their mum as little kids, and that must leave you with a terrible insecurity. Spike was fiercely protective of his family but, probably because I lost Paddy, he was both mum and dad.'

But however angry Jane may have been with him from time to time, that hasn't coloured her feelings for Spike, the great affection she still holds him in and the enormous gratitude she feels for everything he gave her:

'...A river of sensitivity, the most wonderful humour, an appreciation of everything. An incredibly deep and interesting appreciation of life. I can't thank him enough for what he showed me, about history, archaeology, wine, genealogy. He never really did very well financially, considering what he gave us. His appreciation of life was wondrous, he was a philosopher, a poet. He gave me boundless imagination. Obviously, I feel a terrible sense of loss, but that's the way life goes – people die. I've got his genes. I'm very lucky as his child, I can reach up to a shelf and pull out a book and there he is...So for any trauma I went through – losing Paddy or finding out about his affairs...I just think of all the other things.'

When I was younger and a good deal angrier, I used to get fed up with strangers pulling me aside at various functions and telling me, often with tears in their eyes, how wonderful my father was, and how gracious he'd been to visit them in hospital, or to write to their Auntie Doris, or to send flowers to Grandma Smith who was dying of cancer...so much so that I wanted to scream, 'He's not the fucking Messiah!' But these days, mellowed (slightly) by age, I can now appreciate the lovely things people have to say about him. It's always nice to hear how your dad touched so many people's lives.

Sarah Sellers agrees:

'Sometimes people come and talk to you and you know that they really have a love of him and his films and all the rest of it and you think, "That's really nice." And it's nice meeting people that knew him well…

'When I had a stall at Camden Passage, Kenneth Griffiths lived around the corner, so he'd often come and walk by and say hello to me and tell me stories about my dad that were really nice – silly things he'd got up to…silly times when he'd dressed up as people and fooled other people, and that was great.

'I just think the whole thing with celebrity now is dreadful and part of that is always looking for the dirt, always looking for the bad things and there seems to be as much interest in finding out about bad things as looking at what is good. So, sometimes, it's really nice and refreshing when somebody comes up and tells you a really good story…you really know that they loved him and that's good.'

Michael Sellers, too, pays a touching tribute to his father at the end of his book, *P.S. I Love You*:

'The one bequest we have from Dad is shared by millions throughout the world.

'Many of Dad's films are already screen classics. Our children will one day come to see them and our grandchildren, too. And the generations of our family will pass down not only his films but all of Dad's stories, right back to the great Mendoza.

'No one can deprive us of our memories. At last we are a united and peaceful family and we bear the name of Sellers with pride.'

When my dad died, there were many touching tributes paid and a wonderful service at Westminster Abbey, which Prince Charles attended and at which Michael Parkinson and Jimmy Tarbuck both spoke. It was a great occasion, full of love and laughs. Jimmy gave a very funny speech, ending with a warning to the congregation: 'Don't let Ken Dodd anywhere near the collection plate.'

Richard Bentine says of Michael's death:

'Because of the cancer, because of the paranormal, because of Gus [Richard's brother who died in 1971], we had this constant stream – endless letters – and he and Mum used to make enormous efforts to answer every single one.

'And when he died in 1996, the two things I think which touched me most were: 1) that the RAF insisted they wanted to take part in his memorial service, so we had the memorial service in the Actor's Church in St Paul's in Covent Garden and, when we came out at 3.15pm, the Red Arrows had been given permission to fly across London. They flew over the Actor's Church substantially lower than they should have... The fly-past was something that Prince Charles organised; and 2) the number of letters we got from people, saying, "I just wanted to say how much I loved your father, because in 1986, when my wife died, I wrote to him and he sent this fantastic letter back with a little drawing on it..."

'There were all these letters from people we'd never met before – that was the thing I found amazing, because you can read a letter from a relative or friend and know it's emotionally raw, because what you share is something very personal that you know about...But when you get a letter from a stranger – like from that woman in Norfolk who Dad had given his jacket to – it's in those that you find out how you as a family fit into the scheme of things. Because it's very easy to be an influence on people if you appear on a television set and you're seen. But the true measure of a person...is all those things you do that are not seen...things done quietly and unassumingly.

'I'm very glad my children were able to encounter Dad...he built them an *Ark Royal* out of cardboard boxes which he made one summer in Palm Springs, and then brought back on the aeroplane. He made them a steamer, with all the moveable docking cranes and things. He used to make models out of balsa wood...He'd scratch build First World War aeroplanes for them, so they could run around the house with them. And he built a fantastic garden railway – 380 feet of track running round the flower beds – boys running up and down changing the points. He was a big kid, Dad. It would be nice if he was still around now because I always felt he died a little bit too early.

'For so many decades, he was not in England for six months of the year and so I got used to the concept of him being alive somewhere else. And now I feel he's just alive somewhere else. I hope so, anyway. I'd rather believe that than think we just all disperse into cosmic goo – it's more comforting. So I still miss him; I talk to him just as much – I just don't lose as many arguments as I used to.'

For some of us, the aftermath has been occasionally bizarre, as Sarah Sellers explains:

'Since he's died, there have been various societies and whatever, one of them being the Dead Comics' Society. I went along to some of those events, and I did think they were rather sad, I have to say, because...I just found it really bizarre... because I was a celebrity there, and I'm not a celebrity, and people would clap and you'd have to stand up, and then I'd look around at who the other celebrities were, and there was nobody who was a celebrity – there was somebody's aunt or somebody that touched somebody, you know...

'I just couldn't do it after a while, it just seems bizarre that people should be interested in me because of my father. I mean, yeah, they can be interested in him, fine, but I'm a different person, so...I can sit and talk like this for a while, but there's a limit to what I can say...I can't really understand what the great excitement is.'

As I mentioned in the Introduction, I was struck down with

cancer a few years ago. The cancer was on the back of my tongue and the treatment, a combination of radio- and chemotherapy, caused my throat to swell to the extent I could no longer eat normally and had to be fed with a tube directly into my stomach. The fibreless mush I had to ingest resulted in my becoming severely constipated and, in desperation, I sought the help of the district nurse who performed an enema. As I 'assumed the position' – facing the wall with my knees drawn up – the middle-aged nurse, in the very act of inserting the tube, bent over me and said, 'So, you're Harry's boy, are you?'

Dad never went in for philosophising about life, he just got on with it. Not that he never thought about 'bigger issues'; he was both knowledgeable and open-minded about such things, believing that 'truth is a pathless land…' and that each of us finds our own way there by our own means.

David adds:

'I asked Dad once, "What have you learnt from life?" It was quite a serious question and he thought for a while and eventually said, "Never play peek-a-boo with a small child at the start of a transatlantic flight."

'And, a few years ago, I was coming back from New York – we'd not long left JFK – and this child in the seat in front of me peeped over the headrest and looked at me – I ignored it. And that's absolutely true. So I can honestly say that I have acted on his advice.'

Jennifer offers her perspective:

'When it comes to Dad's legacy, there are so many precious things that he's left behind. Physically, I have inherited his tendency to pile on weight (thanks, Dad), an identical laugh, a strong set of lungs and the habit of sticking the end of my tongue out of the side of my mouth when I'm concentrating.

'He instilled in me a love of literature, music and art and a fear of mathematics; he made me understand the importance of kindness and humility; he gave me a highly developed sense of the ridiculous and a low boredom threshold.

'Most of all, he was an honest, good man. He lived his life in an honourable way and gave generously of his wealth and time to good causes without desiring any reward. He had a God-given voice – just listen to his early operatic aria recordings if you don't believe me.

'He was intrinsically funny, intelligent, quick and witty but never cruel. He was the genuine article. He was the best dad you could ever get.

'But the most precious legacy he's left me, apart from all the happy memories, is that every time I look at my three children, I am reminded of him. His legacy carries on.'

For me, there was no passing on of paternal wisdom; we were never sat down and given a fatherly talk. The closest he ever came to this was to quote from Polonius's speech in *Hamlet*. The old man is giving his son, Laertes, advice prior to his setting off on a trip to Paris:

This above all: to thine own self be true,
And it must follow, as the night the day,
Thou cans't not then be false to any man…

I have always tried to act on this, but it's hard advice to follow, especially when you're a struggling actor. When the choice is between working or starving, it's tough to say no to something just because it doesn't comply with your morals or beliefs.

Happily, I no longer have to make such compromises, and am now able to say no to things I don't want to do.

But despite a complete absence of paternal guidance, Dad gave me so many wonderful gifts: an appreciation of music, of humour, history, archaeology, painting, literature. He also taught me to look for the interesting in the apparently mundane and not to judge people by appearances.

But, most of all, when I think of him it's the laughter I remember. It's a cliché, I know, but it's true. He made me laugh – he lit up any room he walked into and could bring the sun out on the dullest of days. He was like a warm fire you wanted to cuddle up in front of, and I miss him. I miss his warmth, his generosity and humanity, and I wish he were still here.

Postscript

And There's More where That Came From!

In this digital age, *The Goon Show* repeats broadcast on BBC Radio 7 are beamed down to us from a satellite and the waves they are carried on no longer escape out into space. But what of those original broadcasts beamed from Broadcasting House all those decades ago? Those radio waves, laden with raspberries, explosions and cries of 'Spon!' have long ago floated free of our solar system and must by now be saturating the airwaves of our neighbouring galaxies. Could aliens on planets circling far-distant suns be settling down by their radiograms with cups of cocoa to listen to the continuing adventures of Seagoon, Bloodnok, Bluebottle and Eccles? What must they make of stories about mysterious Frenchmen hurling batter puddings at unsuspecting English spinsters?

And if, down here on Earth, *The Goon Show* has slipped slightly in popularity, it's doubtless because life has caught up with the crazy world the Goons created. Nowadays, with the emergence of lunatics willing to blow aeroplanes out of the sky with explosive underpants, perhaps the idea of exploding shirt-tails is not quite so funny any more.

But it would be remiss of me to close a book about one of the most joyous comedies ever on such a sombre note. So, here's a final story from my sister, Jennifer, about the great, mad world of Goonery – they're still out there, folks!

'It's part of the British consciousness, but not just the British consciousness, there is a Goon Show Preservation Society that is quite lively in New York.

'I remember Dad arriving in America, and he was met at the airport by a bunch of ultra-orthodox Jews in their black coats and hats, with their ringlets and full beards. And when he saw them he was quite worried, because he thought they might be there to protest at what they perceived as anti-Semitism in *The Goon Show*.

'Then one of them called out, "Hello, Neddie! Welcome to America, buddy!" And they all started doing *Goon Show* voices. It's surreal, isn't it? But this is the kind of thing that happens – you couldn't make it up.'

How long *The Goon Show* will carry on making people laugh no one can say, but I hope for some time yet and, if this book has made you think about donning your best cardboard trousers and dipping your toe into one of the repeats on BBC Radio 7, then I am glad to have been some service in perpetuating its legacy.

I would now like to bid you farewell with a line my father was fond of quoting. I have no idea where it's from, but I think you'll agree it's profound: 'And so, as the sun sets slowly in the west, across the date-fields of Manitoba comes the cry of the Indian fire-walker: "My feet are killing me!"

Thank you and goodnight – or, as Dad would say, 'Hup!'

Goonchildren

(in order of appearance)

Jennifer Giannini (née Secombe) *b.*1949

Marylla 'Fusty' Bentine 1949–1987

Stuart 'Gus' Bentine 1950–1971

Laura Milligan *b.*1952

Andy Secombe *b.*1953

Michael Sellers 1954–2006

Sean Milligan *b.*1954

Sile Milligan *b.*1957

Sarah Sellers *b.*1957

Richard 'Peski' Bentine *b.*1959

Serena 'Suki' Bentine *b.*1960

David Secombe *b.*1962

Victoria Sellers *b.*1965

Jane Milligan *b.*1966

Katy Secombe *b.*1967